THE BIBLE
ON THE BIG SCREEN

THE BIBLE

ON THE BIG SCREEN

A GUIDE FROM SILENT FILMS TO TODAY'S MOVIES

J. STEPHEN LANG

BakerBooks

Grand Rapids, Michigan

Published by Baker Books
a division of Baker Publishing Group
P.O. Box 6287, Grand Rapids, MI 49516-6287
www.bakerbooks.com

Printed in the United States of America

Library of Congress Cataloging-in-Publication Data
Lang, J. Stephen.
    The Bible on the big screen : a guide from silent films to today's movies / J. Ste-
phen Lang.
        p.   cm.
    Includes bibliographical references and index.
    ISBN 10: 0-8010-6804-5 (pbk.)
    ISBN 978-0-8010-6804-1 (pbk.)
    1. Bible films—History and criticism. 2. Bible—In motion pictures I. Title.
PN1995.9.B53L36 2007
791.43'6822—dc22   2007018805

Photo credits: Photofest—6, 20, 57, 64, 84, 103, 121, 146, 187, 198, 215, 234, 246; Library
of Congress—32, 80; Icon Productions—268.

CONTENTS

123 329

The blinded Samson (Victor Mature) visited in prison by the repentant Delilah (Hedy Lamarr) in Cecil B. DeMille's 1949 *Samson and Delilah,* kicking off a decade of lavish and mostly profitable biblical epics in glorious color. The movie also set the precedent of having bad girls of the Bible turning out good on screen.

INTRODUCTION

From the 1897 Passions Till Now

When Mel Gibson's *Passion of the Christ* premiered in 2004, it was only the most recent of a long, long line of biblical films dating back to 1897. In that year, with motion picture technology still in its infancy, three films titled *The Passion* were exhibited—each of them less than ten minutes long and (of course) all silent and in black and white. Cast members were not named. Needless to say, special effects were minimal. But what motivated those pioneer movie producers was what motivated Gibson more than a century later: to tell an old, old story from the Bible in a new and dramatic way—and make a profit. Like Gibson, those early producers took their share of criticism. As early as 1912, a popular movie about Jesus's life was accused of being anti-Semitic—and too violent. Has the world really changed much?

Motion pictures definitely have changed in many ways. From grainy, silent, black-and-white "one-reelers" of only a few minutes, they grew steadily longer and longer, so that a film based on the Bible could show not just an isolated incident like Jesus's crucifixion or one of his miracles but a long, connected story. Sound was added so that actors actually could speak the ancient words of the Bible. And sound improved steadily in quality, so much so that noted composers could create stirring music to accompany stirring events. Color changed from a mere novelty to a thing of beauty, so that ancient Israel could be eye-catchingly beautiful—or menacing.

Audiences changed too. Since 1897 they became gradually more secular, less and less familiar with the Bible. The three *Passion* films released in 1897 not only were silent but also had no "titles," the "word cards" used in silent films from 1907 on. Their producers assumed (probably correctly) that the audience would be familiar enough with the story of Jesus that no words were needed. That is certainly not true today in this biblically illiterate world. Yet movies based on the Bible continue to be produced, and Gibson's *Passion of the Christ* proved there is still a vast audience eager to see the Bible on film. Anyone who thought that a Bible movie could not draw crowds as *The Ten Commandments* or *David and Bathsheba* once did was proved to be wrong.

This book is a guide to Bible films—from those crudely made *Passions* of 1897 to the high-tech, professionally packaged *Passion* of 2004 and beyond. It is intended as a reference guide but also as a continuous story, the story of changes in the film medium itself, in audiences, in styles of acting and scriptwriting and directing. The changes in movies based on the Bible reflect in many ways the changes in our culture, both good and bad.

Some definitions are in order: in this book, *Bible film* and *biblical film* both refer to films in which the main plots and characters are drawn from the Bible. Under that broad definition are various categories:

1. Films that stick closely to the words and narrative flow of the Bible. The most extreme example of this is the 2003 movie *The Gospel of John*, in which every word of the Gospel is either narrated or spoken. A reader sitting with the Bible in his lap and watching this film would find nothing omitted (except that "he said," "he replied," and such were not included, for obvious reasons). Not quite as extreme as this is the 1966

Italian film *The Gospel According to Matthew*, which draws almost all its dialogue from Matthew's Gospel but omits several stories and sayings from that Gospel. In other words, the scriptwriter took Matthew's Gospel and did some editing (mostly for purposes of running time). Another example is the 1965 epic *The Greatest Story Ever Told*, where most of the dialogue and story are drawn from the four Gospels. The popular 1912 *From the Manger to the Cross* had all its title cards taken directly from the Gospels. *The Bible . . . In the Beginning* (1966) has dialogue and narration almost word for word from Genesis. With the exception of the last two films, such films have not usually been very popular with moviegoers. They are "too biblical" for a mass audience, and probably the last film would not be popular if released today, considering its King James English.

2. Films that tell a story from the Bible but add characters and situations not included in the Bible. The 1956 blockbuster *The Ten Commandments* is a good example of this, since it presents the story of Moses from the book of Exodus but also adds several subplots, such as the rivalry of Moses with the pharaoh Rameses and his romance with Nefretiri. *King of Kings* (1961) follows the Gospels in presenting the story of Jesus but adds subplots involving the biblical characters Judas and Barabbas. Cecil B. DeMille's *King of Kings* (1927) has most of its dialogue and story taken from the Gospels but adds material relating to the characters Mary Magdalene and Judas. The popular 2004 film *The Passion of the Christ* fits this category also—following the Gospels but adding material about Jesus's mother and Pilate's wife. *David and Bathsheba* follows the David story from 2 Samuel but adds situations involving the two title characters and in some ways condoning their adultery. Some of the most popular (and thus profitable) biblical films belong to this category.

3. Films that take a relatively minor character or story from the Bible and flesh it out with numerous subplots and characters. *Sodom and Gomorrah* (1962), though based on Genesis, is mostly fiction, most of its characters and story being made up. This is true for the many film versions of *Salome*, in which the daughter of Herodias, whose dance leads to the execu-

tion of John the Baptist, is turned into a major character, though her name is not even mentioned in the Gospels. *The Prodigal* (1955) takes Jesus's short parable of the prodigal son and turns it into a full-length film, fleshing out a story in which the main characters are not even named.

4. Films based on novels, plays, or other literature that tell a biblical story but often depart radically from it. The two musical films of 1973, *Godspell* and *Jesus Christ Superstar*, both fit this category, with *Godspell* using some of the words of Matthew's Gospel in a modern setting and *Superstar* using a stark desert setting, which mixes ancient and modern clothing and weapons. Neither movie included a resurrection of Jesus, which many Christians found offensive, since it is a key point of Christian belief. The best example of this category, though, is *The Last Temptation of Christ*, based on a controversial novel. It included incidents from the Bible but radically reinterpreted them, presenting a Jesus similar to the one in the Bible but also markedly different. *The Passover Plot*, based on a controversial book, presents Jesus as a scheming political radical who fakes his death and resurrection. The most extreme example in this category is *The Green Pastures*, based on a play based on a collection of stories in which rural blacks retold stories from the Old Testament. As a group, these films have not been profitable, since they seem to attract neither people of faith nor people of no faith. Producers assume that the draw of these films is not their tie to the Bible but the renown of the literary work they were based on.

I have chosen not to include films in which biblical events and characters are crucial but subsidiary elements in the film's story. The best example of this is the 1959 epic *Ben-Hur*, which, despite its subtitle *A Tale of the Christ*, is really the story of its title character, a Jewish aristocrat who crosses paths with Jesus more than once and is changed by seeing Jesus crucified. *The Robe* (1953) shows Jesus's crucifixion and how it later affects a Roman soldier and his slave. *Barabbas* (1962) begins with the crucifixion and shows its later effect on the life of the title character. Some of the films in this category have been extremely popular. Also popular but not covered in this book are apocalyptic thrillers like *The Omen* and

End of Days, which are basically horror movies in which biblical concepts of the Antichrist and the end of time are worked into a contemporary setting with little relation to the Bible. Some of these have been highly profitable, though it's doubtful that people were drawn to them by any religious impulse. They are thrillers with a few biblical images thrown in for spice. I do devote a little space to a popular film that parodies the Bible, the 1979 comedy *Life of Brian*, set in the time of Jesus (and briefly showing him) but poking fun at religious people and political zealots and even mocking crucifixion.

The subject of this book is *biblical films shown in theaters for paying audiences*. I am not discussing the many biblical films that have been produced by Christian companies that primarily rent them or sell them to churches or individuals. I call these "church films," and I mean them no disrespect, since some of them are well produced (even on a shoestring budget) and, in the divine view of things, many of them are no doubt of much more value than the high-budget films that make their way into the local theater. Their purpose is primarily to minister, not to make a profit. They are intended to strengthen the faith of believers, or to lead to conversions, or both. However, certain "crossover" films will be discussed in this book, since a handful of "church films" did get released in theaters, the most notable being the 1979 film *Jesus*, which had a limited release in theaters (only some in the South and West) but has had a much longer shelf life as a church film. The same is true of *The Gospel of John*, released in 2003. Both of these were produced and funded by Christian-run companies that primarily produce church films. The theatrical release was done in the hope that the profits would be funneled back into producing more church films, but, sadly, neither film did well in theaters.

For many years the silent films *From the Manger to the Cross* and *The King of Kings* were used by missionaries for spreading the gospel.

With some theatrical films, there is a "backward crossover"—that is, a commercial film that made a profit in theaters is later used by Christians in evangelism and missions. This has been the case with *The Passion of the Christ* and, many years ago, the 1912 *From the Manger to the Cross* and the 1927 *King of*

Kings. These films had a common advantage for showing to non-English-speaking audiences: no dialogue in English. *The Passion* was spoken in Aramaic and Latin, with subtitles in English, and subtitles can easily be substituted in other languages. *The King of Kings* and *From the Manger to the Cross* were silent films, and missionaries found it simple to substitute title cards written in another language.

In today's video age, the line between theater movie and made-for-TV movie is very thin, since both categories end up in video format eventually. In this book I have concentrated on theatrical films, since one important factor in the creation and release of these films is this question: *What kind of biblical or semibiblical film will people pay money to see?* A made-for-TV movie is another matter entirely, since those that air on the major networks are entirely free for the watching. A person can tune in for a few minutes, lose interest, and change channels—or stay glued to the tube for the duration and even record it for future viewing. The person watching TV does not invest his time and money in the way he does when seeing a movie in a theater. (Profit *is* involved in these, of course, thanks to the advertisers. If a biblical film gets high ratings, that increases the likelihood that the networks will produce more of such films—and that Hollywood producers may do the same.)

But even though made-for-TV movies and miniseries are not what this book is about, I have chosen to discuss a handful of them, since doing so sheds some light on just what interested audiences at a particular point in time. For example, the 1970s were terrible years for biblical movies in theaters, yet one of the most popular TV miniseries of all time, *Jesus of Nazareth*, aired in 1977. Why was such a fine film, generally loved by all who saw it, including devout Christians, such a hit on television in a time when Hollywood could not seem to produce a worthy biblical film? In the same decade, several other fine biblical films made for TV were aired. Was their popularity due in part to the *lack* of good biblical films in this decade? I think it was, which is why I choose to discuss *Jesus of Nazareth*, and several other made-for-TV films, in the chapter on the 1970s. Movies and television affect each other, the most recent example being a new crop of biblical TV movies that were produced after *The Passion of the Christ* was such a success in theaters.

The Review Process

In preparing to write this book, I watched every biblical film available to me. Sadly, many are not available. Although many of these films are now available in video format, even more are (pardon the choice of words) gone with the wind. Perhaps in some warehouse or attic somewhere sits a canister containing one of the short films made in 1897 and titled *The Passion*. But most of the silent films about the Bible are long gone and may never be recovered. We should consider ourselves fortunate that some very old films—the 1902 *Life and Passion of Jesus Christ* and the 1912 *From the Manger to the Cross*—are available to us today, even if watching a silent film does require some concentration. Some much more recent films have apparently vanished also. I would like to see the 1954 film *The Sins of Jezebel*, if only because it is the only film ever made about one of the Bible's most interesting characters, the wicked queen Jezebel, who is confronted by one of the Bible's most heroic and admirable characters, the prophet Elijah. But this film, like some other unpopular films, has seemingly vanished. One suspects that if it had been a quality film, it might have been preserved somewhere, but who can say? As time passes, it is possible that every film ever made—good or bad—may end up in video format eventually.

For these films that cannot be viewed, I had to rely on reviews and comments by people who did see the film. In most cases we do not even possess the credits listing actors, writers, directors, and so on. For many we only have the title, the year (sometimes approximate), and the country of origin. Needless to say, with this limited data available, this book does not devote many pages to those films. Happily, for some of the most popular films, much data is available about their production, the script, the producers' motivations, choices in casting, and the like. One of the treasures I consulted in writing this book was director Cecil B. DeMille's *Autobiography*, in which he wrote at length about the making of *The Ten Commandments* (two different versions), *Samson and Delilah*, and *The King of Kings*. We are fortunate that the man most identified with the biblical epic was a fount of information about his work. Several other people associated with biblical films—actor Charlton Heston, director-actor John Huston, and some others—also wrote extensively about their works.

I also read reviews of each film in both secular and religious publications. Some of these are quoted in the book, and I think such quotes are appropriate, since many people are swayed by critics, and sometimes critics are right—but not always. Sometimes audiences stay away from a good picture and flock to a bad one—and vice versa. In the final analysis, my reviews of the biblical movies here are not based on what critics said, or how much profit the film made (or didn't), or what the director or star wrote about the film afterward. Each review is based on my own knowledge of the Bible and Christian theology and on viewing each film more than once. At the risk of sounding immodest, my own knowledge of the Bible is probably deeper than that of critics who review films for secular newspapers and magazines. Reading their reviews, one wonders if it ever occurred to them to ask whether the film was faithful to its source—an issue critics always raise when they review a film based on a popular novel or play. Reviews in secular magazines can contain "groaners," statements that betray the reviewer's appalling lack of familiarity with the Bible—such as a review in the well-respected *Time Magazine*, which referred to Jesus appearing to his disciples "after Pentecost" in the 1961 *King of Kings*.[1] (After *Pentecost*? A reviewer who confuses Pentecost with the resurrection is obviously *not* a close reader of the Gospels.)

For the films reviewed in this book, I followed this procedure: I watched the film straight through in one sitting, with no notes or interruptions—in other words, the way one watches a film in a theater. A few days later I watched the film again, this time taking detailed notes and making frequent use of the pause button, often playing back certain scenes several times. Even the most alert viewer misses things the first time around, so the second viewing was very helpful with every film. Some films seem to improve with a second viewing, while in others more flaws become apparent.

In reviewing each film, I give a synopsis of it and try to answer these questions:

- In what ways did the movie reflect the social/religious/political climate of its time?
- What motivated the producers, aside from profit?

- Why were the particular writers chosen? Did they have any ax to grind?
- Did the movie turn a profit? Why or why not?
- How faithful was the movie to the Bible—not only in the details (dialogue, plot) but also in the general spirit of the story and characters being depicted?
- How did religious leaders and groups react to the film before and after its release? How have later Christian and Jewish audiences received the film?
- How did critics in the secular media react?

Accentuating the Positive

Some well-known movie critics typically review a film and give it a "thumbs-up" or "thumbs-down"—in other words, "do see this movie" or "don't see it." In this book I have not made that judgment, since every film I saw, even some of the controversial ones, had some good things along with the bad. The fact is, every movie ever made had some people who loved it—and some who hated it. A fine film like Mel Gibson's *Passion of the Christ* pleased most people who actually saw it—but not all. Some were repulsed by its graphic violence, while others accepted the violence as depicting what actually happened to Christ. And some who saw the movie carried a bias with them, already expecting the violence to be disgusting, while some heard the film was "too Catholic." (Sometimes we see what others tell us to see.) This film, and every other film discussed in this book, had its fans and its critics.

I tried to view every film with an open mind, even the ones like *The Last Temptation of Christ* that so many people found offensive. I frankly can't recommend *Last Temptation*, since it is deeply flawed in many ways, but there are good things in it, and I tried to point these out in my review of the film. Christians may have qualms about paying money to buy or rent a film like this, so I can recommend my own way of dealing with that problem: find a copy at a local library and check it out without investing money in it.

It is easy to nitpick any biblical film. For example, when I saw *Godspell* in 1973 with my mother and aunt, my aunt was bothered that there weren't twelve disciples in the movie. Looking back, I think that was a minor thing, although I'm pleased my aunt knew how many disciples Jesus had (since according to some polls, many churchgoers don't know that). Jesus not being resurrected at the end of the film was a *much* bigger issue than the number of disciples. The same year, I knew people who saw *Jesus Christ Superstar* and complained that the women in Herod's entourage wore bikinis, which surely weren't worn in biblical times. Probably true—but among the many things wrong with *Superstar*, the bikinis weren't the worst. More recently, some evangelicals avoided seeing *The Passion of the Christ* because they heard it was "too Catholic" in giving such a large role to Mary. When I review the film later in this book, I note that Mary does indeed have a large role, but that as an evangelical myself, I did not find that offensive, since love for one's son is not something specifically Catholic, and one of the Gospels does say that Jesus's mother was present at the cross.

Commercial films are not made for Bible scholars, nor for laymen who know the Bible extremely well. That audience would be very small, even assuming such people all went to the theater. Commercial films are made for the masses, and most people paying to see a biblical film in the theater or on video will not know if the film "sticks to the Bible" or not. One of the purposes of this book is to describe how closely each film sticks to the Bible, both in the details and in the general presentation.

The Age-Old Image Problem

It is a universal human trait: we want to make pictures or statues of people or things we love and admire—friends, loved ones, pets, celebrities, heroes. People have been doing this since ancient times. And yet the second of the Ten Commandments strictly forbids making any "graven image"—or, more precisely, it forbids bowing down to any idol, whether it looks like a human, an animal, or whatever. God in the Bible is an invisible spirit, and no man-made object could represent him. If you're familiar with the Old Testament, you know that God's people, the Israelites, frequently disobeyed the command about idols, and many of them bowed down to idols representing other gods. But in one way they were faithful to the commandment: they never did make idols or images of the true God.

The first Christians were Jews, and they kept their prejudice against idols and images. But Christianity spread throughout the Roman Empire, and many of the new converts saw no reason they should not paint pictures or make statues of Christ, the apostles, the heroes of the Old Testament, and so on. If in the past they had honored their statues of Apollo or Zeus or Venus, surely it was right to honor Christ and the saints, right? They saw their paintings and statues not as idols to worship but as visible reminders of Christ and the heroes of the faith.

A new faith arose in the Near East: Islam, which was even more anti-idol than the Jewish religion had been. Muslims conquered many areas that had been formerly Christian. Interacting with Muslims had an interesting effect on Christians: they became even more attached to their pictures and statues of Christ and the saints, if only because the Muslims were so dead set against them. So for many centuries, churches were filled with pictures and statues of people from the Bible, and no one questioned it.

Muslims will not allow any film to be made showing the prophet Muhammad. Interestingly, many Muslim nations also ban certain films dealing with Jesus, considering them blasphemous—for example, *The Last Temptation of Christ*. While Muslims do not make Jesus the center of their faith, they do consider him a holy prophet. It is ironic that Muslim nations are more sensitive about films blaspheming Jesus than supposedly "Christian" nations are.

At the time of the Protestant Reformation in Europe (the 1500s), some Protestants accused Catholics of "idolatry," saying that people were literally worshiping the images in the churches. Many churches stripped themselves of pictures and statues and concentrated on the spoken word of the sermon. But the human desire for visual aids crept back in again. It's an inescapable fact: people of faith like to have visual reminders around them—statues, pictures, crosses, even the familiar fish decal seen on auto bumpers. In a sense, the fish sticker is in the same category as Michelangelo's biblical paintings on the Sistine Chapel in Rome: visual aids to belief and expressions of belief.

Not all the expressions of belief were lifeless images. Through the centuries, the stories of the Bible were told and acted out, sometimes in theaters, sometimes inside the churches themselves. The early Christians had a low opinion of drama, and rightly so, since the stories were often obscene and characters were often the false gods of the pagans. But people have an urge to tell stories by acting them out, so inevitably the Bible was staged. In the Middle Ages the dramas drawn from the Bible were called *mystery plays*, and we possess a few copies of those. Apparently the first ones were reenactments of the stories of Jesus's resurrection. These later became longer and more complex and were known as *passion plays*, chronicling Jesus's arrest, crucifixion, and resurrection. Since Jesus's death and resurrection are at the core of Christian belief, it was natural they would be at the center of Christian drama. Later there were dramas about the birth of Jesus, with visits from the shepherds and wise men. Then other stories from the Old and New Testaments were turned into dramas, often acted out by traveling drama troupes, some of them having their own stages on wheels. Some of the plays added comic elements, and at times church authorities had to rein in the players and remind them that these were sacred stories and that too much buffoonery was not appropriate.

Composers were drawn to the stories as much as authors were. The words of George Frederick Handel's *Messiah* are drawn straight from the Bible, and many of his other works retold biblical stories: *Solomon*, *Israel in Egypt*, *Jephthah*, *Esther*, *Joseph*, and others. For a long time the Bible was considered too sacred to be performed as opera, but the Camille Saint-Saëns opera *Samson and Delilah* broke that tradition, and others followed.

Stage plays, operas, choral music, and works of art were not the only ways of retelling the stories of the Bible, of course. For two thousand years the stories have been read aloud, paraphrased, and commented on by preachers. They have been told and retold in homes, around campfires, anywhere. They have served as the framework of countless biblical novels, some of them huge sellers. They have found their way into countless hymns and other songs. One old hymn is titled "I Love to Tell the Story." It is natural for people of faith to tell the stories—not just in the words of the

Bible itself but also through the words presented in a different form—in songs, sermons, pictures, plays, and films.

When the new medium of film became available, it was inevitable that there would be films about Jesus and other people of the Bible—after all, the Bible was the most-read book in the countries that pioneered motion pictures, including the U.S.

Worth quoting here are some words from the *New York Times* review of the last movie discussed in this book, the 2006 film *The Nativity Story*: "The challenge in producing a movie like this is to find enough conventional movie elements—suspense, realistic characters, convincing dialogue—without selling out the scriptural source."[2]

The Jesus Problem

The first biblical films were about Jesus, and rightly so, since Christians regard him as the Son of God. But presenting the Son of God on-screen presents a huge problem: however he is acted, and whoever is playing him, not every viewer will be pleased. People who have read the Gospels for years have their own ideas of what Jesus was like. So, unfortunately, do people who have never opened a Bible or entered a church. We pick up our ideas about Jesus from the Bible but also from pictures, plays, films, and what I call "the cultural atmosphere," which includes things that everyone "just knows" about Jesus—or thinks they know. Today, for example, when we are constantly told to be "tolerant" and "nonjudgmental," we think of Jesus as a tolerant, peaceful soul, the one who kept the angry crowd from stoning a woman caught in adultery. But people forget that in that episode, Jesus told the woman, "Go and sin no more" (John 8:11 NKJV). That is, he agreed with the would-be stoners that the woman had sinned. Interestingly, in the 1916 silent film *Intolerance* (note the title), the sweet Jesus of the film does not say "Go and sin no more." (The movie was ahead of its time in that respect.) In 2006, NBC ran a short-lived series called *The Book of Daniel*, in which the main character, a minister, actually had conversations with Jesus—represented as a hip, laid-back, totally nonjudgmental character, a Jesus for the twenty-first century but not much like the Jesus of the Bible who took a whip and ran the money changers out of the temple

What film Jesus could satisfy everyone? Ted Neeley as Jesus in the 1973 *Jesus Christ Superstar* exuded warmth and humanity but not much else.

court and who could lash out with harsh words against the Jewish religious establishment.

The film Jesuses are an interesting group. In the 1927 film *The King of Kings*, he was a sweet-faced, compassionate type (played by a man over fifty) but somehow lacking in fire. In *The Passion of the Christ* he was the suffering servant of God, agonizing spiritually before his arrest, physically afterward, fully human in every way—but, in this film, not given much opportunity to show any emotion but sorrow. In *The Greatest Story Ever Told* he had dignity and exuded power, but he didn't seem to suffer much on the cross. Max Von Sydow, who played Jesus in that film, said that it was a "wonderful failure" because no film could portray Jesus in a way that would satisfy most audiences. In the 1961 *King of Kings* he seemed full of youthful vigor and "star power"—but, again, not much of a sufferer at the end. In *Godspell* he exuded warmth and joy and good humor, seeming to be a man one would be pleased to have dinner with but somehow not the type who could be the Son of God. In *Jesus Christ Superstar* he showed righteous anger at the Jewish authorities and frustration at his thickheaded disciples, as the Jesus of the Gospels did—yet he seemed too self-absorbed to be mankind's Savior. In *The Last Temptation of Christ*, he seemed so full of doubt about himself and about God that we marvel anyone would have followed him—even though he was human in an appealing way. The Jesuses of *The Gospel According to Matthew* and *The Gospel of John* both have fire in them, acting with a sense of urgency, not afraid to confront the establishment—even if it means getting killed, which they sometimes seem to be begging for.

None of these screen Jesuses is quite the Jesus of the Bible—or even the Jesus of the popular imagination. Each of them has some appealing qualities, and each has something in common with the Jesus of the Gospels. But none is "just right" for the obvious reason: none of them is the real Jesus. Whether any writer or actor can give us that Jesus is doubtful. There is some mysterious quality in the Jesus of the Bible, something that can't be captured in any picture, statue, play, or film—a quality that made people who knew him personally think that he was God in the flesh. My personal favorite of the screen Jesuses is the one played by Robert Powell in the TV miniseries *Jesus of Nazareth*. Given the long running time of that program, we saw Jesus running the gamut of emotions found in Scripture. And yet even that Jesus isn't quite right, though many people loved the miniseries.

> "I spent sleepless nights trying to find a way to deal with the figure of Christ. It was a frightening thing when all the great painters of twenty centuries have painted events you have to deal with, events in the life of the best-known man who ever lived. Everyone already has his own concept of him. I wanted to be reverent, and yet realistic. Crucifixion is a bloody, awful, horrible thing, and a man does not go through it with a benign expression on his face."[3]
> —William Wyler, on directing *Ben-Hur*

That is as it should be. The real Jesus, the one millions of people think of as Savior and Lord, couldn't possibly be captured on film. Every movie about Jesus, and every actor playing Jesus, is a failure in some way. But that is not to say all the efforts were wrong or misguided. With all their inadequacies, the actors playing Christ

in films serve to remind us that Christ was fully human as well
as fully divine.

The Anti-Semitism Problem

Filmmakers discovered very early that making a film about the
trial and crucifixion of Jesus involved a problem: it would offend
Jews. Why? Because even though it was technically the Romans
who crucified Jesus, he was condemned by his own people, the
Jews—or at least by their religious leaders. All four Gospels record that Jesus was brought before the high priest, Caiaphas,
and condemned as a blasphemer deserving of death. Jesus was
taken to Pilate, the Roman governor, because the Jews could not
execute a man themselves. Historians tell us that Pontius Pilate
was no saint and that he had been very cruel to the Jews at times.
But the Gospels show that in the case of Jesus, Pilate wasn't eager
to condemn him to death because he saw Jesus was an innocent
man, despised and envied by the priests because of his popularity
with the common people. The Romans, for all their faults, liked
to think of themselves as fair-minded, and Pilate had no desire to
be pushed around by the priests. Still, he caved in to pressure, for
the priests threatened that if he released Jesus, he was no "friend
of Caesar," and every Roman official had to stay in Caesar's good
graces. In effect, Pilate and the priests had something in common:
they wished to get rid of Jesus to hold on to their jobs.

Matthew's Gospel states that Pilate washed his hands in front
of the crowd, saying, "I am innocent of this man's blood. . . . It
is your responsibility" (27:24). Then "All the people answered,
'Let his blood be on us and on our children!'" (v. 25). What did
Matthew mean by "all the people"? Didn't Jesus have admirers
among the people? But Matthew 27:20 states that the chief priests
had persuaded the crowd to ask for Jesus's death. Mobs can be
amazingly fickle, and probably some of the same people who
had shouted "Hosanna!" a few days earlier as Jesus rode into Jerusalem could have been persuaded (by peer pressure) to shout
"Let him be crucified!" An individual human may be rational, but
a mob rarely is.

"Let his blood be on us and on our children"—these words, according to some Jewish spokesmen, have led to brutal persecution

of Jews through the ages. Supposedly, Christians have thought of Jews as "Christ-killers" who are accursed because of what their ancestors said: "Let his blood be on us and on our children." Whether this verse ever really led to persecution of Jews is difficult to prove. Certainly the Old Testament shows that anti-Semitism had existed centuries before the time of Jesus. Christian persecution of Jews is truly shameful, but Jews have faced persecution in many cultures that were not Christian, and certainly the greatest persecutor of all, Adolf Hitler, was no true Christian.

At any rate, the accusation that the Gospels are anti-Semitic does not hold water. Jesus was a Jew, as were his twelve disciples, and the Gospels (with the exception of Luke) were written by Jews. Another Jew, Paul, wrote a huge chunk of the New Testament. It was not the Jews as a group that the Gospels condemned but the narrow-minded priests and officials who saw Jesus not as the Messiah but as a troublemaker whose followers might stir up trouble and bring down the wrath of Rome on the temple bureaucracy. In John's Gospel one of the priests says, "If we let him go on like this, everyone will believe in him, and then the Romans will come and take away both our place and our nation" (11:48). It is very clear that they were much more concerned about "our place" than "our nation"—and giving no thought at all to what God might think of their deeds. Jesus understood that the Jewish leaders would not tolerate him for long, and he warned his disciples that he would die in Jerusalem (see Matt. 16:21; 20:18). Time-serving bureaucrats generally are not spiritual people, and throughout history they have opposed every person who had enough charisma to impress the crowds. (Anyone who has ever worked in the headquarters of a religious denomination, as I have, knows that many "religious professionals" are pretty unspiritual, regarding religion as their job, not the spirit of their lives.) So eager were the priests to be rid of Jesus that they assured Pilate that "We have no king but Caesar" (John 19:15)—shocking words, coming from men who supposedly believed God was their true king and who had no reason to bow down to Rome's Caesar. Non-Christian writings from this period of history do not give a favorable picture of the chief priests, so their depiction in the Gospels is easy to believe. Many Jewish writers of the same period denounced the corruption of the priestly families in Jerusalem.

At one point in Jesus's trial before Pilate, Jesus says to the governor, "He who delivered me over to you has the greater sin" (John 19:11 ESV). The "he" here might be Judas but probably is Caiaphas, since Caiaphas engineered the arrest and urged the death penalty. But Caiaphas isn't getting all the blame here. Jesus tells Pilate that Caiaphas's sin is "greater" than Pilate's—meaning Pilate is not off the hook, morally speaking. Pilate wants to release Jesus, but he caves in to the priests' words, "If you release this man, you are not Caesar's friend" (John 19:12 ESV). You might say that both the priests and Pilate had to be rid of Jesus for fear of losing their jobs. Both parties commit the sin of sacrificing an innocent man to their own desire to hang on to their positions. That is not a particularly Jewish sin but rather a human one, seen throughout history.

> Most movies dealing with the crucifixion of Jesus have been accused of being anti-Semitic.

In summary: The Gospels are not anti-Semitic. Any movie that truly bases its script on the Gospels cannot be anti-Semitic either. But every movie showing the trial of Jesus inevitably provokes the charge of anti-Semitism. Cecil B. DeMille faced this in 1927 with his film *The King of Kings*. In the film, Caiaphas is as spiritually blind as he is in the Gospels, but DeMille added a scene in which Caiaphas prays to God and admits that he alone is responsible for the death of Jesus—an episode not in the Gospels, but a scene DeMille hoped would pacify Jewish critics by showing that one man, Caiaphas, bore the responsibility, not the Jews as a whole. DeMille's film was a runaway success, but it still irked him that after all his precaution with the script, many Jews claimed the film was anti-Semitic.

Mel Gibson faced the same charges when *The Passion of the Christ* was released in 2004, although, as with DeMille's film, the criticisms seemed to have no effect on the film's profits. Even the clearheaded thinker and columnist Charles Krauthammer claimed he was offended by *The Passion* because of its anti-Semitism. However, Jewish film critic and radio host Michael Medved loved the film and encouraged all his listeners, whatever their beliefs, to see it. Perhaps Krauthammer failed to notice that the most bloodthirsty, cruel people in *The Passion* are the Roman soldiers who show sadistic glee in beating and crucifying Jesus.

In the 1970s *Jesus Christ Superstar* provoked cries of anti-Semitism, and its distributor, Universal, felt compelled to issue a statement defending the film. The 1961 MGM epic *King of Kings* deliberately omitted Jesus's trial before Caiaphas, so it faced few accusations of anti-Semitism. The 1977 TV miniseries *Jesus of Nazareth* fended off the accusations by having some members of the Jewish council rise in defense of Jesus and also by having a fictional character, Zerah, be the prime mover in arresting and crucifying Jesus.

The simple truth is, it is extremely unlikely that any play or film has ever led to persecution of Jews. But it is also true that fear of being accused of anti-Semitism is a factor when the story of Jesus's trial is filmed.

Choices of Characters

Below is a list of biblical characters and the number of films made about them. The numbers in parentheses are the totals with made-for-TV films included. The list does not include films in which a particular character is shown briefly in a minor role. The list has many surprises.

Jesus Christ, 39 (42)	Sodom and Gomorrah, 2
David, 10 (12)	Daniel, 2
Salome / John the Baptist, 9	Jephthah, 2
Joseph (Old Testament), 8 (10)	Barabbas, 2
Samson, 6 (8)	Jacob, (2)
Moses, 5 (8)	The creation, 1 (2)
Solomon, 5 (6)	Paul, 1 (4)
Esther, 3 (4)	Peter, (2)
Judith (Apocrypha), 4	Jonah, 1
The prodigal son, 4	Ruth, 1
Noah and the flood, 3 (5)	Elijah and Jezebel, 1
Adam and Eve, 3	Maccabees (Apocrypha), 1
Cain, 3	Jeremiah, (1)
Abraham, 2 (3)	The book of Revelation, (1)

Naturally, Jesus Christ has been the main character in the most films. And naturally the second most common biblical character on film is David, the Old Testament character whose stories take up the most space, with his long and colorful life set out in great detail in 1 and 2 Samuel, 1 Kings, and 1 Chronicles, not to mention the many psalms that are attributed to him. The problem with films about David is that his life was so long and colorful that the whole saga cannot be packed into a film of normal length. The 1985 film *King David* tried to do that and failed. This is why some films chose to focus on a few incidents—his killing of the giant Goliath, his adultery with Bathsheba, the rebellion led by his son Absalom, or others.

The third position may surprise some people: Salome, the daughter of Herodias, mentioned in the Gospels as being the cause of the beheading of John the Baptist. This woman is not even named in the Bible (we know her name from the writings of the Jewish historian Josephus), yet there are more films about her than about several important characters of the Old and New Testaments. The reason for so many films about Salome is not her brief appearance in the Bible but rather her being the subject of a popular play by Oscar Wilde and later an opera by Richard Strauss (remembered for its "Dance of the Seven Veils"). However, every film about Salome is also a film about John the Baptist, who definitely *is* an important character in the Bible, since he was a great prophet and the man who baptized Jesus.

Following Salome, the next position is Joseph of the book of Genesis, whose timeless story of being a spoiled son sold into slavery by his jealous brothers shows a man in terrible circumstances rising to power and finally saving and forgiving the brothers who wronged him. It is a touching and inspiring story (plus the setting in Egypt gives it great visual appeal). But the man holding the next position is hardly inspiring: Samson, the long-haired Hebrew muscleman with a weakness for women. He is hardly a spiritual role model, yet his saga—with violence, lust, and betrayal—seems made for the screen. This explains why there are more films about him (and the treacherous Delilah) than about Moses, the great lawgiver of Israel, who led the Hebrew slaves out of Egypt. (Moses, however, is the focus of one of the most watched biblical movies ever, *The Ten Commandments*.) After Moses there is Solomon, famed for his wisdom and for building the temple in Jerusalem—two things that hardly make for a good film. Rather, the movies about Solomon inevitably revolve around his meeting with the queen of Sheba, told in one chapter of 1 Kings. But that one chapter has been expanded into several films, all of them showing that Solomon had a fling (and in some cases also a child) with the queen. As with the Samson films, these are hardly inspiring.

The list is interesting because of what it reveals about film producers— and audiences also. Producers want to create a film that has "name recognition." People have heard of Jesus, of course, and also Samson and Moses and Noah, and they have at least a vague idea of what those characters were like. But they may know little about the prophet Elijah, perhaps not even his name, which explains why this list includes only one film dealing with the man who was considered the greatest prophet in the Old Testament, the man whom Jews still "set a place for" at their Passover meals. Somehow the story of this fiery prophet, his foe the wicked queen Jezebel, his confrontation with the prophets of Baal, and his miraculous ascent into heaven—none of this has yet grabbed the attention of film producers. Even more noteworthy is that the greatest man in the New Testament (after Jesus, that is), the apostle Paul, has never been the subject of a theatrical movie in the U.S. Two TV movies have devoted much time to Paul, but why have film producers neglected this man who wrote a huge chunk of the New Testament and led an amazing life—persecuting

> "There was a picture I wanted to make about a dynamic, colorful personality who changed history—St. Paul, the savage persecutor of early Christians, who turned right around and became Christ's first and greatest missionary and His thirteenth apostle."[4] So wrote Frank Capra, director of such movie classics as *It's a Wonderful Life* and *Mr. Deeds Goes to Town.* Capra thought actor James Cagney could've played the role of Paul to a tee, but after working with Frank Sinatra on one movie, Capra thought Sinatra could do it also. When Capra let it slip that he was considering Sinatra for the role of one of the great saints of the Bible, newspaper columns reported it, and Capra received tons of indignant letters. Capra never did direct a movie about Paul.

Christians, becoming one, taking the gospel to foreign lands, and surviving a stoning, a flogging, a shipwreck, and being taken as a prisoner to Rome? The one theatrical film about this amazing man was made in Italy in 1909.

A handful of films have been made about Abraham, a man whom both Jews and Muslims regard as their physical and spiritual ancestor and who is regarded by Christians as a great role model of faith. But except for the incident of the near-sacrifice of his son Isaac, his story has been neglected. So has the miracle-filled story of Elisha, friend and protégé of the prophet Elijah. Several of the leaders in the book of Judges are interesting, but except for Samson (and a couple of films about Jephthah), they have been ignored. And yet Judith, a character from the Apocrypha, has been the subject of four films—even though most Bibles do not even contain the book of Judith. But her story seems made for filming: an attractive woman feigns love for an enemy general, then beheads him, while her people rout his army. It is not an inspiring or deeply spiritual story, but it is one that attracted producers, who seem drawn to Samson and Delilah or Solomon and the queen of Sheba, with their exotic settings, foreign women, and suggestions of sex. In fact, Cecil B. DeMille claimed that he sold his studio the idea of doing *Samson and Delilah* by presenting it not as a biblical story but as a story of lust and betrayal. Clearly, importance in the Bible is not the criterion for making films. If it was, the list would look something like this:

Jesus
Paul
Moses
David
Abraham
Elijah
Peter
Elisha
Gideon

The movie industry has the habit of imitating itself. If a certain story was made into a successful film, inevitably it will be remade. We see the pattern starting with the first biblical movies ever made—first several about Jesus (beginning in 1897), then Salome (1902), Samson (1903), Joseph (1904), Moses (1907), David (1908), and Solomon (1909). Thus in the first twelve years of commercial films, the main subjects were already chosen. If a film failed, as the Italian-made 1909 movie about Paul did, chances are producers would shy away from the subject.

1

GRAINY, SILENT BEGINNINGS

From One-Reelers to Feature Length

O ur subject is biblical movies, but in order to cover that subject, we need to take a quick look at how filmmaking began.

Who invented motion pictures? Several people were involved, but much of the credit goes to American inventor Thomas Edison. He was an amazing man, but not one with much ability to see into the future, for he had no idea that film would become such a powerful force in the world. Edison understood the physical phenomenon that makes films possible: *persistence of vision*. A film consists of thousands of still images run in sequence, but the brain runs all the images together, so we see fluid motion, not individual frames. He invented the kinetoscope, which a person looked into to view moving images of a man walking, a horse running, or the like. It sounds boring to us, but remember that in the late 1800s, this was an amazing novelty. But Edison had so little ambition for his kinetoscope that when he filed the patent in 1891, he didn't bother to

A very thoughtful-looking Thomas Edison (1847–1931), who more than any other individual was responsible for the development of motion pictures.

pay the additional $150 that would have granted him international copyright. He was soon to regret this, for inventors in Europe would use and refine his invention without having to pay him a penny.

The first kinetoscope parlor opened on Broadway in New York in April 1894. The kinetoscope was basically a peep show, with a coin dropped in a slot providing about fifteen seconds of image. Edison didn't think a projected image would catch on. But in France, the Lumière brothers Louis and Auguste disagreed. They patented their Cinématographe in 1895. The first time an audience paid to see projected moving images is said to be December 28, 1895, in Paris, courtesy of the Lumière brothers, who exhibited a twenty-minute program consisting of ten brief films, all showing everyday occurrences. (However, some sources say the first projection of a motion picture for a paying audience was on November 1, 1895, in Berlin, Germany.) On April 23, 1896, Edison gave the U.S. its first public showing of a projected motion picture at Koster and Bial's Music Hall in New York.

These early movies were one part of a vaudeville show—that is, people were paying the admission price not just to see the short film but to see various live acts as well. Some wax museums and traveling carnivals also showed films. The very earliest movies made by Edison and others were fifty feet in length, running less than a minute. By 1895, when the Lumière brothers began projecting them, a reel was about one thousand feet. The novelty value of seeing movement was all that mattered at first—parades, street scenes, trains moving, and so on. Audiences tired of this before long, so producers began casting around for something more ambitious, even telling a story, although a short one.

Enter the Bible

At this point the history of biblical films begins. In 1897 at least three different movies, all titled *The Passion*, were released:

two were produced in France (one from the pioneering Lumière brothers), one in Austria. We know that one of the French films ran about five minutes, and probably the others did also. The films were silent and in black and white, of course. They did not have titles, the word cards inserted between scenes of a film. (These were not introduced until 1907.) We have no copies of these three films, alas, but we can assume they showed the crucifixion of Jesus and included some form of movement, since people weren't paying money to look at still images.

On January 30, 1898, the first American biblical film was shown. It was titled *The Passion Play* and produced by the R. G. Hollaman company of New York. Hollaman, born in Britain, ran the Eden Musee, which had been a wax museum, then a music hall, then a motion picture theater. His film was a three-reeler, directed by L. J. Vincent. It was the first biblical movie to list cast members: Frank Russell as Jesus, Frank Gaylor as Judas, Fred Strong as Pilate. Though it had no titles, a narrator spoke at each showing. It was nineteen minutes long, with twenty-three scenes. Hollaman ran it twice daily for three months, and clergy generally praised it highly. Supposedly some fragments of the film are kept in the George Eastman Archives in Rochester, New York.

> Many film historians think the Hollaman company's 1898 *Passion Play* may have been the first attempt to tell a story on film.

In 1898 another film titled *The Passion* was released, directed by Sigmund Lubin and filmed in Philadelphia. The following year, French director Georges Méliès, a former magician himself and known for his venturing into "special effects," directed *Le Christ marchant sur les flots* (*Christ Walking on the Water*), not only the first special-effects biblical movie but also the first not on the passion theme.

Let's pause here to ask an obvious question: why was Jesus's passion—his trial, flogging, and crucifixion—the first biblical story to be filmed? The answer is obvious enough: it is the most important story in the Bible, since the sacrifice of the innocent Son of God is, Christians believe, the act that saves sinners and reconciles them to God. Aside from that, Jesus's crucifixion was familiar to millions of people, whether they had ever read the Bible or not. Crucifixion makes for an interesting visual image, though we can safely assume that these passion films of the late 1890s were nowhere near as realistic as Mel Gibson's 2004 *Passion of the Christ*. Gibson's film ended in the right way: Jesus is raised from the dead, which for Christians is the most important part of the story. Since these early passion films no longer exist, we don't know if they ended with Jesus's resurrection or not, though they probably did.

Let's ask another important question at this point: what was the motive of these early filmmakers in releasing films about Jesus? One obvious answer: money. Lots of people identified themselves as Christians, and even those who did not were reasonably familiar with the story of Jesus—so much so that even without spoken dialogue or title cards projected on the screen, the story could be told with the audience mentally filling in the words from the Bible. (Mel Gibson was tempted to release *The Passion of the Christ* with no subtitles, in the hope that the audiences of 2004 would also be able to follow the story without words. Wisely, he did not do so. The audiences of 2004 were not nearly so familiar with the Bible as the people in the 1890s were.)

Aside from the profit motive, we can assume those early filmmakers liked the challenge of presenting a story set in ancient times, attempting to give the audience sets and costumes that looked like the ancient world—or at least what people *thought* the ancient world looked like. Whether the producers had any spiritual motivation for the films is anybody's guess. In the divine scheme of things, a film could serve a spiritual purpose even if its producers and actors were just doing a job.

Oddly, the next biblical film would not be about Christ but about a woman who would be the subject of numerous biblical films: Salome, the daughter of Herodias, whose dancing pleased her stepfather, Herod, so much that he offered to give her whatever she asked. Prompted by her mother, she asked for the head of the imprisoned prophet John the Baptist. Salome is not even named in the Bible (where she is simply called the "daughter of Herodias"), but her name became famous because of a play about her written by Oscar Wilde. Though a very minor character, Salome is the most-filmed woman of the Bible, with at least ten films of that name in the silent era, made in Italy, France, Germany, the UK, and the U.S. The German film *Salome*, directed by Oskar Messter, was released in 1902.

But a much more important biblical film was released in 1902, one that happens to be, so far, the oldest biblical film available on video: *La vie et la passion de Jesus Christ, notre Sauveur* (*The Life and Passion of Jesus Christ, Our Savior*). Directed by Ferdinand Zecca for the Pathé brothers company of France, the film had no titles at all. It was simply assumed that the audience in 1902 was familiar enough with the Bible—or at least with the story of Jesus—that no words were needed. It opens with the Annunciation: Mary enters carrying a water jug and kneels in prayer. A winged angel appears, and we gather from his hand motions he is telling her she is to bear the child Jesus. In the next scene, Joseph and Mary arrive in Bethlehem, the street all abustle with people. They arrive on foot, not on donkey. Joseph is turned away by the innkeepers. Next we see shepherds in the fields, with painted clouds overhead. Sheep are in a pen, and one shepherd awakes to see a golden star in the heavens. (The prints of the film were actually tinted by hand to show certain colors.) A gold-winged female angel appears, then several more, some of them child angels, one carrying a banner with the Latin words *Gloria in excelsis Deo*—Glory to God in the highest.

> A great boost to the young film industry was the stage actors' strike of 1900. Theater owners had to show films in order to lure audiences in.

Next, wise men with a caravan enter, the three on camels. In Bethlehem, Mary and Joseph kneel and pray over the infant Jesus in the manger, the gold star over them. The donkey and cow munching on hay add an interesting touch to the scene. The wise men's caravan arrives at the stable. Mary lifts up the baby and shows it to them. In the next scene soldiers with swords enter, pursuing women carrying infants. Some of the women struggle. Gold-winged angels play harps over the infant Jesus. Joseph lies down to sleep and an angel appears, telling him to flee with the child to Egypt. They leave on a donkey, and seconds later the soldiers arrive. The family stops on the road to rest, and the soldiers show up, but an angel in armor drives them off with a sword. (This angel protector isn't mentioned in the Bible, but it does add a nice touch of drama to the scene.) Fleeing to Egypt, the family pauses to rest in front of the sphinx, with pyramids in the background.

Back in Nazareth, Joseph chops down a tree while the boy Jesus helps. The scene of the three doing their daily chores is rather nice. In the next scene, the boy Jesus chats with the teachers of the law. Joseph and Mary arrive, obviously distressed. John the Baptist preaches by the river. Jesus arrives and is baptized (by sprinkling), and a golden dove appears over his head. At the wedding at Cana, Jesus turns the water into wine. All the people are amazed. In the next scene, a long-haired Mary Magdalene enters while Jesus is at supper. She kneels at Jesus's feet. In the next scene, Jesus goes to a well, where he talks with the Samaritan woman. Some of the disciples arrive and chide him for talking with her. In the next scene, various cripples present themselves for healing. Jairus speaks to Jesus, then learns his daughter is dead, but Jesus goes to the house and raises her. Next we see a storm-tossed sea, and Jesus literally rises up from the water and walks, ghostlike. The next scene is the miraculous catch of fish by the disciples. Jesus goes to their boat—walking on the water—and tells them to lower their net, which is quickly filled with fish. Next the two sisters weep at the tomb of Lazarus. Jesus arrives and has men move the stone away. Lazarus raises up at Jesus's command.

Next is the transfiguration: Jesus and three disciples go to a hill. A sort of halo envelops Jesus, and his clothes become dazzling white, with Moses and Elijah speaking with him. Next he enters Jerusalem on a donkey as people wave palm branches and throw down their garments. Jesus enters the temple court and drives the money changers out—not with a whip but with his hands (which looks a bit silly, frankly, as if he were slapping someone for being late for dinner). The Last Supper appears like most paintings of it. Jesus announces that one disciple will betray him, and they are distressed. Judas leaves to do his dirty work. In Gethsemane, Jesus prays and appears to be in real agony. A winged angel appears to comfort him. Judas enters and kisses Jesus. Peter draws a sword, but Jesus stops him. Jesus is brought before Caiaphas. (Apparently at this point in history, film studios were not afraid of being accused of anti-Semitism, so showing the Jewish high priest as a villain was all right.) In the courtyard outside, Peter denies Jesus. Jesus is brought before Pilate. He is stripped to the waist while four bare-chested soldiers flog him; then the crown of thorns is pressed onto his head. Pilate washes his hands.

Mary and Mary Magdalene are present at the cross, along with John. There is thunder and lightning. After the burial, the Roman soldiers doze away at the tomb, which is a stone sarcophagus. Four angels appear and lift the lid off it. Jesus rises up (as if standing on a small elevator), to the astonishment of the soldiers. The women arrive at the tomb and an angel speaks to them. Jesus blesses the disciples and ascends into heaven, surrounded by a gold halo and ring of cloud. We see him in heaven, surrounded by angels.

As with almost all of the earliest films, there are no close-ups, so it is as if we were watching a stage play, and the camera hardly moves. Without close-ups to communicate much emotion, the actors have to gesture very broadly. This is an interesting film to watch today, because in spite of being silent and in spite of having costumes and painted sets that look like some local church's play, the story is still appealing—maybe because the story of Jesus is sublime even without spoken words, close-ups, or special effects. Jesus ascending to heaven on a wooden, painted cloud may sound silly, but it is actually rather charming, and it certainly impressed the original viewers.

We aren't certain how long the original 1902 film ran. In 1905 Pathé released an expanded version of the film with some new scenes, bringing it to a running time of forty-four minutes, which is what today's video version has. For 1905, that was a *long* film. Films had lengthened considerably since the early days of fifteen seconds of motion in a peep show.

In 1902 or 1903, the Pathé brothers released *Samson and Delilah*, which was also directed by Ferdinand Zecca. It ran about fifteen minutes, and as far as we know, it was the first movie based on the Old Testament. As with Salome, the Samson story would be filmed several times in the future. Filmmakers early on began the pattern of refilming a profitable story. Unfortunately, we have no idea just how much of a connected story these early films told, since they no longer exist.

The Great Train Robbery, produced in 1903 by Edison's company, ran about ten minutes and had fourteen scenes—all long shots, except the close-up of the gang leader firing point-blank at the audience. This movie is often considered the first narrative on film. It wasn't, but its popularity did make it a breakthrough in the evolution of editing and storytelling. From this point on, films would get gradually longer and their stories more involved.

The following year, 1904, the second Old Testament film was released in France, *Joseph vendu par ses freres* (*Joseph Sold by His Brothers*). As with stories of Jesus's passion, Salome, and Samson and Delilah, the Joseph story would be retold many times in future film. The Joseph story seems made for film, having an exotic setting (ancient Egypt) and the deep emotion of a man being sold by his brothers as a slave, rising to high office, and then, years later, forgiving his brothers and saving them from a famine.

A dramatic change in movie exhibition came in 1905, when John Harris and Harry Davis of Pittsburgh turned an old storeroom into a ninety-two seat auditorium and charged a nickel admission, leading to the term *nickelodeon*. The catchy name, the price, plus the popularity of *The Great Train Robbery* and other films with a story resulted in the creation of 8,000 nickelodeons within four years. But for several more years, the brief movies were just one element in a vaudeville show built around live acts.

In 1906 a French film, *La vie du Christ* (*The Life of Christ*), was released. We can assume from its title that it must have covered other events besides Jesus's crucifixion. In the same year, from Italy, came *Guiditta e Oloferne* (*Judith and Holofernes*), based on the book of Judith in the Apocrypha. Most Protestants are probably not even aware of the Judith story, but it was a natural for film, telling the story of a beautiful and virtuous Jewish widow who saves her city by seducing the Assyrian general Holofernes and then beheading him. It would be filmed several more times in the future.

In 1907 an important innovation was introduced: titles. For the first time, audiences saw words projected on the screen to help explain the action and provide dialogue. This would allow films to become longer and stories more complex. In this same year, another French-produced *Samson* premiered. Also in that year, France released *Moses et l'Exode de l'Egypt* (*Moses and the Exodus from Egypt*). Moses is the most important character in the Old Testament, and God's deliverance of the Hebrew slaves from Egypt is considered the supreme event of the Old Testament. Several more versions of the Moses story would be filmed in the future, notably one of the most popular biblical films ever, the 1956 epic *The Ten Commandments*.

For the next couple of years, the U.S. would be the source of biblical films. The Kalem company released *Jerusalem in the Time of Christ* in 1908. In the same year there was another *Salome*, starring the noted actress Florence Lawrence and directed by J. Stuart Blackton, who would go on to direct several more biblical films.

In 1908 the U.S.-made *David and Goliath* was released, marking the first film telling of the colorful life of David. This was directed by Sidney Olcott, who would go on to direct other biblical films. In 1909 the Vitagraph company released *The Life of Moses*, featuring a parting of the Red Sea that cost $10,000—a huge sum in those days. It was done in five installments, one reel per week, on the assumption audiences could not sit through something longer than fifteen minutes or so. (Some time later, it was released as one film.) It was directed by J. Stuart Blackton, who had directed two other biblical films released that year, *The Way of the Cross* and *The Judgment of Solomon*, the first film telling the story of the famous King Solomon. (We can assume from its title that the film related the story of 1 Kings 3, in which Solomon shows his wisdom in deciding who was the true mother of an infant.) Also in 1909 Vitagraph released *Jephthah's Daughter*, telling the tragic tale of the Israelite judge Jephthah, who made a rash vow to God resulting in the sacrifice of his young daughter (see Judges 11). The first screen telling of the Christmas story was released in 1909, an American film titled *The Star of Bethlehem*. The David story got another telling that year in *Saul and David*. And for the first time, the second most important person in the New Testament, the apostle Paul, was featured in the Italian film *San Paolo* (*St. Paul*).

> Florence Lawrence was one of the first real "stars" of films, and she set a precedent of glamorous women playing the role of the biblical Salome.

While 1909 was a banner year for American-made biblical films, 1910 saw a wave of French-made films. Louis Feuillade directed two of them: *Esther*, the first film telling of the story set in ancient Persia, and *Le festin de Belshazar* (*Belshazzar's Feast*), based on the book of Daniel's story of the Babylonian ruler Belshazzar being conquered by the Persians. (Presumably this film had the episode of a disembodied hand writing words of doom on the palace wall.) In the same year, both France and Britain released versions of the Salome story. The British film is notable because the UK has released very few films based on the Bible—in fact, a grand total of three. Due partly to law, partly to tradition, the British have been reluctant to depict biblical characters—especially Jesus—in plays, operas, or films, regarding it as blasphemous. (It is somewhat ironic that one of the best film Jesuses, Robert Powell of *Jesus of Nazareth*, was English.)

In 1911 the U.S. studio Vitagraph released *Cain and Abel* and *The Deluge* (about Noah and the flood), from France came *Jesus of Nazareth*, and Italy produced *I Maccabei*, released in English as *The Maccabees* and based on the Apocrypha. In 1912 Italy released *David* and *Herod the Great*. But the most important biblical film of that year was *From the Manger to the Cross*, which will be discussed in detail later in chapter 2.

The listing of these biblical films may give the impression that movie producers either were very religious or found biblical films very profitable. But in fact, what was going on in these years was simply a huge volume of new films being released. The days of the thirty-second peep show were long past, and people were flocking to the movie theaters in droves. Since all the films were silent, films were especially popular with the new waves of immigrants, many of whom knew little English.

Within a few short years of its birth, the cinema had already supplanted live theater and the novel as the primary way people experienced the art of storytelling. Born at the end of the nineteenth century, film would be the great storytelling medium of the twentieth century and beyond.

Building Babylon in California

We'll pause here to look at another important immigration that had taken place: the American film industry, which began in the Northeast, had moved to California—specifically, to a place called Hollywood. Ironically, Hollywood began as a religious settlement, founded in 1887 by devout Methodists named Horace and Daeida Wilcox, who hoped to make it sin-free. Incorporated as a city in 1903, it banned not only slaughterhouses and oil prospecting but also liquor sales and (ironically) movie houses. But a shortage of water forced it to incorporate with Los Angeles in 1910 and lose its autonomy and religious character. Despite the landslides, earthquakes, and Santa Ana winds, the climate is mostly benign and predictable. It also offers a wide range of scenery within a short distance (mountains, desert, ocean), making it ideal for filming outdoors, so beginning in about 1907, filmmakers set up shop in the area. The natives did not like these new movie people, and in 1913 over ten thousand Los Angeles citizens signed a petition to ban moviemaking within the city. Labeling themselves Conscientious Citizens, they claimed the movies would lead to immorality. The petition went nowhere, but the immorality came to stay.

Historian Paul Johnson has stated that "movies were the product of a marriage between California and Ashkenazi Jews."[1] (The Ashkenazi Jews were those of Germany and eastern Europe, many of them speaking Yiddish when they arrived in the U.S.) Many of the new Jewish immigrants had earned their fortunes in the New York entertainment industry, where Jews owned many of the nickelodeons patronized by the urban working class, particularly new immigrants who knew no English. They eventually moved to California with its more predictable weather and lenient tax laws.

Carl Laemmle, first of the Jewish movie tycoons, moved his Universal Studios from New York to California in 1912. Laemmle was typical of the Jewish moguls: large family, poor, eastern European. He had beavered away at odd jobs until somehow getting hooked into the nickelodeon business. And other movie moguls fit this pattern: Louis B. Mayer, Sam Goldwyn, Harry Cohn, Jesse Lasky, Adolph Zukor, Joseph Schenk. Zukor loved America, speaking for them all when he said, "I arrived from Hungary an orphan boy of sixteen with a few dollars sewn inside my vest. I was thrilled to breathe the fresh, strong air of freedom, and America has been good to me."

America was good to the movie industry in general. By 1920 there were 100,000 people in the Los Angeles area involved in movie production, grossing a billion dollars a year. Producers, directors, and stars could live like emperors. Building a palatial home in Beverly Hills, actress Gloria Swanson announced, "I will be every inch and every moment a star." These newly rich tried to outdo each other in putting their wealth on display.

Many a preacher spoke out against the immoral "Babylon" that had been built in California. It is definitely true that where there is wealth, immorality follows (as the Old Testament prophets frequently said). Early movies were all G-rated (by today's standards, anyway), but people were aware that among the movie crowd, wealth and wildness went hand in hand. The Jewish studio heads pretty much left the religious element of their heritage behind them. To put it in Jesus's terms, they chose to serve mammon rather than God, and this was generally true of the whole industry. They did not see biblical films as having any particular moral or spiritual purpose; they were just good entertainment, and the stories of the Bible were not copyrighted, meaning no one had to pay the authors a percentage of the profits. The studios' choices of biblical subjects to make into films had nothing to do with the stories' spiritual importance but simply with presenting an entertaining story, preferably one with an exotic setting and involving violence and sex—or at least suggestions of sex. This explains why some important Bible characters were neglected (Paul, Elijah, Abraham) while fairly unimportant people and stories were filmed often (Samson, Salome, Judith, Esther). Scriptwriters played fast and loose with the biblical stories, more interested in making an entertaining film than in sticking closely to the Bible. It's doubtful that any of the actors or other people involved in these biblical films altered their behavior in any way due to being involved in a story based on the Bible. It was "just a job." Still, some of the films are inspiring to watch.

In the late 1920s, the film industry heard enough complaining about the immorality in Hollywood that it imposed on itself the Hays Code, a self-censorship code that was in effect for several decades. We will look at the code in more detail later.

Let's pause here to ask an obvious question: how did Christians respond to these new things called "motion pictures"? Christians had a long-running suspicion of theater, and rightly so, considering how obscene and violent drama was in the days of the Roman Empire. It got cleaned up considerably in the Middle Ages, but actors always had a reputation (partly deserved) for not having the highest morals. In the late 1800s, most stage plays were reasonably "family friendly," but the bawdy burlesque shows tended to put all theatrical people in a bad light, so lots of Christians (though not all) generally avoided the theater. The earliest motion pictures were, remember, simply one piece in a vaudeville show of singers, jugglers, and actors. One of the earliest films, produced by Thomas Edison's company, showed a thirty-second kiss between a man and a woman, and many people were scandalized. It sounds silly to us, but stop and consider: here projected on a wall were a man's and woman's faces, not life-size but wall-size. Such scenes kept some Christians away from motion pictures for many years. Certain branches of Christianity—Holiness, Pentecostals, and some of the more conservative Baptists—simply made it a rule that their members would not patronize motion pictures, not even the most wholesome ones. Even as late as the 1960s, there were stories (many of them true) about conservative Christians driving to a town several miles away to see *The Sound of Music* or *Mary Poppins*. (Seeing the film at their local theater would've meant running the risk of having a fellow church member see them standing in line.)

Interestingly, one denomination that saw a more positive role for films was the Salvation Army. The Army decided early on that film could be used for evangelistic purposes, and it created a Limelight Department to produce slides and films. The brief films showed how people who had gone astray were rescued by the Army. Films also showed the deplorable conditions of slum dwellings in order to challenge the audience to respond. The Army also exhibited the 1897 French film *La vie et la passion de Jesus Christ*. Being less tradition-bound than many Christian denominations, the Army was quick to see the religious potential of films. In time, most denominations would begin producing their own films for purposes of ministry and outreach, even as those same denominations cast a cold eye on Hollywood films.

2

FROM FULL-LENGTH
TO THE ERA OF SOUND

1912—1929

During these early years, films were getting longer, their stories more involved. A dramatic leap came in 1913: on April 12 the nine-reel (almost two hours) Italian epic *Quo Vadis* opened at the Astor Theatre in New York. Admission was one dollar, which was a lot of money at that time. Directed by Enrico Guazzoni, the film had a cast of five thousand (and thirty lions). It was the first real blockbuster film in America and Europe. An interesting new idea had been born: if you're building expensive sets and hiring lots of actors, you may as well get full use of them and make a really long movie—and charge more to see it, of course.

Quo Vadis was based on a popular novel by Polish author Henryk Sienkiewicz, and it told the story of Christians being persecuted under the Roman emperor Nero. The apostles Peter and Paul were part of the story. Given the success of this ancient epic with its religious elements, it was inevitable that an American film studio would produce a long film with an ancient setting. The result would be the most popular and most important biblical film until Cecil B. DeMille's *King of Kings* in 1927.

From the Manger to the Cross: *The Leap into Feature-Length*
Biblical Films

Released October 1912	**Jesus:** Robert Henderson Bland
Kalem Company	**Mary:** Gene Gauntier
70 minutes	**Mary Magdalene:** Alice Hollister
Silent, black and white	**Pilate:** Samuel Morgan
Filmed in Palestine and Egypt	**John the Baptist:** James Ainsley
	Judas: Robert Vignola
Director: Sidney Olcott	**John:** Jack Clark
Screenplay: Gene Gauntier	**Joseph:** Montague Sidney
Photography: George K. Hollister	

The film's subtitle is *Jesus of Nazareth*. The first title reads "A review of the Savior's Life according to the Gospel narrative," which is quite accurate, because the titles are taken directly from the King James Version of the Gospels. In fact, the titles are so faithful to the Bible that they use ellipses where words were omitted. The screen shows a map of the Holy Land in the New Testament period. A title reads, "With scenes filmed at Jerusalem, Bethlehem, and other authentic locations in Palestine."

In the first scene, Mary is shown carrying a water jug. Later, while dozing, she rises up to see the angel—who is not shown. (This actually works better on-screen than the rather silly looking winged angels of some earlier films.) The angel who appears to Joseph in a dream is also not shown. Mary and Joseph try to find lodging in Bethlehem and end up in a stable. The angel who appears to the shepherds is not shown. The three wise men, on camels, meet at a crossroads (meaning they are from different regions, obviously). The wise men go to Herod, who seems sullen and uneasy about the news of a "king of the Jews" being born. After the wise men visit Jesus, the family makes a stealthy getaway to Egypt, where they pause to rest in front of the great pyramids and sphinx. Some scenes of the boy Jesus doing his chores are shown. At age twelve, the boy Jesus amazes the teachers in the temple.

A very shaggy-haired John the Baptist preaches in the wilderness. He identifies Jesus as the Lamb of God, which seems a bit silly, since Jesus is too far away to be seen. For some odd reason the actual baptism of Jesus is not shown, nor his temptation. Jesus calls the disciples, who are waist deep in water as they fish. As usual, the disciple John is shown beardless—an old tradition in paintings, for some reason. Jesus performs some miracles of healing, then goes to the wedding at Cana (which is slightly wrong, since the turning of the water into wine is described in the Gospel of John as his first miracle). The episode of cutting through the roof of a house to lower a paralyzed man is shown (see Mark 2). Jesus heals him, then raises the dead man of Nain, who is being carried out for burial (see Luke 7). At a Pharisee's house, the sinful woman anoints Jesus's feet with the precious ointment.

Pressed by the crowd, Jesus teaches from a boat. Later that night, he walks on the water. He heals more people, then stays awhile at the house of Mary and Martha, where Mary sits at his feet while Martha is busy with the chores. Later, when Jesus learns that Lazarus is dead, he weeps—profusely. The men struggle to move the heavy stone from Lazarus's tomb. Lazarus comes forth, quivering and unwrapping his graveclothes. At a dinner, while people recline on low couches (which is historically correct), a woman anoints Jesus's feet with perfume and wipes them with her hair. Judas protests this "waste." Judas goes out after Jesus scolds him, suggesting it was at this point that he decided to betray Jesus.

Jesus enters Jerusalem, with people shouting Hosanna and waving palm branches. In the temple, Jesus uses his own belt as the whip to drive out the money changers. After this the priests and scribes connive to destroy him. There is an interesting shot of Jesus alone on the Mount of Olives, looking at Jerusalem in the distance. Judas, looking very sneaky and sinister, goes to the priests.

At the Last Supper, Jesus washes his disciples' feet. At the actual supper, the disciples recline on low couches. Judas leaves before Jesus passes around the bread and wine. The title refers to this as "the First Communion." In fact, the disciples kneel as Jesus gives them the cup, much like a minister serving communion. Afterward, the scene in Gethsemane appears to be broad daylight, which is odd. After the betrayal and arrest, Judas goes back to the priests, who are amused at his sudden guilt. Judas hangs himself. Interestingly, the film omits Jesus being brought before the priests—an episode that many films have omitted for fear of being charged with anti-Semitism.

Jesus is taken before the toga-clad Pilate. Then he is taken to Herod, where Herod's men mock him, then returned to Pilate, who has him scourged—two Roman soldiers flailing away while the people jeer. He is fairly bloody when returned to Pilate. The crowd clamors for Jesus's crucifixion. Pilate washes his hands. The episode of freeing Barabbas is omitted. The soldiers mock Jesus, crowning him with thorns, spitting in his face (something the Gospels mention, though most films do not show it), menacing him with spears. He carries his T-shaped cross through the streets. The placard over his head seems to have the full inscription (in three languages), not the usual *INRI* shown in many films. The soldiers cast lots for Jesus's robe. Jesus promises the repentant thief he will be in paradise. Jesus says, "I thirst," and a soldier lifts up a sponge on a spear. Jesus does indeed seem covered in blood. After he dies, the title bears John 3:16 ("For God so loved the world that he gave his only begotten Son, that whosoever believeth in him should not perish, but have everlasting life"). The film ends and, oddly, there is no resurrection.

From the Manger to the Cross is the second-oldest biblical film available for viewing today, and it's an important one for several reasons. It was the first to be filmed in the Holy Land itself, with the crew filming scenes in Bethlehem, Nazareth, and Jerusalem—which certainly look better than the painted backgrounds of the earlier films. It was also the first U.S. film about Jesus to achieve great success, and not just in America. It is a solidly biblical film, since scriptwriter Gene Gauntier (who also played Jesus's mother) drew the titles straight from the Gospels. We can puzzle over why she did not choose to show Jesus's baptism—or, more importantly, his resurrection from the tomb. But for the most part it is a fine film, faithful to the Bible, with sets and costumes that look reasonably authentic. At this stage in film history, close-ups and a mobile camera were still in the future, so watching it is very much like watching a stage play, with no chance to zoom in on the face of Jesus or another character—something that bothers us but would not have bothered the audience in 1912, since the close-up had seldom been used before.

It turned out to be a highly profitable film, and it had a long second life as a church film used by many missionaries and evangelists—probably the first commercial film to be used that way.

The two-hour Italian epic *Quo Vadis* impressed everyone who saw it, notably American director D. W. Griffith. Between 1908 and 1913, he directed more than five hundred one-reel films for the Biograph film company. Griffith believed that longer films were the wave of the future, as proven by an eight-reel French film of 1912, *Queen Elizabeth*, starring the noted actress Sarah Bernhardt. The success of *Quo Vadis* in 1913 confirmed Griffith's faith in longer movies. Griffith had seen a stage play based on the book of Judith in the Apocrypha, and in 1914 he released *Judith of Bethulia*, running a little over an hour. His version followed the Apocrypha closely, with one notable change: Judith actually falls in love with the Assyrian general Holofernes, even though she had determined to seduce and then murder him in order to save her people. Being in love with him creates dramatic tension (will she or won't she go through with her plan?). This was neither the first nor last case of a script adding a romantic element that the book of Judith lacked. Filmmakers had learned early on that the "boy and girl fall in love" formula helped sell a picture.

From the Manger to the Cross was director Sidney Olcott's third religious film. He had already directed the earliest versions of *Ben-Hur* and *David and Goliath*.

In the same year *Judith* was released also came *Jephthah's Daughter*, another *Salome* from Italy, *The Wife of Cain* (it would be interesting to know the story in that), *Daniel*, and *Joseph in the Land of Egypt*. Then in the following years came an Italian-made *Christus*, another U.S. *Samson*, another U.S. *Salome* (starring the famous screen "vamp" Theda Bara; Christians who saw the film were somewhat scandalized by her scanty attire), *The Bible* (we're not sure how much this covered), and a German-made *Sodom and Gomorrah* directed by future Hollywood director Michael Curtiz.

Intolerance: A Thoroughly Modern Jesus

Released September 1916
Wark Productions
Black and white, with color tints
Kino International's video version is 177
   minutes, but other longer and shorter
   versions exist. No one will ever know
   just what the original release print was
   like or how long it ran.
	Director: D. W Griffith
	Screenplay: D. W. Griffith, Anita Loos
	
	Jesus: Howard Gaye
	Mary: Lillian Langdon
	Mary Magdalene: Olga Grey
	Pharisees: Erich von Stroheim, Gunther
	   von Ritzan

Intolerance was, for its time, the most expensive movie ever made—and a colossal failure. Ninety years after its initial release, it is still fascinating and frustrating to watch, pleasing and puzzling a viewer today as much as it pleased and puzzled those who saw it in 1916. It is interesting as a curio in the history of film, but for the purposes of our present book, it is especially interesting for the extremely modern view of Jesus Christ presented in it.

Pathbreaking silent film director D. W. Griffith made *Intolerance* after his incredible 1915 success, *The Birth of a Nation*, an epic story about the Civil War and Reconstruction, which is still watchable today. The movie pleased audiences and dazzled movie critics, but it was banned in some states and caused some race riots because of its sympathetic depiction of the Ku Klux Klan in the Reconstruction South. (Griffith was the son of a Confederate veteran, and he grew up listening to his father's exaggerated tales of his exploits as a soldier in gray.) Incensed by the negative reaction, Griffith published a pamphlet called *The Rise and Fall of Free Speech in America,* which linked censorship with intolerance. In his pamphlet (which was probably ghostwritten for him), he said that "the motion picture is a medium of expression as clean and decent as any mankind has ever discovered. A people that would allow the suppression of this form of speech would unquestionably submit to the suppression of what we all consider so highly, the printing press."

Griffith had in fact cut certain scenes from *The Birth of a Nation* in order to mollify its critics. Cut was a segment referring to the hypocrisy of Northern abolitionists who were descended from slave traders and to a letter in which Lincoln stated that blacks were inferior to whites. However, Griffith stood by his finished product and saw his critics as meddling killjoys, a type of person he despised, as would be seen clearly in the film *Intolerance.*

Intolerance is a four-part film, with the four stories set in different periods of history, each of them tied together by the theme of the title. The film was actually an expanded version of a short film he had begun shooting before *Birth of a Nation*, titled *The Mother and the Law*, which is the modern story in *Intolerance*.

Griffith detested what he called "meddlers," especially when they saw themselves as saintly. So including Jesus in the epic was not out of any sense of religious conviction but in order to use Jesus's own sad fate as an illustration of Griffith's theme. Griffith himself was not religious at all. He had been brought up by a devout Methodist mother who frowned on swearing and drinking, and in his childhood he had a curious experience. As a child in Kentucky, on a winter day outdoors, Griffith had a vision of Christ in the sky. Griffith politely introduced himself to Christ and told him, "I love you and always have." But despite this and despite his mother's influence, he seemed to have absorbed little of the Bible (or its morals—he was a notoriously unfaithful husband). However, he had no qualms about using Jesus as a symbol of love and peace, or of something even more significant for us in the twenty-first century: *tolerance*.

The film opens with these words: "Each story shows how hatred and intolerance, through all the ages, have battled against love and charity." In fact, the film has a subtitle: *Love's Struggle Through the Ages*. The opening (and recurring) image of the film is a woman rocking a cradle, showing that human emotions are the same through the ages. The four stories are:

1. The Modern Story, The Mother and the Law, dealing with a poor couple persecuted by the law and meddling socialites
2. The Judean Story, dealing with Jesus and his enemies
3. The French Story, dealing with the 1572 massacre of Protestant Christians in France
4. The Babylonian Story, dealing with the conquest of "tolerant" Babylon by the Persians.

Obviously the Judean Story is our main concern here. It is also the shortest of the four stories, the bulk of the film being taken up with the Modern and the Babylonian. The opening of the Judean Story includes these words: "the Man of Men, the greatest enemy of intolerance." Some pious Pharisees pray in the streets of Jerusalem, making a great show, wearing their phylacteries, while the laborers along the street have to cease all work during the prayers. One even prays in the exact words of the Pharisee in Jesus's parable of the Pharisee and the tax collector (Luke 18): "I thank thee, God, that I am not like other men."

The film cuts to the other stories, then to the wedding at Cana in Galilee. Outside the home of the wedding, Jesus greets the two Pharisees, who snub him. Inside, Jesus greets his mother. The Pharisees outside claim there is too much merriment among the people—obviously a link to the other stories. These words appear: "The first miracle: the turning of water into wine. Note: Wine was deemed a fit offering to God; the drinking of it a part of the Jewish religion." The servants open one of the huge water jugs, smell it, realize it is wine, and look at Jesus in wonder.

A title reads, "And the Pharisees said, 'Behold a man gluttonous and a winebibber, a friend of publicans and sinners.' St. Matthew 11:19." Jesus is dining at the house of a publican (tax collector).

Then the film shows a Bible story that liberals love to quote today: The Pharisees bring Jesus a woman caught in adultery, telling him that the law of Moses mandates stoning her. Jesus writes in the sand, then says, "He who is without sin among you, let him first cast a stone at her." They drop their stones in horror and walk away, one pausing to look at the Hebrew letters he wrote in the sand. Jesus asks, "Woman, where are thy accusers?" The titles do *not* give us Jesus's very important words "Go and sin no more," but judging from the woman's body language, Jesus has said, "Neither do I condemn you." The philandering Griffith took the modern view of the story—forgiveness granted but no repentance needed. With his long string of mistresses and his hatred of "meddlers," he wasn't about to include "Go and sin no more." Griffith had long ago tired of his wife, Linda, and after she found in his possession a love letter from another woman, he wrote her a long letter of confession stating that there had been women before then and would be more in the future and that marriage, to him, was not a moral state to live in.

After the poor mother in the Modern Story has her child taken away by "reformers," the film cuts to Jesus saying to a crowd, "Suffer little children."

The Judean story does not resume until, appropriately, the Modern Story segment has the boy unjustly convicted for murder.

Jesus is shown bearing his cross through the streets of Jerusalem, and then the film cuts again to the Modern Story, with the boy sentenced to hanging. He is saved literally at the last minute—the noose is already around his neck—after the governor, learning he was innocent of the murder, pardons him.

Jesus carries around his neck the placard listing his crime, which is historically correct though never featured in other movies of the crucifixion.

Rather frustratingly, the actual crucifixion is not shown—at least, not in the video version available today. The original film did show Jesus on the cross. Griffith bowed to pressure from the Jewish group B'nai B'rith to remove close-ups of Caiaphas and the other priests from the crucifixion scenes, placing the blame for it solely on the Roman soldiers.

The multipart film ran so incredibly long that Griffith had to do some major cutting, and the Judean Story (which could be subtitled "Jesus of Tolerance") was cut more than any of the others. In fact, Griffith's original rough cut for the film was a staggering eight hours, but he got the message right away that no movie house had any intention of showing a film that long, not even in two parts. Thirty scenes with Jesus were in the original script (which has vanished); only six were in the film that was released.

As should be obvious by now, Griffith had no intention of presenting the full story of Jesus. He and his coauthor (novelist Anita Loos) picked and chose those parts of the Gospels that seemed to illustrate the theme of intolerance, so the movie gives us not the Christ or the Savior but the great preacher of tolerance (and victim of intolerance). But even in the other stories, the script quotes the Bible: for example, during a dance in the Modern Story, a title reads "To everything there is a season . . . a time to mourn and a time to dance. Ecclesiastes 3." When Babylon is falling to the Persians, a title half-quotes Revelation: "Babylon, that mighty city, is falling." In the French story, France's queen mother demands the extermination of the Protestants for their past atrocities against Catholics, and she quotes the Old Testament: "An eye for an eye, a tooth for a tooth." Viewers were expected to know that that Old Testament law had been superseded by the New Testament's teaching about mercy.

The movie is very modern in that it sides with the young and vivacious against the middle-aged and dull. Jesus in the movie is not young, but he seems to be on the side of the young and vital—even merrymakers and adulterous women—while the killjoy Pharisees seem old and dull. Of all Jesus's many miracles, the only one shown is his turning water into wine. In the Modern Story stuffy, middle-aged socialites try to stop the young working-class folks from enjoying dances and drinking. In the Babylonian Story the stuffy priests of Bel are jealous of the frolicsome maidens who worship the goddess Ishtar. Griffith was on the side of the fun crowd.

Howard Gaye, who played Jesus, had the small but important role of Robert E. Lee in *Birth of a Nation*. Gaye became Griffith's "full-time Christ," not only in *Intolerance* but in other Griffith movies where Christ would appear out of the clouds to forgive some person who had sinned. As in *Intolerance*, he always seemed a bit too sweet-faced and mild, rather lacking in the vitality we find in the Jesus of the Gospels. During the filming of *Intolerance*, he did his own makeup at home, then drove to the studio down Sunset Boulevard in his Model T Ford—Jesus behind the wheel.

> Novelist Anita Loos, who collaborated with Griffith on the script for *Intolerance*, was best known for her comic novel *Gentlemen Prefer Blondes*.

The Babylonian Story is not directly based on the Bible, but since it does have some characters mentioned in the Bible, it is worth discussing briefly. The story takes place in 539 BC, the time of Belshazzar. The movie's view of Belshazzar is certainly different from the Old Testament account, where Belshazzar is a decadent pagan, feasting from vessels the Babylonians had plundered from Jerusalem's temple and receiving his just punishment from the hand of God. (This is told in the book of Daniel; at a feast Belshazzar is horrified to see a ghostly hand writing on the wall, foretelling his conquest and doom, which is immediate.) In the movie, Belshazzar is good and tolerant—the "apostle of tolerance and religious freedom," the victim of Persian imperialism and the plottings of the intolerant priest of Bel, in league with the Persians. For Griffith, the Persian king Cyrus epitomizes killing in the name of God. The Persians are beaten—which is definitely not the case in the Bible or in history. In fact, Cyrus took Babylon with no battle at all.

Throughout the Bible, the name Babylon symbolizes decadence and idolatry, and the Persians are generally presented favorably. Even aside from the Bible, few historians have praised Babylon as a "tolerant" civilization. (Few ancient empires were "tolerant" in our modern sense of the word, but the Persians were certainly more tolerant than the Babylonians. The Babylonians had taken the Jews into exile and burned their temple, while it was the Persians who allowed the Jews to return home and rebuild their temple.) We can assume that Griffith chose the Babylonian story because it gave him an excuse to construct some awe-inspiring sets for the temples and the city walls—sets so amazing that they were tourist attractions in Hollywood for many years afterward.

Intolerance opened in New York on September 2, 1916. It had cost almost $2 million, which was a huge amount in those days, twenty times the cost of *Birth of a Nation*. When it opened, Griffith fully expected it to pay off, since reviewers loved it, and it ran for four months at the New York theater where it opened. Griffith toured the country, attending premieres in various cities, with a stump speech about free expression. Griffith's name and publicity machine had a lot of pull—but only temporarily. Ticket sales slumped off soon enough, and the movie he intended as the spectacle that would outperform *Birth of a Nation* did not break even. Audiences were puzzled by the four-part structure, and people in 1916 weren't quite as obsessed with the theme of intolerance as we are today. To try to recoup his losses on the expensive film, Griffith edited the Modern and Babylonian stories and released them as individual movies.

Without realizing it, Griffith's Jesus had set the pattern for the Jesus beloved by modern liberals, including those who despise Christianity: this is the Jesus who encounters the woman caught in adultery and says, "Let he who is without sin cast the first stone," and says to the woman, "Neither do I condemn you." This liberal, tolerant Jesus does not conclude the scene with the crucial words found in the Gospel: "Go and sin no more."

The failure of Griffith's *Intolerance* did not encourage the making of more films set in ancient times—or at least not long epics. The next biblical film would be a German film in 1917, *Der Galilaer* (*The Galilean*), another telling of the passion story. The next from the U.S. would be another *Salome* in 1918, this one starring

the famous screen "vamp" Theda Bara. Then in 1921 came another American film titled *The Bible* (we do not know what this
covered, though certainly not the entire Bible) and *The Queen
of Sheba*, another wild elaboration on the meeting of Solomon
and the queen. In this version, directed by J. Gordon Edwards,
the queen kills her wicked husband, for which her country is
grateful. She visits Solomon and wins a chariot race for him.
The night before she leaves Jerusalem, Solomon visits her, and
a child results. Back home in Sheba, the child is accepted as the
child of the dead king. At age four, she sends him to visit Solomon, who is pleased to see him, but Solomon's brother Adonijah
is not pleased, fearing that Solomon plans to make his son heir.
A coup is planned, and the queen sends her army to support
Solomon and rescue their son. With the conspiracy smashed, the
queen and her son head home. The silly plot bears the scantest
resemblance to the Bible, although it is true that Solomon and
Adonijah contested the throne of Israel. This bizarre plot would
show up in a similar form in the successful 1959 film *Solomon
and Sheba*.

In one year (1922) there were three versions of *Salome*: two
from the U.S., one from Germany. Also from Germany came
Sodom and Gomorrah, released in the U.S. as *Queen of Sin* and
directed by future Hollywood stalwart Michael Curtiz. (The plot
of the story did not even hint at the actual sin of sodomy, and this
oversight would be repeated in a film of the same name in the
1960s.) Also from Germany came another *Joseph and His Brothers*. From Austria that same year came yet another *Samson and
Delilah*. Apparently people could not get enough Samson, for a
British-made *Samson and Delilah* was released in 1923, the same
year as the German-made *INRI* (released in English as *Crown of
Thorns* and, of course, showing the crucifixion of Jesus). *INRI*
included some scenes shot in Palestine. Also that year was *The
Shepherd King*, directed by J. Gordon Edwards and telling the
story of Saul, David, and Goliath. (The "shepherd king" of the title
was David, of course.) Though filmed in Palestine and Egypt, it
did not draw a huge audience. Happily, 1923 was also the year
that one of Hollywood's most respected directors (and showmen)
turned his attention to the story of Moses—and not for the last
time, as it turned out.

The Ten Commandments: *Mr. DeMille Warming Up*

Released December 1923
Paramount
Silent, black and white with color
  segment
135 minutes

Director: Cecil B. DeMille
Screenplay: Jeanie Macpherson
Photography: Bert Glennon, Peverel
  Marley, Archibald Stout, J. F.
  Westerberg

Moses: Theodore Roberts
Rameses: Charles De Roche
Miriam: Estelle Taylor
Aaron: James Neill
Dathan: Lawson Butt
Taskmaster: Clarence Burton

At this point we pause for a brief look at the background of the one man most identified over the years with biblical films, Cecil Blount DeMille. Born in 1881 to a family of Dutch extraction, DeMille was raised Episcopalian and grew up listening to his father read from the family Bible. The Bible affected DeMille in another way, visually, for it was one of many Bibles filled with the famous illustrations by artist Gustave Doré. It is no accident that DeMille's biblical films have a certain "Doré look" about them. (Doré and other artists influenced biblical films, just as biblical films influence people's ideas about biblical people and events.) DeMille's parents had both been actors, and he and his brother William both acted and wrote plays before becoming involved with the fledgling film industry. Cecil became associated with the enormous Paramount studio, but he had such incredible clout that for all practical purposes he was an independent producer-director.

DeMille's wife, Constance, was adored and treated well, but this didn't keep Cecil from having several mistresses throughout his sixty years of marriage. Constance learned to play the game played by many women married to successful men: accept that there is another woman in his life and be glad if he treats you with respect and doesn't desert you. In fact, DeMille was a model husband and father in many ways, and his family members and servants adored him. Most actors and technicians recall working with him as demanding but rewarding. He was courteous but such a perfectionist that he could sometimes speak sharply to his crew.

The script for *The Ten Commandments* was written by Jeanie Macpherson—who happened to be one of DeMille's mistresses.

"Mr. Biblical Epic" himself, director Cecil B. DeMille, setting up the golden calf scene for the 1923 *The Ten Commandments*. The woman touching the golden calf is Moses's sister Miriam (Estelle Taylor). The woman in the hat is scriptwriter (and also DeMille's mistress) Jeanie Macpherson.

She was a talented writer but also stubborn and high-strung, and she and DeMille had some heated verbal battles over the script. It is ironic that two of DeMille's biblical films—this one and the later *King of Kings*—list her name and DeMille's over everyone else's (one wonders if either of them bothered to notice that "Thou shalt not commit adultery" is one of the commandments). Actress Julia Faye, who played the part of Pharaoh's wife in the film, was also a member of the DeMille "harem."

DeMille was a master showman in many ways, aware of what caught and held an audience's attention. He had directed melodramas, westerns, and comedies. In the early 1920s he decided, as a publicity stunt, to have the subject of his next Paramount picture be decided by a contest, with $1,000 going to the person with the best idea. Letters came in from all over, and someone suggested Moses and the Exodus—or to be precise, eight different people suggested the same story, so DeMille ended up awarding $1,000 to each.

DeMille took the story seriously, even to the point that he gave each crew member a Bible and told them to read the book of Exodus carefully. He employed hundreds of Orthodox Jews as extras for the crowd scenes, and one of the mess tents served strictly kosher food. Men and women crew members ate in different mess tents, and married ones had to leave their spouses at home while the film was in production. Prohibition was in force, and DeMille insisted that no liquor be on the set. Some people in the press snickered about this very strait-laced movie production, but DeMille would have the last laugh, as the movie was a great success.

The opening title shows stone tablets over the words "Cecil B. DeMille's Production of The Ten Commandments." The credits refer to Moses as "the Lawgiver," Rameses as "the Magnificent," and Dathan as "the Discontented."

The opening title reads, "Our modern world defined God as a 'religious complex' and laughed at the Ten Commandments as OLD-FASHIONED. Then, through the laughter, came the shattering thunder of the World War. And now a blood-drenched, bitter world—no longer laughing—cries for a way out. There is but one way out. It existed before it was engraven upon tablets of stone. It will exist when stone has crumbled. The Ten Commandments are not rules to obey as a personal favor to God. They are the fundamental principles without which mankind cannot live together. They are not laws. They are the LAW." DeMille recognized that the world was becoming more secular, that in the Roaring Twenties it was becoming chic to mock religion or even mock God. This film was intended to show, in both its modern and ancient stories, that forgetting God and his law was not wise.

Most of the titles in the film are drawn straight from the book of Exodus. To give the titles a more "ancient" feel, the letters resemble the Hebrew alphabet. The first title is from Exodus 1:13–14, telling of the Egyptians enslaving the children of Israel. The first shot shows a burly, hirsute taskmaster standing in front of a huge statue of Pharaoh. The slaves are drudging away at a temple, hauling in a sphinx figure. Moses's sister Miriam is shown carrying a yoke on her shoulders, bringing water to the taskmaster while the slaves groan for a drink. An Egyptian official tells the "dogs of Israel" to kneel to the image of the conqueror, "the king of Kings," Rameses. The slaves grovel, then are forced back to their grind. (The actor playing Pharaoh isn't nearly as charismatic as Yul Brynner in the same role in 1956.) One of the slaves is literally ground into the dust as the other slaves haul the sphinx statue. Miriam goes to the dead slave, then prays to God for deliverance.

Unlike the 1956 version, the film omits the story of Moses being found as a baby by an Egyptian princess and raised in the pharaoh's court, as well as the story of his killing an Egyptian slave driver. In the next title, we learn that God sent "Moses the Lawgiver," shown as an intense but fairly aged man with a long, white beard. Aaron is introduced as the "Priest of Israel," although at this point in the biblical story he was not yet called that. (He was made Israel's first high priest after the Israelites had departed Egypt.) The two men enter Pharaoh's palace. Pharaoh's young son reminds Pharaoh that "this man has already tormented us with nine plagues." (Sadly, this film does not show any of the plagues.) Pharaoh orders them to kneel, but Moses says he kneels to no one but God. Off to the side we see a priest bowing to statues of the animal-headed Egyptian gods. Moses warns Pharaoh that God will strike down the firstborn as the next plague. Pharaoh's son strikes Moses with a whip. Pharaoh scoffs. Moses exits, the son still whipping him. As Moses and Aaron leave, the Egyptian court loses itself in music and a dancing girl.

The next title tells of a great cry in Egypt at the death of the firstborn. Pharaoh is brought the body of his dead son, while his wife and her maids wail. Pharaoh takes the boy in his arms, then sees Moses standing there. He finally tells Moses to take the children of Israel away. He lays the body of his son before an idol of the sacred scarab beetle. He prays for the gods to bring his son back to life.

The next title says that the Israelites took gold and jewels from the Egyptians, who were glad to be rid of the slaves (see Exod. 12:35–36). The Israelites depart in a bustle, people carrying loads and herding their livestock. Moses leads them forth into the desert, with the long double column of sphinxes behind them. This crowd scene is truly impressive, especially with its occasional close-ups of children laughing and families rejoicing at their freedom. DeMille knew how to use the camera to turn a horde into individuals.

Pharaoh grows angry when his gods do not restore his son to life. He vows to his son's corpse that the Israelites will be ground under the wheels of his chariots. He bangs a gong to summon his troops. His aides arrive and clothe him in armor. The scene shifts to Moses leading the huge column of people through the desert.

The title from Exodus relates that Pharaoh massed six hundred chariots to go after the Israelites. There is an interesting contrast between the Egyptians' gilded chariots and plumed horses and the humble livestock of the Israelites. The Israelites are peacefully camped out near the Red Sea. They go running to Moses when they see the chariots approaching. Rallying around Dathan, the chronic griper, they ask Moses, "Were there no graves in Egypt?" Moses assures them they will witness a miracle. The "pillar of fire" appears, causing the chariots to halt (see Exod. 14:19–20), although it actually is an image of a wall of flame superimposed over the chariots. Dathan has already picked up a stone to hurl at Moses, but the people see the flame and relent. Then Moses stretches out his arms, and the roiling seas part (an effect made by running the film in reverse). Pharaoh sees and is awed. The flames vanish, and he orders his troops to pursue the Israelites, who panic once again. Moses tells them to wait and see the salvation of the Lord. He brings his hands together and the waters close in on the Egyptians. We see air bubbles as the horses and men sink into the sea.

The Red Sea segment had literal red in it, since this part of the film used a very primitive form of color film—primitive to us, that is, but dazzling to the original audience. This was the first biblical film to use color. Twenty-three years later, DeMille would direct the first all-color biblical film, *Samson and Delilah*.

In the next scene the people are camped out at Sinai. Moses makes his way up the bleak mountain, the wind rushing and the lightning flashing. Amidst what appear to be fireworks, the Ten Commandments, written in English, appear one by one. Moses is a sort of secretary, seeing the commandments in the sky, then engraving them into stone on the mountainside.

Back in the Israelite camp, the people grow restless and force Aaron to make them a golden calf idol. Interestingly, we see the people making the idol immediately after the second commandment, the one against making idols, appears. The Israelites cavort around their calf idol while musicians beat drums. (DeMille knew how to suggest an orgy without actually showing it.) Moses covers his face as the Lord strikes the mountain with lightning, creating the tablets that Moses may carry down. He tells Moses that the people below have "corrupted themselves." A scantily clad Miriam gyrates and guzzles wine in front of the calf idol, which the title refers to as the "golden god of pleasure." Rather jarringly, Dathan strokes her breast, then sees that her skin is affected by leprosy. (In the Bible, Miriam is punished with leprosy later in the story for rebelling against Moses.) Moses comes down from the mountain. In anger, he throws down the tablets and they shatter. Miriam bows to Moses and asks for forgiveness. Lightning strikes the calf idol. The wind howls and lightning strikes many of the people.

At this point, fifty minutes into the film, the modern story begins, with a woman reading the Exodus passage aloud to her two adult sons. One son mocks the story as "bunk" that was "buried with Queen Victoria." The story follows the contrasting fortunes of the successful but immoral Dan and the morally upright Johnny. Dan becomes a highly successful contractor but loses his soul in the process, breaking all ten of the commandments, while John is a humble carpenter. At the end, Dan is wanted for murder, and when he tries to skip the country in his boat named *Defiance*, the boat strikes some rocks and he dies.

DeMille had the last laugh on Paramount studio head Adolph Zukor, who had balked at the idea of a biblical movie, saying that people had no desire to see "old men in tablecloths and beards." In fact, DeMille would prove several times that "tablecloth and beard" movies could be very profitable.

As expected, *The Ten Commandments* was a rousing success. It cost Paramount $1.2 million (a huge sum in those days) but earned back many times that amount. The modern story seems a bit corny and melodramatic to a viewer today, but the story of Moses is still impressive, even though it pales in comparison with the version DeMille did in 1956. The scenes with the Israelites and later the Egyptian troops passing through the huge row of sphinxes are awesome, and they do not seem "over the top" the way the Babylonian sets in D. W. Griffith's *Intolerance* did. Critics generally had high praise for the film but thought the ancient story far superior to the modern second half. (A suggestion to anyone who buys or rents the film today: stop the video when the Moses section ends.) When DeMille remade the film in the 1950s, he would have enough clout to do what he had hoped to do with the original version: film it in Egypt.

As this synopsis shows, the film stuck reasonably close to the book of Exodus, though for reasons of running time it had to omit the details about Moses's birth and upbringing, as well as skip showing the plagues on the Egyptians. Also, it showed Miriam, Moses's sister, as the leader in worshiping the golden calf idol, which is not found in Exodus. Still, as Hollywood's first movie about the Moses saga, it is very commendable. In 2006 it was released in DVD format, packaged with the 1956 version's fiftieth anniversary edition, giving viewers the chance to compare just how much filmmaking had changed between 1923 and 1956.

In between *The Ten Commandments* and DeMille's next biblical film, *The King of Kings*, the German film *Passion Play* was released, as was an American film *The Wanderer*, based on the parable of the prodigal son. MGM released the second version of *Ben-Hur*. Like the versions of 1908 and 1959, the 1925 version showed Jesus from behind or from afar instead of showing his face, which let the audience focus on how people reacted to him. In the next biblical film the audience would get a full-face view of the Christ, as served up by DeMille.

Let's pause here for a brief glimpse at the decade of the 1920s. It has been called the "Jazz Age" and the "Roaring Twenties," a time when traditional morals were loosening up. Probably the most famous man in America in this period was automobile manufacturer Henry Ford, who had grown up on a farm but made his fortune in the big city. Many would follow this path, finding in the city not only job opportunities but also a place away from the moral guidance of parents and churches. (The automobile—Ford's Model T being the top seller, as he intended—had dramatically changed the rituals of courtship, dating, and sex, of course.) Though Prohibition was in force for most of the decade, people found it relatively easy to secure illegal liquor and also found it easy to scoff at the Christians who had helped secure Prohibition in the first place. Religion took some major hits in the decade, the most famous being the 1925 "Monkey Trial" in Tennessee, where a young schoolteacher was found guilty of teaching evolution to his students. He lost, legally speaking, but the real loser was conservative Christianity, for the press turned the trial into a showdown between enlightened modern thought and backward religion, typified by former statesman William Jennings Bryan, a great man made to appear the buffoon when he testified to his belief in the literal truth of the Bible. Modern urbanites thumbed their noses at a religion that people like Bryan would profess, just as they thumbed their noses at a federal law (Prohibition) that made Christians appear to be meddling killjoys.

But there was still plenty of vitality left in American Christianity, and one of the best Bible films ever made would premiere in 1927.

The King of Kings: *The DeMille Christ*

Released April 1927	**Jesus:** H. B. Warner
Pathé-DeMille	**Judas:** Joseph Schildkraudt
112 minutes	**Peter:** Ernest Torrence
Silent, black and white, some sequences	**Mary:** Dorothy Cumming
in color	**Mary Magdalene:** Jacqueline Logan
	Caiaphas: Rudolph Schildkraudt
Producer-Director: Cecil B. DeMille	**Pilate:** Victor Varconi
Screenplay: Jeanie Macpherson	**Matthew:** Robert Edeson
Photography: J. Peverell Marley	

In 1926 legendary producer-director Cecil B. DeMille decided his next big project would be *The Deluge*, the epic story of Noah and the flood. His plan changed when he learned Warner Brothers studio was already beginning production on *Noah's Ark*, which will be discussed later in this chapter. One of the writers working for DeMille sent him a memo, asking, "Why skirt around the one great single subject of all time?" The writer even suggested the title *The King of Kings*, taken from Revelation 19:16, where Jesus is called "King of Kings and Lord of Lords." The film would prove so successful that the MGM studio reused the title in its own Jesus film in 1961.

The actual writing of the script was assigned to another writer, Jeanie Macpherson, DeMille's longtime mistress (one of several), who was, however, a dedicated worker, putting in sixteen-hour days as she labored to produce a filmable life of Christ based on the four Gospels. DeMille wanted to add a love interest to the story by suggesting a love story between Jesus and Mary Magdalene.

H. B. Warner, already past age fifty, as Jesus in Cecil B. DeMille's 1927 silent classic *The King of Kings*, which was used for decades by missionaries to present the gospel. John is on the left side of the picture, a very uneasy-looking Judas on the right.

Thankfully, that idea did not make its way into the final film, although some films closer to our own time (notably *Jesus Christ Superstar* and *The Last Temptation of Christ*) made that doubtful relationship an important part of their plots.

DeMille faced a challenge that every director of a Jesus movie faces: namely, who to cast in the crucial role of the Son of God. A star too familiar to the public is an unwise choice, since people already have an idea of the characters that person has played (and probably an idea of some unsavory incidents in his private life as well). Using an unknown is a good option, but DeMille preferred to work with someone tried and tested. So he tapped H. B. Warner, a star of stage and early silent films but almost forgotten by Hollywood in 1926. Warner was the ripe age of fifty-one when filming began, whereas the Bible says Jesus was around thirty when his ministry began. But DeMille thought Warner's lean body and, more important, his warm, expressive, and slightly sad face would be perfect for playing the most challenging role ever.

In his autobiography DeMille wrote, "All my life I have wondered how many people have been turned away from Christianity by the effeminate, sanctimonious, machine-made Christs of second-rate so-called art, which used to be thought good enough for Sunday school."[1] DeMille assumed Jesus had to be a strong man to endure forty days of fasting during his temptation and to endure the flogging and crucifixion, not to mention day after day of walking, enduring the elements. Jesus had to be a masculine figure, a strong man, but also played sensitively, since this was a man who "noticed things like lilies of the field and how they grow, or mother hens and how they keep their chicks warm under their wings."[2]

The challenge of finding the right Christ was met, but the other challenge was reducing all the stories about Jesus in the four Gospels to a film of reasonable length. Simply put, that can't be done—not the whole life of Jesus in two hours, anyway. Fifty years later, television would cover the life of Jesus reasonably well in the long, long miniseries *Jesus of Nazareth*, spread out over several nights. But an ordinary movie-length film about Jesus has to make some choices—meaning omitting a lot. DeMille and Macpherson chose to begin the film with Jesus in the middle of his adult ministry, omitting the familiar stories of the virgin birth, the wise men, the shepherds, the boy Jesus in the temple, the baptism by John, the temptation, the choosing of the disciples. *The King of Kings* would begin in midstream, so to speak, with Jesus already having a reputation as a healer and teacher.

The other wise choice in the script was having the film begin not with an incident from the Gospels but with the totally fictional episode of Mary Magdalene, a wealthy courtesan, lounging in her pleasure palace with some of her clientele. DeMille knew this would catch the audience completely off guard and have them wondering for several minutes just where the movie was headed. His knowledge of human nature and of how to pull an audience into a story was amazing.

Having picked his cast and put a script together, DeMille invited them all to his home for a marathon read-through of the script. He told them that they were telling on film the greatest story ever told, but they had to make it interesting and entertaining since so many people, especially the young, seemed very ignorant of the most basic facts about the life of Jesus. (One can only imagine what he would say about the biblical illiteracy of today.) The film would also have to avoid offending people, particularly Jews, who, he said, had been unfairly blamed for bringing about the death of Jesus. How DeMille managed that difficult (and perhaps impossible) task will be discussed in more detail below.

DeMille was aware that America had a love-hate relationship with Hollywood, being fascinated by its glamour but regarding it as a moral cesspool, which it was. He ordered cast and crew not to drink, smoke, gamble, or swear during the filming of the movie. (How well they abided by these rules is not known.) He was especially protective of his Jesus, H. B. Warner, and the sometimes boozy Warner had to be on his absolute best behavior during filming. DeMille suspected, with good reason, that reporters on the pay of other Hollywood studios would have been overjoyed to catch Warner in some moral indiscretion during the months of filming. In fact, one minor scandal did erupt: the actress playing Jesus's mother, Mary, started divorce proceedings against her husband while the film was in production, even though DeMille specifically forbade it.

To craft the overall "look" of the film, DeMille told his chief photographer, Peverell Marley, to study paintings, especially those of the Renaissance, to set up the lighting for the film. DeMille was not the first or last director to strike a responsive chord by having the movie shot to resemble famous paintings. People who saw the movie, both then and later, stated that in some odd way it "looked familiar" to them—meaning that it looked like many of the classic paintings they had seen. DeMille was correct in assuming that people's images of Bible stories are drawn not just from the Bible itself but from familiar paintings and sculptures. He himself had grown up fascinated by the famous illustrations by French artist Gustave Doré, and more than a few of the shots in the film were set up to look like Doré's images.

In the synopsis that follows, the quoted sections are direct quotations from this silent film's title cards. Many of them are direct quotations from the Bible, with the chapter and verse being provided on-screen. DeMille wanted his audience to know that his film was based solidly on the Bible itself.

There are no credits at the beginning or end of the film except those listed with the title itself: "Cecil B. DeMille's The King of Kings, by Jeanie Macpherson." Then follows these words: "The events portrayed by this picture occurred in Palestine nineteen centuries ago, when the Jews were under the complete subjection of Rome—even their own High Priest being appointed by the Roman procurator. Cecil B. DeMille." (DeMille's actual signature was used.) Then: "This is a story of Jesus of Nazareth. He Himself commanded that His message be carried to the uttermost parts of the earth. May this portrayal play a reverent part in the spirit of that great command." DeMille was letting his audience know that though this was entertainment done for profit, there was a spiritual motivation as well.

Then came the jarring, teasing opening that DeMille knew would pull the audience into the story: "In Judea—groaning under the iron heel of Rome—the beautiful courtesan, Mary of Magdala, laughed alike at God and Man." Mary's home is a pleasure palace, with musicians, lavish furnishings, and rich food. A monkey frolics among the guests. The bare-shouldered (and nearly bare-breasted) Mary has a pet leopard that she caresses. She misses her favorite man, Judas, but another man tells her he has taken up with a "band of beggars" led by a carpenter from Nazareth. The most famous title card in the movie has Mary saying, "Harness my zebras, gift of the Nubian king!" The men tell her the carpenter has healed people, even raised the dead. Mary laughs. Four zebras do indeed pull Mary's chariot. This first sequence is tinted, with very bold reds.

The scene moves from the gaudiness of Mary's home to a village street, where a blind girl gropes about, asking to be taken to Jesus. Then we meet "Judas Iscariot, the ambitious, who joined the disciples in the belief that Jesus would be the nation's King, and reward him with honor and high office." Judas, who is beardless (unlikely for any Jewish man of that era), tells people Jesus will throw off the yoke of Rome. Some Roman soldiers hear and are not amused. A boy comes forth, showing his healed leg. He is identified as Mark, the future author of one of the Gospels.

Enter the other villains: "Spies of the High Priest—Pharisee, Scribe, and Temple Guard—driven by the fury of religious hatred." One of them tells the boy, "Be thou warned, this man is not of God! (John 9:16)." Then "Peter, the Giant Disciple, a man quick of temper but soft of heart" shoos away the critical Pharisee. The disciples are all introduced individually, as is mother Mary.

The blind girl is led by Mark to Mary's house. Mary leads the girl to Jesus. The girl says, "Lord, I have never seen the flowers nor the light. Wilt Thou open my eyes?" A title reads, "I am come a light into the world." The first we see of Jesus, almost twenty minutes into the film, is through the eyes of the girl. His face is truly striking, even though he is clearly a good bit older than thirty. (Luke 3:23 says Jesus was about thirty when he began his ministry.) The girl embraces Jesus. Peter is elated, but Judas tells him Jesus would get further by healing the rich than the poor.

> The two main villains in the film, Judas and Caiaphas, were played by son and father, Joseph and Rudolph Schildkraudt—both Jews.

Mary Magdalene rides into town with her zebras and African attendants, asking, "Where is this vagabond carpenter?" She barges into the house, stares at Judas, then goes to confront Jesus, but she is made uneasy by his gaze. Jesus says to her, "Be thou clean" (Matt. 8:3). We see the phantoms of the seven demons that were driven from her—Lust, Greed, Pride, Gluttony, Indolence, Envy, Anger. "We teach thee to forget and to hate and to consume." Thus the movie identifies her seven "demons" (Luke 8:2) with the seven deadly sins. Jesus banishes them with a wave of his hand. Feeling suddenly uneasy in her skimpy clothing, she gathers her cloak around her, goes to Jesus, and caresses his feet.

"The high priest, Caiaphas, who cared more for revenue than for religion, and saw Jesus as a menace." Pharisees enter and smugly tell him that they saw Jesus healing on the Sabbath. Caiaphas looks at the coin in his hand and sees Caesar's face on it. He tells his men to take Matthew the tax collector and some Roman soldiers and ask Jesus if he pays the tax.

In a village, a man has a "lunatic" child who is literally climbing the walls. Judas tries to heal him as Jesus healed Mary, but he has no effect. The boy bites his hand. Matthew's account says the disciples failed (see Matt. 17:16), but the movie individualizes it to Judas.

Jesus is shown working with his carpentry tools. Men arrive and ask Peter if Jesus pays taxes to Caesar. Jesus sends Peter to fish, telling him he will find a fish with a coin in its mouth. Peter is amazed, as are the others. The Pharisee asks if it is lawful to pay taxes to Caesar. Jesus utters his famous words, "Render unto Caesar the things that are Caesar's, and to God the things that are God's." Matthew the tax collector is awed by this. Jesus asks Matthew to follow him.

The father of the lunatic boy is a carpenter himself. He tells Jesus he makes crosses for the Romans, and they pay him well for it. Jesus stands by one of the crosses the man has made, as if he sees the instrument of his own death.

Children flock around Jesus, and Judas tries to shoo them away, but Jesus tells him to let the children be near him. There are *lots* of children in this movie, an element that DeMille knew would appeal to both children and parents in the audience.

In Bethany, Mary and Martha come to Jesus, telling him their brother Lazarus has died. In this version, Lazarus lies in a stone sarcophagus inside a cave. Some men move the lid away. Jesus tells Lazarus to "come forth," but in fact Lazarus raises up from the stone slab he lies on, his hand moving first. There is a literal halo around Jesus's face. Mary hesitates as she unwraps the cloths from Lazarus's face.

The temple guards bring Caiaphas a woman convicted of adultery. Caiaphas tells them to take her to Jesus and see how he responds. If Jesus tells the woman to go free, he is breaking the law of Moses.

"The Temple . . . to the faithful of Israel, the dwelling place of Jehovah. But to the High Priest Caiaphas, a corrupt and profitable marketplace." The temple set is awesome, showing the priests going about their work of slaughtering cattle. Men bring the adulterous woman to Jesus. Some of the people are already holding stones in their hands, looking eager to kill. As in John's Gospel, Jesus "wrote with his finger on the ground" (John 8:6 ESV)—but in the film we see Jesus writing the names of the sins that the would-be stoners are guilty of. (Was the scriptwriter aware that in some old manuscripts of John's Gospel, the text reads "Jesus wrote with his finger on the ground the sins of each of them"?) Jesus tells them that the one who is without sin should cast the first stone. One by one they walk away. Unlike the Jesus in D. W. Griffith's 1916 *Intolerance*, this one says, "Go and sin no more," as in the Gospel.

Jesus sees the money changers cheating the people. He makes a whip out of cords but mostly overturns tables. In this version huge numbers of sheep and cattle are released from their pens. Caiaphas sees and bangs on a gong in the shape of the star of David. The guards are summoned and accompany him to see Jesus. Before the guards can seize Jesus, his devotees enter waving palm branches and flowers. Obviously the chronology isn't quite right here (the triumphal entry into Jerusalem preceded the cleansing of the temple), but it works beautifully. Judas is ecstatic, thinking this is the moment to crown Jesus king. But Jesus withdraws, as stated in John 6:15.

With Jesus by himself in a court of the temple, Satan, in a black cloak, tells Jesus he will give him power over the world's kingdoms—if Jesus will worship him. The actual temptation by Satan took place at the beginning of Jesus's ministry, but it does seem to fit this part of the story well, since the crowd has hoped to make Jesus king at this point.

Jesus shows himself to the crowd again, holding a lamb in his arms and telling the people, "My kingdom is not of this world." Judas, his hopes of an earthly kingdom shattered, goes to the priests to betray Jesus. We see the coins counted out one by one. This scene is beautifully filmed and lighted, with Caiaphas grinning triumphantly.

The Last Supper is almost like the Leonardo da Vinci painting, except that Judas is at Jesus's side, John on the other. (John is beardless, as he so often is in paintings.) The bread is the authentic flat unleavened bread of Passover. Judas is clearly very uneasy throughout the scene. The scene moves very slowly, but this allows tension to build. We almost think Judas will have a nervous breakdown. He can't bring himself to eat the bread or drink the wine. He departs, with the other disciples asking Jesus, "Is it I, Lord?" Jesus predicts Peter's denial but puts his arm around Peter as he slumps on the table.

The group that Judas leads to Gethsemane is very menacing. Interestingly, at this point Matthew is shown writing something down (the first draft of his Gospel?) while the boy Mark rests on his lap. Gethsemane seems full of large boulders, as often seen in paintings. After Judas's infamous kiss, all the disciples rise up and fight, Peter cutting off a man's ear, but Jesus stops them and heals the man's ear. Jesus submits meekly to his captors. He tells them to let the disciples go (see John 18:8), a detail forgotten in most films.

A literal rooster crows after Peter's third denial. Peter's eyes meet those of Jesus.

Interestingly, we see Jesus enter the Sanhedrin's hall for questioning, but the actual trial there is not shown. DeMille was trying to avoid the charges of anti-Semitism that inevitably are heard when a film shows the Jewish leaders condemning Jesus. The scene moves immediately to Pilate, who sits in front of a huge Roman eagle statue, very much the power figure. Probably no such eagle existed, but it's a nice touch. He is obviously not thrilled at Caiaphas bringing Jesus to him. (According to the Gospels, the priests would not have entered Pilate's palace, since it entailed ritual impurity.) Pilate is a somber figure, rather amazed that Jesus will not answer him. He cynically asks, "What is truth?" with a flippant smile. He tells Caiaphas he will chastise Jesus and let him go (see John 19:1). Caiaphas tells his men, "Bribe rogues to cry his death! Confuse the people! Scatter his friends!"

> DeMille's researchers went to great lengths to find actual branches from the species of bush that, according to Bible scholars, was probably the source of the crown of thorns.

Pilate's wife, called Claudia Procula in the film, goes to Pilate and asks where Jesus is. A curtain is drawn and she sees he is being lashed. She tells Pilate not to do anything to Jesus, for she has suffered on account of him in a dream. While she seems to be having some influence on him, Caiaphas points out that if he lets Jesus go, he is no friend of Caesar. Pilate asks an aide to bring out Barabbas. Judas sneaks in and is in agony as he sees Jesus being whipped. Jesus's back shows gashes but he does not seem to be suffering much. The Roman soldiers are a vulgar crowd, fashioning the crown of thorns and hailing Jesus as king. Judas watches, recalling he wanted Jesus to be a king. With the crown of thorns and old robe on, the actor Warner looks exactly like a thousand paintings of this horrible scene. Finally the captain brings the mockery to a halt.

Out in the streets, the priests' henchmen work up some of the local layabouts to call for Jesus's death as a blasphemer. One man says he cannot be bribed to call for the death of an innocent fellow Jew. Obviously this was added to show that not all the Jews wanted Jesus crucified. In his autobiography DeMille wrote, "We went to great lengths in *The King of Kings* to show that the Jewish people of Jesus's time followed and heard Him gladly, that His death came at the hands of a few unrepresentative, corrupt religious leaders and the cowardly and callous Roman government."[3]

Pilate shows Jesus to the people. Barabbas is a surly, burly beast of a man. Pilate reminds the people of the Passover custom of releasing one prisoner. The rogues scream for Barabbas's release. When Pilate asks the crowd what he should do with Jesus, Caiaphas, right at his shoulder, says, "Crucify him!" The men in the crowd take up the cry. Some in the crowd shout, "The high priest speaketh not for the people!" And some in the crowd, mostly women, are pleading for Jesus. Mary Magdalene pleads, but one of the priests' men asks the people if they will listen to "the harlot of Magdala." Pilate still hesitates, asking, "Shall I crucify your king?" Caiaphas taps him on the shoulder and with a smirk says, "We have no king but Caesar!" Pilate washes his hands. "I am innocent of the blood of this just man—see ye to it." He stomps away in disgust.

As so often seen in Bible films, Jesus carries a full cross, while the two thieves carry only the arm pieces. He sees his mother and John in the street. Interestingly, some lepers call out to him, and he heals them as he pauses a moment. Simon of Cyrene volunteers to carry Jesus's cross after he falls; he is not "compelled" as in the Bible. Simon realizes how heavy the cross is, then looks with admiration on Jesus.

Judas hangs himself as the workmen drive their nails into Jesus's hands. An interesting camera angle is used: with the rope around his neck, he can see the three crosses. The placard on the cross does indeed have Jesus's charge written in Latin, Greek, and Aramaic. Caiaphas comes right up to the cross to mock Jesus. The actor H. B. Warner had a very lean, muscular physique, so he looks like the Jesus of so many paintings. He says, "Father, forgive them, they know not what they do." The interchange with the two thieves takes place. The repentant thief dies at peace, with only his faithful dog at the foot of his cross. At the foot of Jesus's cross, Mary shares sorrow with the mother of the unrepentant thief. Darkness falls, perplexing everyone. Lightning flashes. Jesus says, "It is finished! Father, into thy hands I commit my spirit." His death is peaceful;

his eyes close as if falling asleep. Rain falls. Judas's body swings from the tree. The earth quakes, sending Caiaphas into a panic. The good soldier calls out, "Truly this man was the Son of God." The huge curtain in the temple is ripped from top to bottom by lightning. Seeing the curtain ripped, Caiaphas falls to his knees and prays, "Lord God Jehovah, visit not thy wrath on thy people Israel—I alone am guilty!" This is not in the Bible, and from what we know of Caiaphas, it's unlikely he felt guilt over Jesus's death, but by including this scene DeMille was trying to defuse critics who would accuse him of blaming Jesus's death on all the Jews.

The Easter segment is tinted. The tomb is tightly sealed with a large stone secured by thick ropes. The Roman guards are mystified as a blinding light surrounds the stone. It rolls away, and a glowing Jesus walks out in a clean white robe. The area of the tomb is, interestingly, abloom with lilies, and doves are everywhere. The women arrive—carrying flowers, not spices as in the Gospels—and see the tomb is open. Jesus greets Mary, and she recognizes him. Later Jesus goes to his disciples, passing through the shut door in a blaze of light. The boy Mark is among them. The risen Jesus literally glows.

He tells them to preach the gospel to every creature. We then see him against the background of a modern city. He says, "Lo, I am with you always," his last words in Matthew's Gospel.

DeMille thought that in H. B. Warner he had the perfect actor to play Jesus. Audiences today might not agree, since he not only seems too old for the part but also seems a bit too placid and mild, even in the scene of cleansing the temple, where a bit more fire and anger would have helped. Still, he does project a great deal of love, especially in the many scenes with children, and he has a certain dignity that has been missing in the Jesuses of more recent films. The other roles are well acted, though by our standards today, the acting in almost all silent films seems a bit "hammy."

> DeMille stated that entertainer Will Rogers told him, "You will never make a greater picture because there is no greater subject."

The King of Kings was released in April 1927, with tickets in New York being presold and a near-riot on the day of the premiere. In Hollywood that May the film was chosen for the opening of Grauman's Chinese Theatre, later to be famous for its footprints of movie stars.

The movie was released in two versions. The "blockbuster" version that played in New York and other large cities ran 155 minutes and included several color sequences. The general release version that most Americans saw ran 112 minutes and had color only in the Easter scene. As usual for a DeMille film, it was not well received by the critics, but the public loved it, not just in the U.S. but in Europe as well. The *New York Times* reviewer admitted that "hardly a whispered word was uttered among the audience." Though the film pleased audiences, including almost all Christians who saw it, it was protested by certain Jewish groups, despite the film's effort to shift the blame for Jesus's death onto the Romans and the high priest Caiaphas instead of the Jews at large. For the most part Christian leaders were ecstastic about the film. In fact, DeMille had engaged several high-profile Christians to serve as religious advisors on the film, including Bruce Barton, author of a best-selling book about Jesus called *The Man Nobody Knows*. Another advisor was Daniel Lord, a Catholic priest who often disagreed with the dictatorial DeMille about details of the script. At one point DeMille got so aggravated that he told Lord to "go to hell." Lord supposedly replied, "I already have a reservation elsewhere."

In his autobiography, published in 1959, DeMille speculated that *The King of Kings* was being screened somewhere in the world every day since its release and had been seen by an estimated 800 million people. Not all these were *paying* customers, for missionaries used it for evangelistic purposes, taking advantage of the fact that in a silent film it is fairly easy to substitute titles in other languages (both easier and cheaper than the dubbing or subtitles used in sound films). DeMille was possibly correct in writing that "probably more people have been told the story of Jesus of Nazareth through *The King of Kings* than through any other single work, except the Bible itself."[4] Or at least that was true until the 1979 film *Jesus*, which has also been widely used by missionaries and evangelists (see page 222).

One closing, and pleasant, footnote: DeMille claimed he gave all his profits from *The King of Kings* to charity.

Who Wants to Hear Actors Talk?

A seismic shift in the movie industry occurred on October 6, 1927. This was the release date of *The Jazz Singer*, often described as the first movie with synchronized sound. It wasn't, and in fact, it was a silent movie with four sound interludes, which featured several songs and bits of dialogue by the star, singer Al Jolson. Audiences lined up to see one of their favorite celebrities singing at them from a movie screen. Warner Brothers had gambled on this "part-talkie" film, and the gamble paid off handsomely. All the other studios began production of "talkies." A gangster picture, *Lights of New York*, which premiered in July 1928, was the first all-talking film. By the end of 1929, almost half the twenty thousand theaters in America were wired for sound. Sound films and the Great Depression came into being at the same time. The sound films would help many people escape, momentarily at least, the dreariness of that period.

Let's pause here to mention a little-known fact: the groundbreaking film *The Jazz Singer* was actually based on a story and play with the very biblical title *The Day of Atonement*. The story concerns a Jewish cantor who wants his musically talented son to follow in his footsteps (singing in the synagogue worship service, that is). But the son (played by Al Jolson) wants to become a pop singer, and the drama in the story comes from father and son learning to accept each other. Jolson sings several pop songs in the film, but he also sings the Jewish *Kol Nidre*, the prayer that is sung in every Jewish synagogue on the annual Day of Atonement (Yom Kippur). The "atonement" in the play's title had a double meaning—not only the reconciliation of God and man (which is what Yom Kippur is all about) but also the reconcilation of father and son. In a sense the movie symbolizes what happened to the Jews who created the film industry: leaving behind their religion in order to achieve fame and fortune. People reared in Christian homes pretty much did the same thing when they settled in Hollywood.

Oddly, from the very beginning, sound was a possibility for film. In fact, Thomas Edison originally thought of film as an adjunct to another of his inventions, the phonograph. In some ways it is remarkable that sound was so long in coming. Once it was established, audiences loved it. Supposedly one of the movie moguls had asked the question, "Who wants to hear actors *talk*?" Apparently the public said "We do!" with great enthusiasm. The old movie cameras were bulky and noisy, meaning the film included the noise of the camera itself, but producers quickly overcame this problem. A few stars with bad voices found themselves out of work (a situation that is spoofed in the film *Singin' in the Rain*), but a new wave of stars became as familiar from their voices as from their faces. Scriptwriting changed dramatically, of course, with writers having to provide lots more dialogue than the old silent films required. A new job category was established: film composer. In time some noted composers provided background music for films, and the use of music was a key element in film storytelling, including the biblical films.

The coming of sound did not mean that all the old silent films were thrown on the scrap heap. On the contrary, many of them were rereleased with synchronized soundtracks, giving them a new lease on life. Among the rereleases were *From the Manger to the Cross* and, of course, DeMille's *King of Kings*.

When *The Jazz Singer* was released in October 1927, all film studios still had numerous silent films in production. One, released in 1928, was yet another version of the story of Judith, this one made in Italy. Another was Warner Brothers' *Noah's Ark*, directed by Hungarian-born Michael Curtiz. In 1928 producer Daryl Zanuck had just joined Warner Brothers, and he promised "the greatest picture ever made." He hired boy wonder Curtiz, who had directed the 1922 *Sodom and Gomorrah* in Austria. *Noah's Ark* opens with a view of a tower like the tower of Babel. Curtiz was on a fairly tight budget, so instead of hiring animals to be brought in, he sent photographers to zoos to film the beasts, then matted the images into one frame, which contained as many as eighteen shots, making it look like the animals are all boarding at one time. For the flood, a huge holding tank held six hundred gallons. The aim was to empty the huge tank onto a pagan Babylonian set, drowning the heathen. Three hundred extras were on the set, plus another hundred men to create wind, lightning, rain, and the flood, along with fifteen cameras. Buildings were rigged with dynamite and detonation wires. The studio spent $40,000 on special effects that ran only a few seconds on film. Several of the extras were injured, and one lost a leg, leading to new safety regulations in Hollywood. The film includes shots of frightened pagans clinging to the high walls of the ark amid the pounding waves. The evil Babylon lies as a flooded ruin. The pagans' costumes were based more or less on authentic Babylonian designs. The scene in the pagan temple of Hadrashar was stunning.

Obviously the film took some major liberties with the Noah story in Genesis—or, more precisely, added a lot of material, since the story as it stands in Genesis would probably fill up only a half hour or so. Since Genesis says that God sent the flood because mankind had become so wicked, it made sense for the film to show just how wicked people were. In the film, Noah's son Japheth is blinded by the pagans and chained to a mill, and his future wife, Miriam, is about to be sacrificed by the wicked pagans. (The scriptwriter must have borrowed the blinding and chaining from the story of Samson in Judges.) Then a great wind blows the temple doors open and announces Noah. A ring of fire protects the ark against pagan troops. When Noah hears God's warning about the flood, he encounters God in a burning bush and sees the words in a flaming book on a mountainside. (Here the writer was borrowing from the Moses saga, apparently. A lot of Bible readers in the audience may have been scratching their heads and saying, "Hey, wait a minute!") The film could have been subtitled *Bible Mish-Mash*.

Like several films made after *The Jazz Singer*, this one was a "part talkie." It had been filmed as a silent, using titles, but after the shooting was done, the actors were herded back into a recording studio so that some parts of the dialogue were audible.

Despite all the expense, the producer's promise of "the greatest picture ever made," and the advertising tagline of "The Greatest Drama of the Age," the movie did not make a huge profit. Following the great success of the 1956 epic *The Ten Commandments*, Warner rereleased *Noah's Ark* in 1958, eliminating the titles and badly recorded dialogue and using a narrator on the soundtrack. It was not a success.

Noah's Ark was, it turned out, Hollywood's last attempt at a biblical film for many years, the 1930s and 1940s being "the lean years" for the Bible on-screen.

3

THE LEAN YEARS

The 1930s and 1940s

Every movie buff knows that the 1930s and 1940s were Hollywood's heyday, with films being released in huge quantities and (generally speaking) of high quality. The silent film had died a quiet death; people embraced sound, and with each passing year sound improved in quality. Yet, oddly, for two entire decades Hollywood did not release one single film based on the Bible (not counting Cecil B. DeMille's *Samson and Delilah*, released late in 1949 and earning most of its profits in 1950). One film very loosely tied to the Bible was *The Green Pastures*, which will be discussed in more detail later in the chapter, but it barely qualifies as the kind of biblical film discussed elsewhere in this book.

Germany released three biblical films in the 1930s: *Joseph and His Brothers*, *The Sacrifice of Isaac*, and *Joseph in the Land of Egypt*. Britain released *Her Strange Desire*, the story of Joseph and Potiphar's wife. And from France came *Golgotha*, director Julien Duvivier's depiction of the Passion week. It has the distinction of being the first sound movie about Jesus. A 1923 German-made film about Jesus, *INRI*, was rereleased in 1934 with a new soundtrack and with the English title *Crown of Thorns*. In sum: for two decades there were two films about Jesus, three about the Joseph of Genesis, and one about Abraham and Isaac—none of them produced in the U.S. Why this dearth of biblical movies, especially since Cecil B. DeMille had experienced such huge success with his 1927 film *The King of Kings*? Didn't the Great Depression and the horrors of World War II make people want to turn to spiritual subjects?

The numbers say yes, since more people went to church in 1940 than in 1930, and even more in 1950. And bookstores certainly got the impression that religion was important. One bestseller of the 1930s was *The Life of Our Lord*, a book written in the 1800s by novelist Charles Dickens for his children. Beginning in 1939, Jewish-Christian novelist Sholem Asch cranked out a string of biblical best-sellers, *The Nazarene*, *The Apostle* (about Paul), and *Mary*. Lloyd Douglas, a Lutheran minister, continued his second career as a successful novelist with his 1943 semibiblical book *The Robe*, following it up with the 1948 story of Peter, *The Big Fisherman*. (Both these would make it to film in the 1950s.) Fulton Oursler's retelling of the life of Christ, *The Greatest Story Ever Told*, was a huge seller in 1949 and later. In 1942 the bestselling book was A. J. Cronin's *Keys of the Kingdom*, the story of a priest, and in 1943 it was *The Song of Bernadette*, the story of a peasant girl who became a Catholic saint. On the other hand, Alfred Kinsey's *Sexual Behavior in the Human Male* was a big seller from 1948 on, indicating that some Americans had things on their minds besides faith.

In fact, during these two decades Hollywood did not shy away from religious subjects. *Boys Town*, the story of the priest Father Flanagan, was extremely popular, and Spencer Tracy won an Oscar for playing the priest. *The Keys of the Kingdom* and *The Song of Bernadette* were both made into extremely successful films, and the whole point of *Bernadette* was that even in the modern world, God still works miracles. The huge hit of 1944 was *Going My Way*, with Bing Crosby as a singing priest who manages to turn some scapegrace street kids into a church choir. This was followed a year later by a sequel, *The Bells of St. Mary's*, again with Crosby and with Ingrid Bergman as an appealing nun. *Come to the Stable*

Will H. Hays, for whom Hollywood's self-imposed Hays Code was named. In all his photos, Hays looked dour and moral—which he was. Hollywood preferred having this straitlaced Presbyterian layman monitoring its films to having the government play censor.

(1949) had nuns as its heroines. *Joan of Arc* (1948) centered around one of the Catholic church's most popular saints. Religion found its way into other successful films, such as *Mrs. Miniver*, showing an English town in wartime, the film ending with a minister delivering a sermon in a bombed-out church. Frank Capra's *It's a Wonderful Life* depicted a man saved from suicide by a watchful angel. World War II did indeed seem to turn people back to God—but not to films about the Bible.

The simple fact is, Hollywood thrives on imitation. Had one of the studios released a biblical film in these two decades, the others probably would have followed suit—assuming the first one made money, that is. But the last successful biblical film had been DeMille's *King of Kings*, which was a silent. No precedent existed for making a sound film based on the Bible, and no one was willing to set the precedent—until DeMille himself made *Samson and Delilah* at the end of the decade. During these lean years for the Bible on film, audiences had to be satisfied with two silent movies that were rereleased with synchronized soundtracks: the 1925 *Ben-Hur*, rereleased in 1931, and the 1912 *From the Manger to the Cross*, rereleased in 1938. *The Last Days of Pompeii*, released in 1935, was an "almost biblical" movie, with Pontius Pilate among its cast of characters.

The 1930s and 1940s may have been lean years for biblical movies, but biblical morality in films was probably at its peak. This was in no small part due to William Harrison Hays, usually known as Will, a strict Presbyterian and, as it happened, national chairman of the Republican party. After helping Warren Harding get elected president in 1920, Hays was given the job of U.S. postmaster general but resigned to become the "czar" of Hollywood self-censoring. Several scandals in the 1920s had given Hollywood an image as an immoral cesspool (which it was, frankly). Summer 1921 brought the scandal of comic actor Fatty Arbuckle, who was accused of killing an actress/prostitute who was present at one of his wild parties. On September 23, 1921, *Variety* ran the headline "Worldwide Condemnation of Pictures as Aftermath of Arbuckle Affair." Some states, including New York and Massachusetts, began to make noises about passing film censorship laws. The thriving film industry had no desire for any government—federal, state, or local—to play censor, so several studio heads got together and chose the wiser course of *self*-censorship. The highly moral Will Hays seemed just the man to keep would-be censors off producers' backs. So beginning in 1922, Hays headed the Motion Picture Producers and Distributors of America (MMPDA). On assuming his new post, Hays announced that he hoped to develop the highest moral and constructive efficiency in films, but wished to be neither a censor nor a reformer. In fact, he was both.

Criticism of films' immorality continued through the 1920s, so in 1930 Hays had Martin Quigley, a Catholic publisher, and Daniel Lord, a Jesuit priest, draw up the Production Code, which came to be known as the Hays Code. The Code set out in considerable detail the limits to be observed in depicting crime and sexuality. Criminals, adulterers, and other wrongdoers had to be punished; family life had to be seen as a positive force; religious and ethnic groups were not to be offended. Films were to avoid "all low, disgusting, unpleasant though not necessarily evil subjects."[1] Directors were to follow "the dictates of good taste and regard for the sensibilities of the audience."[2] Needless to say, no profanity or obscenity was allowed. Rhett Butler's final "damn" at the end of *Gone with the Wind* had to be given the Hays office's approval, with all the studios understanding that this one exception would *not* set a precedent. (In 1948 the film version of the long-running play *Life with Father* was not allowed to conclude with the play's famous last line, "I'm going to be baptized, damn it!")

> The Hays Code prohibited depicting clergy in comic or villainous roles. Films were not to ridicule any religious faith.

People today may snicker at the strictness of the Hays Code. But on the positive side, during the Hays Code era, American movies stressed patriotism, loyalty, truth, family, religion, courage, fidelity, the rewards of virtue, and the punishment of vice. In a sense the movies were a more effective form of social engineering than Prohibition had been. The movies were a formative influence on

American society and had a huge influence on how foreigners perceived Americans. Life imitates art, and as scandalous as some of the movie people were in their private lives, they were clean on-screen, and evil was always punished. With about two-thirds of the American people going to see at least one film per week, the movies could not help but be an influence—and, with the Code at work, a mostly positive one.

In his autobiography, director Cecil B. DeMille wrote approvingly of the Code: "What all those who worked on it and adopted it had in common, and shared with the overwhelming majority of the American people, was a belief in the natural moral law and in the Ten Commandments as an expression of that law. That is the basis of the Production Code. To my mind, it stands as an example of the effective unity which can be achieved by men of very different beliefs, but of common fundamental principles and shared good will."[3]

The Production Code Administration was felt at every stage of filmmaking, from selection of a story to script approval to approval of the final film. From 1934 on, no member of the MMPDA could release a film without the PCA's seal of approval.

Also in 1934 the Legion of Decency was formed, inspired by Roman Catholic bishops and approved by a papal encyclical of 1936. The Legion approved or disapproved of certain films and had the power to influence large groups of people to boycott certain films. While thought of as being strictly Catholic, the Legion's influence was approved by many Protestant Christians as well.

Hays retired in 1945 but stayed on as an advisor to the MMPDA for five more years. With the Hays Code and the Legion of Decency watching every film carefully, all films of these two decades safely fell into what would now be a G rating. No parent had to puzzle over the question, "Will this be all right for my kids?" because every film was family-friendly—and highly moral.

One other item worth mentioning: by the 1930s, most Americans regarded moviegoing as a necessity, not a luxury. Movies were a fixture of pop culture, and people of all classes went to see them, many people attending once a week or more. That being the case, the Hays Code served the useful purpose of making movies appealing to as wide an audience as possible—including children and religious folk. If there were few depictions of Bible stories in the 1930s and 1940s, at least the films were inoffensive and also grounded in a moral foundation of which Christians would approve.

The Green Pastures: *Fish Fry Heaven*

Released July 1936
Warner Brothers
93 minutes
Filmed in Hollywood

Producer: Jack Warner
Directors: Marc Connelly and William
Keighley
Screenplay: Marc Connelly, Sheridan
Gibney
Photography: Hal Mohr
Based on the play by Marc Connelly,
which was based on Roark Bradford's
book of stories called *Ol' Man Adam
an' His Chillun*

De Lawd/Adam/Hezdrel: Rex Ingram
Gabriel: Oscar Polk
Noah: Eddie Anderson
Moses/Sexton: Frank Wilson
Deshee/Isaac: George Reed
Pharaoh: Ernest Whitman
High Priest: George Randol
Abraham/King of Babylon/Magician: Billy
Cumby
Zeba: Edna M. Harris
Master of Ceremonies/Man on Ground: Slim
Thompson
Mrs. Noah: Ida Forsyne
Cain: Al Stokes
Eve: Myrtle Anderson
Joshua: Reginald Fenderson

In this age of political correctness, when Walt Disney's *Song of the South* has not been released on video because of its depiction of plantation slaves, it is rather amazing that this curio from 1936 is available, given the dialect the characters speak in. Given how little known it is to the general public, perhaps it is "under the radar." In any case, it is an enjoyable and interesting film, one that holds the distinction of being the only U.S.-made film of the 1930s that was based—*loosely*, anyway—on the Bible. More precisely, it is the film version of Marc Connelly's Pulitzer Prize–winning stage play, which ran on Broadway from February 1930 to August 1931. The play was adapted from Roark Bradford's 1928 book *Ol' Man Adam an' His Chillun*, a collection of stories he had published in *New York World*. He followed it up with *Ol' King David an' de Philistine Boys* in 1930. Born in Tennessee, Bradford grew up listening to tales told by black workers on his father's land, and he picked up further stories living in Georgia, Mississippi, and Louisiana. Many of the stories were from the Bible but paraphrased the way black preachers often told the stories to their congregations. So you might say the movie is about three steps removed from the Bible itself.

Marc Connelly was a member of the Algonquin Round Table, a New York gathering of sophisticated (and cynical) wits that included Robert Benchley and Dorothy Parker. Connelly had no religious purpose at all in the play, just the desire to entertain an audience with comedy. Nonetheless, for all its comedy, it isn't completely irreverent. In reviewing it at the time of its release, the *New*

God ("De Lawd") with a white beard and frock coat, amiably played by Rex Ingram in the 1936 film *The Green Pastures*. The all-black cast presented Old Testament stories and depicted heaven as an eternal fish fry. It was Hollywood's only biblical film of the 1930s and 1940s, until 1949's *Samson and Delilah*.

York Times said the movie gave "a strange nostalgic feeling that it ought to be true, and if it isn't, we are, somehow, the worse for it" and that it had "the irresistible compulsion of simple faith."[4]

The movie opens with the title embossed on a book. African American spirituals are sung as titles roll by on clouds and old worn pages. Words appear on the screen: "God appears in many forms to those who believe in Him. Thousands of Negroes in the Deep South visualize God and Heaven in terms of people and things they know in their everyday life. *The Green Pastures* is an attempt to portray that humble, reverent conception."

In the first scene we see a small country church, the white-haired pastor ringing the bell. Children are seen preparing for Sunday school. Old Mr. Deshee is teaching the "begots" (geneaologies) from Genesis. One child asks what God looks like, and Deshee says he always imagined him as a fine old preacher he knew. Deshee explains that before the world was made, the angels sang and had fish fries all the time. The choir sings, "Rise and shine and give God the glory." We see white-robed, winged angels at a grand fish fry, skipping rope, playing, and eating. The angel Gabriel, who is very tall, arrives and announces God: "Gangway for the Lord God Jehovah." The Lord is white haired, bearded, in a black frock coat. With a smile the Lord says, "Let the fish fry begin."

God is a lovable character but also exudes great strength. The Lord decides to "rah" (rare) back and "pass a miracle." He makes the firmament —"a whole mess o' firmament"—the earth, and the sun "to dry things out." The angels watch as the newly formed earth begins to spin. The Lord says, "It's a good earth; maybe I ought to put someone down there to enjoy it." He decides to make man in his own image. The newly formed man is the same actor, Rex Ingram, but looks younger. He is shirtless, not nude. God tells Adam he needs a family, "caze at heart you is a family man." He gives Adam and the pigtailed Eve "the run of the whole garden." He warns them against the fruit from one tree and says, "I got a hundred thousand things to do before you take yo' next break." Back in Sunday school, the children recall that Adam and Eve sinned and "got driv' out of the garden."

The New York Times later named The Green Pastures one of the ten best films of 1936—and lots of fine films were released that year.

In the next scene Cain, "who was a mean rascal," stands over the dead body of his brother Abel. The Lord tells him to "get yo'self down the road and far away." The Lord says, "I don't like the way things is going at all."

The Lord has an office and uses Gabriel as a secretary. We see that God has an entire universe to hold together. God remembers "the poor little earth," saying, "I wasn't any too pleased with that job." He decides to return to earth and "see how them poor humans is makin' out." Wearing his hat and carrying a cane, God sees a loose woman, Zeba, plucking her ukulele on a Sunday. God scolds her, but she says people now just use Sunday to get over Saturday. God is appalled to see how immoral man has become. He sees men on their knees and thinks they are praying, but they are shooting dice and boozing. The whole village is full of drinking and carousing. God meets the local preacher, who is lamenting that his church was empty that day. He invites the Lord to Sunday dinner. The preacher is Noah, and he and his family seem to be the only decent people on earth. Noah feels a twitch in his knee—"might be a sign of rain." Noah realizes he is talking to God, who says, "I'm a God of wrath and vengeance; that's why I'm gonna destroy this world." He tells Noah to take two of every bird and animal on the ark—and seeds and sprouts too (something the Bible overlooks). Noah recalls there was a circus in town, so he may be able to "rustle up" giraffes and elephants. The "ark" turns out to be Noah's house with a boat built around it. The locals tell him he's crazy. The animals parade—labeled—into the ark. Noah wears a slicker. The rain finally subsides, and a rainbow appears over the ark. A dove returns with a green twig in his mouth. God appears on the ark and tells Noah he was watching over everything. "I'm startin' all over, Noah."

But back in Sunday school, Mr. Deshee tells the children, "The minute the Lord turned his back, they was bad as ever." The Lord and Gabriel return from having surveyed the earth, sorrowing over man's sins. Gabriel suggests he "doom 'em all again" as with the flood. The Lord has a new idea. The patriarchs Abraham, Isaac, and Jacob, now angels, enter God's office. He tells them he wants to give their descendants a fine piece of land, Canaan. They remind God that their descendants are in bondage under Pharaoh, but their descendant Moses will lead them out. The Lord emphasizes that the leader needs holiness more than brains. If he is holy enough, God will take care of the brains.

Moses is tending sheep in Midian. The Lord approaches him in the burning bush and says, "Maybe you notice the bush ain't burned up." God walks in with his cane. Moses has a slight stammer, but God cures it and says, "I'm gonna make you the best tricker in the world. . . . I'm sick and tired of the way King Pharaoh keeps treatin' my children." Moses's tricks (miracles), God says, will convince Pharaoh. Moses asks that his brother Aaron aid him. God causes Aaron to appear out of thin air. God shows that Moses's cane can do tricks. The choir sings, "Let my people go!"

The fat Pharaoh enters his palace, which looks like a gaudy Masonic lodge. He has a bevy of magicians. Pharaoh asks how the killing of the Hebrew babies is proceeding. One of the magicians suggests making the bricks without straw in addition to killing babies. The two "country boys," Moses and Aaron, are ushered in, bringing their "wonderful walkin' stick," which morphs into a snake. Pharaoh is impressed until he learns they are Hebrews. He orders his men to put them to the sword, but the soldiers' swords can't touch them. Moses tells Pharaoh to free the Hebrews, but he refuses. Moses tells Pharaoh that his next big trick will be worked by the Lord. He says the "oldest boy" in every house will be struck down. Aaron raises the cane and men begin to fall dead. Men bring in Pharaoh's own oldest son.

The ragged Israelites wander the wilderness. It has been forty years and the white-bearded Moses tells the young, spunky Joshua that he will lead the people into Canaan and conquer Jericho. Then "the Lord will take charge. . . . He ain't gon' fail us now." Moses will stay behind while the Israelites press on. He tells Aaron to take care of the ark of the covenant. As the people pass Moses, they all pat his shoulder. Left alone, Moses meets the Lord again. He recalls that he angered the Lord once, but the Lord says Moses is a good man. He takes Moses to another place: "It's a million times nicer than the land of Canaan."

Up to this point, the movie has re-created various familiar stories from the Old Testament. From this point on, it seems to go off in its own direction, not quite tied to any particular characters or books of the Bible. In the next scene, set in the royal ballroom of Babylon, dancing girls gyrate lewdly, but a prophet enters and warns that God sees "nothing but sin throughout the whole earth"—which is probably a fair summing up of what the prophets in general said.

The next scene concerns a man named Hezdrel (not named in the Bible), who is in Jerusalem and learns from his soldiers that King Herod plans to burn down the temple and the ark of the covenant with it. (Herod in fact *rebuilt* the temple, and the ark had long been vanished when Herod lived.) God goes down and talks to Hezdrel (they are played by the same actor) and learns from him that mercy is now seen as more important than wrath. Hezdrel says that his preacher, "old Mr. Hosea," tells them to have faith in their "new Lord," not "that old God," the one of wrath. The new God is the same as the old one, but now he's a God of mercy. Man learned about mercy through suffering. God feels he has learned what faith is. God says, "I guess I was so far away, I was just way behind the times." The theology in this scene is puzzling, to say the least.

Back in heaven, God in his rocking chair is surrounded by his choir. God is reflecting on Hezdrel's words about mercy and learning through suffering. God wonders if it's true that even God must suffer. The angels look over the fence of heaven and see a man (obviously Jesus) carrying a cross up a hill. An angel notes that the burden is too much for one man to carry. At this, God has a flash of insight. "Yes!" he says with a smile. Back in Sunday school the children smile and depart. This last scene is inspiring but, like the one before it, rather puzzling.

As this synopsis indicates, the play and movie (and the stories they were based on) played fast and loose with the Old Testament. Some of the characters, notably Hezdrel, are not in the Bible at all. Aside from that, some people may question whether depicting God in human form is a good thing—especially given the second of the Ten Commandments. In fact, when the movie was released, it was banned in Great Britain and several other countries because they considered it blasphemous to represent God on-screen in this way. The movie did not raise much of a stir in the U.S., where it was not a huge success. Few Christians protested it because it was marketed as a comedy, not a serious movie about the Bible. Still, despite the spoofing nature of the film, God does come across as a thoroughly fine and noble character, and actor Rex Ingram rose to the challenge of portraying the Maker of all things. The image of heaven as a continual fish fry with fun and fellowship may seem a bit shallow, but it might help to recall the New Testament using the images of a feast and a banquet to describe the indescribable joys of heaven.

The title of the film, by the way, is from Psalm 23: "He maketh me to lie down in green pastures" (v. 2 KJV).

In concluding this chapter on the 1930s and '40s, it is worth mentioning that other Bible films were being produced during this period, although not by the commercial film studios. Several Christian denominations and independent Christian producers released a number of films, most of them on the life of Jesus. These were what I refer to as "church films," designed to be rented or sold to churches or other groups, presumably for showing (free of charge) to members. As noted in the introduction, these films are outside the concern of this book. But the church films of this time period are worth noting, if only because they indicate that many Christians had obviously overcome their antipathy to motion pictures or at least considered motion pictures to be a valid way of presenting the truths of the Bible.

4

THE GOLDEN AGE

The Fabulous 1950s

This chapter could have been titled "Big Screen versus Small Screen," for the biggest effect on moviemaking in the 1950s came from the "new kid on the block," television. Thanks to TV, Hollywood had to do some serious rethinking about how to keep audiences lining up to see films.

Before 1947, television was centered in New York, since that was the one place where a lot of people—but still a minority—actually owned televisions. Programs were all live. Advertisers at first weren't drawn to TV, since the audience was so small. A major change occurred with the 1947 World Series. An NBC executive suggested airing the games, since the teams were the New York Yankees and Brooklyn Dodgers. It was a ratings smash and helped the sales of television sets in New York and beyond.

NBC and CBS both started airing regular programs, since they couldn't count on the occasional "special" like the World Series to hold an audience. In 1947 only about 2 percent of American households owned televisions. By 1956, 70 percent did. In 1949 there were 28 TV stations broadcasting to 172,000 television sets. This had jumped to 15.3 million sets by 1952 and 32 million by 1955.

Hollywood felt threatened in a big way, and the major studios initially prohibited their contract actors from working in TV. The movie execs may have hoped—foolishly—that TV would simply starve from having no talent and fade away. But in fact plenty of stage and radio actors were willing to take a chance in the new medium, and many future stars, directors, and writers cut their teeth on live TV dramas like *Studio One*. And plenty of failed movie stars—such as Lucille Ball—found TV to be a perfect showcase for their talents.

Hollywood realized that TV was not going away, so it had to do something. One step was taken in June 1952 by Twentieth Century-Fox head Darryl Zanuck, who announced his studio would cease production of "B" movies, and Jack Warner (of Warner Brothers) soon followed suit, with both studios vowing to concentrate only on "major" films. The change could be seen in the number of films released—534 in 1953, down to 392 in 1955. The studios' logic was something like this: thanks to TV, people can be entertained in the privacy of their homes, but people still enjoy going to a theater for an obvious reason—because it gets them out of the house. To make them want to leave the house, films had to offer something TV couldn't—higher quality, big-name stars, color, and, as of 1953, an enormously wide screen. The first widescreen film was the phenomenally popular *The Robe*, released in September 1953, with the studio (Twentieth Century-Fox) using the process called CinemaScope. Paramount called its wide-screen process VistaVision and decided that only Cecil B. DeMille could crank out a really successful VistaVision epic, which would be the 1956 spectacle *The Ten Commandments*.

Other innovations were less successful, including two introduced in 1952 by producers hoping to pull the audiences in: Cinerama and 3-D. *This Is Cinerama* opened in New York. *Bwana Devil*, in 3-D, opened a few weeks later. (One novelty that never caught on was Smell-O-Vision, used but once, in the 1960 film *Scent of Mystery*. Special "odor projectors" were used.)

The innovations were only partially successful. By 1959 revenue from films had dropped below $1 billion for the first time since

World War II. Blockbusters like *The Ten Commandments* brought in the money but also cost a lot. And some blockbusters, like the 1956 film *War and Peace*, were flops.

Some of the new films had an epic look but were done on the cheap—usually filmed in the cradle of epic films, Italy. Between 1957 and 1965, Italy produced more than a hundred "sword and sandal" epics, many in conjunction with American, French, and Spanish companies. The 1957 *Hercules* cost a mere $120,000 and earned $18 million, making a star out of bodybuilder Steve Reeves, who had been considered for the lead in the 1949 *Samson and Delilah*. Italy cranked out more silly fluff featuring some muscleman fighting monsters or tyrants in practically any era of history or prehistory. Typically there was a beefy hero—Reeves, Reg Park, Gordon Scott, and others—plus usually a blonde, buxom, virtuous heroine he rescues; a pointy-bearded villain; a dark-haired, seductive, dragonish villainess; at least one monster to fight; a race or other chase scene, and the like. Sets and props were usually plastic (and viewers could tell), and

> Many of the cheaply made Italian "sword and sandal" epics had heroes named Samson or Goliath, even though their adventures had little or no connection with people of the Bible. At least one film included not only Samson and Goliath but also the Greek hero Hercules. Apparently the fans of these films were not wise in the Bible or ancient mythology.

things were often given a vague "Middle Eastern" feel without accurately reflecting any particular ancient culture. Films like these could not afford teams of researchers like those employed by Cecil B. DeMille.

Not all the films made in Italy were cheapies, however. Labor had become expensive in California, and studio space and labor in Italy were cheap. In the 1950s, Rome's Cinecitta studio was known as "Hollywood on the Tiber." *Ben-Hur* would be filmed there, and, as later chapters will show, Italy would be the chosen locale for many other ancient and biblical films.

Aside from the movies versus television competition, what else of note was going on in the 1950s? In the U.S. people appeared (at least on the surface) to be religious—or, at any rate, churchgoers. In 1910, 43 percent of Americans were attached to churches, roughly the same as in the 1920s, but by 1940 it was more like 49 percent, indicating that the Depression had made people turn to religion. By 1950 it was 55 percent, then 69 percent by 1960. So the 1950s really was a religious decade.

In 1954 the phrase "under God" (borrowed from Lincoln's Gettysburg Address) was added to the Pledge of Allegiance. Most Americans wanted to identify themselves as believers in God, especially since atheistic communism seemed to be on the march globally, with the Korean War (1950–53) being the first war pitting American soldiers against communists. Even when that war ended, the Cold War lingered on, and no American could forget the menace of communism.

As if to symbolize the wholesome decade, Disneyland opened in California in 1955. It was no accident that its central feature was Main Street, U.S.A.

Billy Graham's first big crusade was in 1949, drawing 350,000 people over eight weeks. His 1953 book *Peace with God* was a huge seller. On the Catholic side, Fulton Sheen's *Peace of Soul* was published in 1949, selling well and leading to his TV series *Life Is Worth Living*, with an audience of 30 million. Norman Vincent Peale's 1952 *The Power of Positive Thinking*, saturated with upbeat verses from the Bible, was also a huge seller. Some other bestsellers of the decade: the novel *Moses* by Sholem Asch; Catherine Marshall's *A Man Called Peter*; Fulton Oursler's *The Greatest Faith Ever Known*; *The Prayers of Peter Marshall*; Jim Bishop's *The Day Christ Died*; Taylor Caldwell's novel *Dear and Glorious Physician* (about St. Luke). Lloyd Douglas's 1943 novel *The Robe* shot back to the bestseller list thanks to the 1953 film version. J. B. Phillips's translation of the New Testament sold well, as did the new Revised Standard Version of the Bible, giving some competition to the venerable King James Version. In fact, the RSV was the bestselling nonfiction book for three years running (1952–54).

But the decade wasn't totally wholesome. Alfred Kinsey's *Sexual Behavior in the Human Male* (1948) was a huge seller, followed in 1954 with *Sexual Behavior in the Human Female*. Suddenly lots of people were reading about sex and, even more important, finding out that lots of unconventional sex was taking place—or so Kinsey led them to believe. Kinsey's assertion that 50 percent of husbands and 26 percent of wives had committed adultery certainly got their attention. Even though the old Hays Code was still in effect, Hollywood had let a fairly benign view of adultery slip through in *From Here to Eternity* (1953). In 1956 there was *Baby Doll*, described in *Time* as "just possibly the dirtiest American-made motion picture that has ever been legally permitted." (It is a very tame movie by today's standards, but it was indeed considered dirty when it was released.) In December 1953 Hugh Hefner launched *Playboy*, which would make dirtiness highly profitable. The steamy novel *Peyton Place*, written by a dowdy housewife, sold 6 million copies in the years 1956–58 and was made into a highly successful film. In 1959 the long-suppressed D. H. Lawrence novel *Lady Chatterly's Lover* was finally published legally in the U.S.

The music scene also changed dramatically, with preachers denouncing something called "rock 'n' roll." Acts like Elvis Presley and Bill Haley and His Comets seem extremely tame by today's standards, but the scolding preachers were correct: there was a definite sexual element to this new form of music and the dancing that accompanied it. Only gradually would the sexual element become blatant.

For the most part, films of the 1950s were squeaky clean, especially by today's standards. The effects of *Playboy*, rock 'n' roll, Kinsey's books, and the like would not really show up in films until the 1960s, when the Hays Code was pretty much retired. Most films of the 1950s were "family friendly," and the most successful ones provided what TV could not: a huge screen, glorious color, and stereophonic sound. The most profitable films included several from the Disney studios (*Cinderella*; *Alice in Wonderland*; *Old Yeller*; *Peter Pan*; *20,000 Leagues under the Sea*; *The Shaggy Dog*), musicals (*The King and I*, *Gigi*, *Show Boat*, *South Pacific*), comedies (*No Time for Sergeants*, *Mister Roberts*, *How to Marry a Millionaire*), westerns (*Shane*), and war epics (*Battle Cry*, *The Bridge on the River Kwai*). Only a handful of top-grossers pushed morality to the edge: *Peyton Place*, *From Here to Eternity*, *Auntie Mame*, *Cat on a Hot Tin Roof*.

Biblical and semibiblical films, so rare in the 1930s and 1940s, would enter a golden age.

Top grossing films in particular years:

1950:   *Samson and Delilah* (second-highest-grossing film of the year)

1951:   *David and Bathsheba* (highest-grossing)

1952:   *Quo Vadis* (second-highest-grossing)

1953:   *The Robe* (highest-grossing)

1957:   *The Ten Commandments* (highest-grossing)

1960:   *Ben-Hur* (highest-grossing), *Solomon and Sheba*
        (seventh-highest-grossing)

[Note: *The Ten Commandments* was released late in 1956 but made most of its profits in 1957. *Ben-Hur* and *Solomon and Sheba* were released late in 1959 but made most of their profits in 1960.]

The decade would also see the only instance (so far) of a biblical film being nominated for a best picture Oscar: *The Ten Commandments*.

One other development deserves mention here: a crop of science fiction films, many of them now considered classics. The Cold War made it inevitable that Americans would flock to films about evil invaders. One film that stands out, however, was about a very saintly invader, the gentle alien hero of *The Day the Earth Stood Still* (1954). I almost included this film in this book because it clearly parallels the story of Christ in many ways: a man from "another world" comes to earth, preaches peace, assumes the name "Mr. Carpenter," and is killed, then brought to life again. Many people write off science fiction as mindless fluff for the kids, but this film had some moral and spiritual substance—more substance, in fact, than the first biblical epic of the decade, *Samson and Delilah*.

Samson and Delilah: *Let the Epics Begin!*

Released December 1949
Paramount
128 minutes

Producer-Director: Cecil B. DeMille
Screenplay: Jesse L. Lasky Jr., Fredric M. Frank
Photography: George Barnes
Music: Victor Young

Samson: Victor Mature
Delilah: Hedy Lamarr
The Saran: George Sanders
Semadar: Angela Lansbury
Ahtur: Henry Wilcoxon
Miriam: Olive Deering
Saul: Russell Tamblyn

Released in December 1949, DeMille's *Samson and Delilah* did most of its business in 1950, and in a sense it belongs to the 1950s, for it set the tone for a certain type of Technicolor biblical epic that reached its peak in the decade. Happily, its producer-director wrote at great length in his autobiography about how the film came to be. DeMille claimed he had wanted to film the Samson story for many years, calling it not only "one of the greatest love stories in history or literature" but also "a poignant drama of faith."[1] He neglected to mention that the Samson story had been filmed many times before, including a French film of 1903 that was probably the first film based on the Old Testament. At least five Samson films were made during the silent era, and clearly DeMille was thinking that another one should be done with sound and color.

From the biblical novel *Judge and Fool* by Vladimir Jaboinsky, DeMille got the idea of having Delilah be the younger—and rejected—sister of Samson's Philistine bride. The Bible does not name the sister, but if Delilah was that woman, she had a motive for wanting to destroy Samson, a motive much deeper than merely being offered a bribe by the Philistine lords. Essentially, Samson is given over to the Philistines because of the fury of a scorned woman—who still loves him, which adds some true drama to the latter half of the film.

DeMille met resistance from his studio, Paramount, which did not think audiences would be interested in a biblical epic, even if it was in gaudy color. (Remember that the 1930s and 1940s were lean years in Hollywood for biblical movies.) Paramount had profited from two religious films DeMille directed in the 1930s: *The Sign of the Cross*, dealing with Roman persecution of the early Christians, and *The Crusades*, but a biblical epic sounded like a long shot. So DeMille got his artist Dan Groesbeck to do some sketches of a slinky Delilah and hunky Samson. The executives liked the sketches. DeMille sold it to them more as a passionate love story than as a religious picture. Regarding this human angle, DeMille wrote, "I am sometimes accused of gingering up the Bible with large and lavish infusions of sex and violence. I can only wonder if my accusers have ever read certain parts of the Bible."[2] He is correct: people do tend to forget that the Bible, the Old Testament in particular, is pretty sexual and violent and does not need much "gingering up." DeMille said too many people read the Bible through a "stained-glass telescope which centuries of tradition and form have put between us and the men and women of flesh and blood who lived and wrote the Bible. Clothing them in what we think is reverence, we have too often stripped the men and women of the Bible of their humanity, and I believe that same process strips them of much of their religious value too."[3]

The film actually opens with an orchestral overture, a signal to the audience that this is no ordinary motion picture. The first image is a huge stone statue of the Philistine god Dagon. A man's hands unroll a scroll with the words "Cecil B. DeMille's Samson and Delilah." The credits note that the screenplay by Lasky and Frank is "from original treatments by" Harold Lamb and Vladimir Jabotinsky, "based upon the history of Samson and Delilah in the Holy Bible, Judges, 13–16."

The earth spins in the void, and as the ugly images of idols are seen, a voice states that man has struggled against the "dark forces" that enslave man's mind with "shackles of fear," leading him to be superstitious and to worship "devil gods." Then soldiers march by in armor, as the superstitious inevitably leads to tyranny. But deep in man's heart still burns "the unquenchable will for freedom."

The scene switches to the village of Zorah in the land of Dan, "a thousand years" before the birth of Christ. In the man Samson, the narrator says, there burned the "bold dream" of liberty from bondage. In the village, an old man tells children the story of Moses confronting Pharaoh. Armored Philistine soldiers enter and threaten the old man. The women mock them for roughing up old men and women. The soldiers literally grind the old man's face in the mud.

Samson's mother, at home, laments that her son plans to marry a Philistine woman. Samson likes to drink with the Philistines and chase women. His mother wants him to marry the sweet neighbor girl Miriam. Samson says he prefers "forbidden fruit." (Samson's hair is not nearly long enough for a Nazirite, and if he is really drinking with the Philistines, he is not keeping his vow of abstaining from wine.)

Cut from the humble family home to the Philistine lord's home, where the lord is gazing at jewels and silk. The daughter Semadar practices throwing spears at a lion skin. She is the unnamed "woman of Timnah" of Judges 14:1–4. In the movie the Philistine governor of the territory is Samson's rival. He refers to the Philistine king (the saran) as "ruler of the five cities," which is historically accurate. Samson easily bends his spear, shaming the man. A trumpet heralds the saran's approach. Semadar's sister Delilah flirts with Samson. She has her arms clasped tightly around him as they ride out in a chariot to hunt down the lion. Samson turns down the offer of a spear; he kills the lion bare-handed. The scene of him struggling with the lion is rather fake looking, frankly. Delilah watches, terrified and delighted. She showers him with kisses, but he has his mind on her sister. The saran arrives, skeptical at hearing the lion was killed with no weapons. He challenges Samson to fight one of his brawny soldiers. Samson spins the big brute in the air easily. The saran gives him the gold ring, the prize for killing the lion, but Samson says he wants Semadar as his prize.

The wedding feast is held, the Philistine men boozing and making cracks about Samson's supposed strength. Samson tells the riddle: "Out of the eater came forth meat, out of the strong came forth sweetness." If they guess the riddle, he will give all thirty of them a rich set of clothes. Delilah tells the men that womanly wile can wheedle the answer out of Samson. Ahtur asks Semadar to find out the riddle—and threatens to burn the house down if she does not. Semadar weeps because Samson hides the answer from her. He finally tells her the bees built a honeycomb in the lion's bones. At the wedding, Ahtur reveals the answer. Samson is furious. He says, "If you had not plowed with my heifer, you would not have solved my riddle." He rejects Semadar, calling her a "cat from the alleys of Timnah." Her father gives the bride to Ahtur. Samson robs some Philistine men of their fine clothes and brings them back to Semadar's household, literally flinging them in the men's faces. (Judges 14:19 says he "struck down" the men before taking their clothes, meaning he killed them, but the movie softens this—and makes it amusing—by having him simply rob them, leaving the men running about naked, covering themselves with foliage.) The father tells Samson he gave Semadar to Samson's "companion" Ahtur, though Ahtur has seemed more like a rival than companion. Her father offers him Delilah, but he has no interest in her. She admits it was she who told the men to wheedle the riddle out of Semadar. She is madly in love with Samson in spite of him rejecting her. The men run amuck and kill both Semadar and her father, then set the house on fire. Samson swears vengeance on the Philistines, which is in keeping with Judges 14:4. Standing by the burning house, Delilah strikes a Scarlett O'Hara pose and swears she will make Samson curse the day he was born.

The film has definitely altered the account in Judges 15, where, after the incident of the clothing, Samson returns to get his wife but finds she has been given to his friend, and he is offered her younger sister. In retaliation, he sets foxes with torches tied to their tails loose in the Philistines' grain fields. In vengeance for this, they "burned her and her father to death" (Judg. 15:6). Samson takes vengeance again, killing many of them and hiding out in a cave.

The film continues: Samson goes into hiding and the Danites won't squeal on him. The saran decides to overtax the Hebrews so they will give Samson away. This isn't in the Bible, but it does serve to make the Philistines seem like worse villains. In the Bible, men of the tribe of Judah hand Samson over—he goes peacefully—to the Philistines. In the movie, we see he has been handed over; he walks behind a Philistine chariot with his hands bound. Then "the Spirit of the LORD came upon him in power" (Judg. 15:14)—a literal wind suggests God's breath—and he breaks his bonds and kills many of his captors. A dwarf had been taunting him with the skull of an ass, and as in the Bible, Samson uses the jawbone as a weapon of death. The movie omits the miracle of God opening up a spring of water for the parched Samson (see Judg. 15:18–19).

The incident is reported to the saran and his chieftains. Delilah, who has become the saran's well-dressed mistress, enters waving an ostrich feather and suggests Samson can be beaten by a woman if not by an army. In the Bible it is the chieftains who persuade her to betray Samson, but in the film it is her idea, vengeance for spurning her. She asks for eleven hundred pieces of silver from each of them for giving them Samson (see Judg. 16:5). She insists he not be killed but be made to work like a beast of burden.

She goes with a treasure-laden caravan and camps in the valley of Sorek (see Judg. 16:4), suspecting Samson will raid them. Samson raids her tent, telling her he is not stealing but merely recouping the taxes the Philistines have taken. There is some romantic banter, she being clearly in love with him, he aware of the "silk trap baited with a woman" but not immune to her charms. She admits she came to trap him. He falls in love with her, and there is a brief romantic idyll. She tries to wheedle the secret of his great strength. The movie omits the three incidents of Judges 16 where he supposedly tells her his secret but she discovers he lies. He finally admits his strength comes from Israel's invisible God. God's power, he says, can "make men greater than themselves." His

strength is in his hair. He tells her he was dedicated to God, and
though he has broken many of his vows, he has kept his hair long.
(Samson was a Nazirite, though the word is not mentioned in the
film. The Nazirite rules are found in Numbers 6. It is unfortunate
that the movie totally omits the fascinating story of Samson's birth
found in Judges 13.) She is clearly pleased at knowing his secret,
but she suggests the two of them go to live in Egypt.

Soon her love turns to hate again when they are interrupted by
Miriam, who tells Samson the Philistines have killed his father and
beaten his mother. Delilah warns him the Philistines are setting a
trap for him. Delilah hates having a rival. Before Samson departs
to save his people, Delilah gives him drugged wine and with a
knife shears off his locks. Judges 16 states that "having put him
to sleep on her lap, she called a man to shave off the seven braids
of his hair" (v. 19), and obviously "put him to sleep" could imply
drugging him.

Samson awakes surrounded by Philistine soldiers armed with
spears. He calls her "Philistine gutter rat." Delilah suggests he call
on his God. But she reminds Ahtur that Samson's blood is not to
be shed. He keeps the promise literally: Samson is blinded with
a hot iron. Samson prays, "O Lord, now you take away my sight,
that I may see more clearly."

The Philistine lords count out their payment of silver for Delilah.
The saran thinks Delilah still loves Samson and insists she go to the
prison to see Samson grinding away at the mill wheel like a beast.
Only then does she learn Samson is blind. A guard trips Samson and
denies him water, while the Philistines mock him. Delilah insists on
giving him water. Her conscience will not let her sleep. She prays
to Samson's God for help. In prison Samson prays also, using the
words of some of the psalms, including Psalm 22, the "desperation
psalm." Delilah goes to him. He lifts her to dash her against the
wall, and they both realize his strength has returned as his hair has
come back. She says with all her money she can bribe their way
out of the city and flee to Egypt. He insists on letting the Philistines
take him to the temple of Dagon as they had planned.

The temple of Dagon has a huge statue of the god with a furnace
in its belly. Delilah enters the temple, wearing a gown of peacock
feathers, to the people's great applause. Miriam and the boy Saul
arrive to plead for Samson's release. Samson tells Saul that perhaps
some day he will be a great king to lead the people of Israel. (Saul

would not have been alive in Samson's lifetime, but it is a nice touch having young Saul be a devotee of Samson.) Costumed dwarves enter and taunt Samson, to the Philistines' delight. Instead of being led to the pillars by the boy, as in Judges, Samson is led there by Delilah with a whip. He warns her to flee the temple, telling her he still loves her. The people await the crucial moment of Samson bowing down to Dagon. Samson prays to God for strength as he pushes against the two pillars. The people are awed to see that the stones of the pillars begin to split. Samson prays, "Mine eyes have seen thy glory, O God; now let me die with thine enemies." The Dagon idol falls, crushing people. The movie does not mention Samson's burial by his family (see Judg. 16:31). At the end, Miriam tells Saul that men will tell Samson's story for a thousand years.

Victor Mature was not a great actor, and he hardly looks brawny enough to be the strongman of the book of Judges. But he does have a certain sincerity and is a perfect contrast to the effete, snobbish saran. Hedy Lamarr was radiant as Delilah, and the combination of love and hate she feels for Samson does give the film some emotional weight. A review in *Newsweek* (which made the film its cover story) stated, "The dialogue wavers between the consciously simple and the slightly ridiculous."[4] And yet, as corny as much of the dialogue in the film seems, the love-hate story is an engaging one. The Bible says nothing about Delilah

> To promote the film, Paramount marketed a four-volume *DeMille's Tales from the Bible.*

repenting over what she did to Samson, but the film certainly makes her a more sympathetic character. Interestingly, the most religious figure in the film is the cynical, worldly saran, who is keen enough to observe that Samson and his God are genuine while the Philistines' god Dagon is merely another idol.

Despite its departures from Judges, the movie is not a bad telling of the Samson story. DeMille liked to boast that his army of researchers made the film historically correct, but the truth is that historians knew little about the Philistines and still do not. The movie is correct in using the title of *saran* and in calling him "lord of the five cities."

DeMille had his researchers find, in the writings of the ancient Roman author Pliny, a description of a temple that, like the one in Judges, could be destroyed by the dislodging of two pillars.

The temple set was forty feet high, and the idol was twenty feet high—yet this was technically a miniature of the actual temple, which on film appears much larger. The scene in which the temple was destroyed took more than a year to prepare and cost more than $100,000 to film, using both real extras and miniatures of people used in a scale model. In his autobiography DeMille wrote, "If the scene is spectacular, credit is due to the Book of Judges, not to me."[5] The temple destruction was, of course, the most talked-about scene of this epic, with the movie literally ending with a bang.

Paramount spent $3 million on the film and another million on advertising. They even arranged lecture tours by historian Arnold Toynbee and other academics. There were numerous product tie-ins: Kellogg's sold "Samson-sized Cornflakes" and several department stores sold "ancient" clothing around the time of the film's release. Paramount promoted the movie through an art contest, offering $2,500 for the best painting illustrating the Samson story. All the marketing activity paid off handsomely: *Samson and Delilah* grossed $11 million in 1949 and 1950 and was the second-highest-grossing film of 1950. It was nominated for five Academy Awards: art direction (won), costumes (won), cinematography, score, and special effects. The smashing success sent a clear message to DeMille's colleagues in Hollywood: the public will line up to see attractive stars wearing fancy costumes in a Technicolor epic based (however loosely) on the Bible. *New York Times* critic Bosley Crowther ended his review of the film by saying, "If you'll settle for gold-plated pageants, muscular episodes, and graphic inducements to wolf-whistling, then *Samson and Delilah* is for you."[6] Even a secular critic like Crowther was aware that in this very watchable film, the Bible had clearly taken a backseat to visual pageantry.

David and Bathsheba: *Oh, Handsome King*

Released August 1951
Twentieth Century-Fox
116 minutes

Director: Henry King
Screenplay: Philip Dunne
Photography: Leon Shamroy
Music: Alfred Newman
Producer: Darryl F. Zanuck

David: Gregory Peck
Bathsheba: Susan Hayward
Nathan: Raymond Massey
Michal: Jayne Meadows
Uriah: Kieron Moore
Abishai: James Robertson Justice

"A kingdom torn apart by an unholy love!"—so ran the advertising tagline for this film, the top-grossing movie of 1951. Another line was "For this woman, he broke God's own commandments! The fire and tempest of their love still flames across 3000 years!" Clearly the marketing people were selling the movie on the basis of romance (and sin), not the Bible itself. Given the film's profits, they must have succeeded.

The story of David is one of the most fascinating in the Bible and in the whole world. His story is told in 1 and 2 Samuel, 1 Kings, and 1 Chronicles. He is a multifaceted character: shepherd boy, musician, poet, warrior, husband, lover, father, king, and, as the Bible puts it, a "man after God's own heart" (see 1 Sam. 13:14). He replaces Israel's failed first king, Saul, but has enough trouble in his own reign. As the old saying goes, "Bad luck makes good stories," and David had enough good and bad luck to keep artists, playwrights, and novelists coming back to his saga for centuries. He attracted moviemakers early on too, the earliest version of his life being *David and Goliath*, a short film directed by Sidney Olcott in 1908. A U.S.-made *Saul and David* followed in 1909 and an Italian *David* in 1912. Given the appeal of his story, it is amazing that Hollywood then neglected the saga until 1951, when Twentieth Century-Fox decided that the success of Paramount's *Samson and Delilah* deserved imitating. A movie with a man's and woman's names in the title, along with suggestions of sin, seemed to sell. They counted on the formula to work, and it did.

In the Bible, people's physical appearance is rarely referred to. David is one of the few called "good-looking" (1 Sam. 16:12 NKJV), which tells us his looks really impressed those who knew him. Twentieth Century-Fox had an obvious candidate for the handsome king, the actor whose looks (and also his voice and acting talents) had been setting hearts aflutter for several years, Gregory Peck. In 1947 Darryl Zanuck, head of Twentieth Century-Fox, bought the film rights to a Broadway play, *Bathsheba*. It was, obviously, focused more on Bathsheba than David. Zanuck decided he just had to do a movie about the fascinating king of Israel, and he asked writer Philip Dunne to research the project. Dunne had adapted numerous classics for the screen—*The Count of Monte Cristo*, *The Last of the Mohicans*, *Forever Amber*, and others—but was not at first enthusiastic for a biblical story. But he got intrigued by the complex character of David. "You could call him a mirror of

The Bible—or steamy Technicolor soap opera? Whatever it was, *David and Bathsheba* holds the distinction of being the only biblical movie to be the top-grossing film the year of its release. In an eleven-year period (1949–1960), audiences turned out in droves to see several biblical couples: Samson and Delilah, David and Bathsheba, and finally Solomon and Sheba.

mankind," said Dunne, "the difference being that David actually did what most of us merely think about doing."[7]

Zanuck wanted Peck because "he has a biblical face." Peck wasn't interested at first, not wanting to star in an epic such as

Cecil B. DeMille excelled in making. Zanuck told him it would be a character study of a complex man, and Peck grew more interested. Instead of spectacle, most of the film was shot at the Fox studios, but the production did involve a $250,000 re-creation of ancient Jerusalem near Nogales, Arizona, not far from Mexico. Less than two weeks of shooting was spent at this location. Compared to DeMille's *Samson and Delilah*, the David movie was fairly low-budget. Peck wore his hair slightly longer than usual for the role, though probably much shorter than the biblical David would have worn his. Not until the later part of the film did he sport a very thin beard.

The movie's opening has a biblical look to it, with the credits shown as words on ancient parchment. These words appear: "Three thousand years ago, David of Bethlehem ruled over the United tribes of Israel. This story of King David's reign is based on one of the world's oldest historical narratives, written by an anonymous chronicler in the Second Book of Samuel of the Old Testament." We learn already that the story is skipping over some of the early incidents related in the *first* book of Samuel. Writer Dunne was wise in choosing to concentrate on only a few incidents in David's life, for the 1985 film *King David* would fail when it tried to compress David's entire life into two hours.

The story opens with David at war with the Ammonites, Israel's army under the command of Joab. David has been out doing reconnaissance and has a slight wound, but he is glad to be wounded in the line of duty again. Ironically, David says—to the soldier Uriah—that in wartime, the best are the first to die. David assures him that peace is better than war and life at home is better than dying in battle. Back in Jerusalem, the prophet Nathan makes his appearance early on. Nathan makes it clear that though it is good to bring the ark to the city, David will not build the Lord a temple. (Raymond Massey gave a commanding performance as Nathan, a dynamic and even intimidating presence, a man you could almost believe was speaking on behalf of God himself.)

Back in the palace, David encounters his first wife, Michal, daughter of Saul. Their relationship has soured; David clearly no longer loves her. Michal walks out, and David goes onto the roof and on a house below sees a woman bathing—with a screen, so we see her only from the shoulders up. Down in the street, David inquires about the house and its owner. It is Uriah's, and the woman is his wife, Bathsheba. David sends a servant to summon her. The servant leaves with a knowing grin. David is anything but subtle, explaining to Bathsheba that the Hebrews are a desert people whose blood runs hot. Bathsheba tells David she has been married seven months and has only spent six days with Uriah. It was an arranged marriage, so she barely knows him and did not marry for love. David gives her a necklace, all the while mocking the practice of royalty going through such rituals. He places it on her neck, saying, "That is for virtue," then kisses her. She is not pleased. She makes it clear that she is simply fulfilling her duty to meet the king. David says he will not take anything by force—not the throne, not a woman. He tells her that Uriah must be a fool to neglect such a woman for the joy of battle.

> During the filming of *David and Bathsheba*, Gregory Peck's own marriage to his first wife was falling apart.

Suddenly things change: Bathsheba admits that she has been watching him for weeks, that she planned to be on the roof so David would see her, and that she hoped she would be the one woman who would please him. She makes it clear she will not be the type of woman to please him and then be sent away. David tells her he has no true friends, that people only want favors, that he is not close to his own children. "I am only a man, Bathsheba. I need someone to understand that." She says, "The man I watched from my window was not a king, but a man, whose heart is well worth the sharing."

Here, alas, is the movie's key departure from the Bible: It tries to "explain" (actually *condone*) David's adultery. His wife has turned into a nagging harridan, and Bathsheba's husband prefers war to loving his wife. So who could blame these two attractive people, caught in unhappy marriages, for finding solace in each other's arms? The Bible, of course, makes no excuses for David's behavior. Nonetheless, the Hays Code ruling Hollywood at the time required that adultery could not go unpunished, so, happily, the Code forced the story to show the punishment, even though the audience had already been led to sympathize with David and Bathsheba. But the movie takes its time getting to the punishment, seeming to enjoy the adultery for quite a while. David and Bathsheba make no secret of keeping company with each other. They return from a chariot ride and meet the procession bringing the ark into Jerusalem. (According to 2 Samuel 6:5, David was part of this joyous procession, not just meeting it by accident.) Outside the city walls, a group is bringing out an adulteress dressed in red. The wife of the man casts the first stone. Presumably the woman is stoned to death. David meets the prophet Nathan before the ark and reflects on the people the ark has outlived: Moses, Aaron, and Joshua. David almost touches it, but Nathan tells him the ark is too sacred to be touched. Immediately we see how right he was, for when the ark seems about to teeter off its cart, a man named Uzzah tries to right it and immediately falls dead. The people are awed and bow down. Nathan takes it as a sign that the ark should not be brought into the city yet but must dwell in a tent for the time being. Naturally the movie omits the account of David "leaping and dancing" as the ark is brought into Jerusalem and Michal chastising him afterward. The studio must have thought the handsome Peck would have looked quite foolish dancing, and certainly Richard Gere did so in the 1985 *King David*.

The stoning of the adulteress is not found in the Bible, but it was inserted to let the audience know what punishment awaited Bathsheba if she was caught. She turns out to be bearing David's child and fears stoning. David offers to get rid of Uriah, but Bathsheba will not hear of such a plan. Later, at a palace banquet, a dancer gyrates as lewdly as allowed on-screen in 1951. Presumably David has hired the dancer to put Uriah in an amorous mood, hoping he will go home and sleep with his wife. He does not: as in the Bible, he will not go to the comfort of his home while his own soldiers sleep in the field (see 2 Sam. 11:11–13).

In the Bible, David's adultery is compounded by his ordering that Uriah be sent to the forefront of the hottest fighting, in the hope he will die in battle (see 2 Sam. 11:15). In the movie, Uriah himself requests such an assigment, so he can show his true devotion to his king. Obviously the script is making the loveless Uriah ask for his own death. Uriah is killed, and when David hears the report of the battle dead, he sends word to Bathsheba to prepare for their marriage after her month of mourning. They wed, but punishment follows. Hot, dry winds blow over the lands; sheep die for lack of water. A whirlwind seems to symbolize God's anger. The son Bathsheba bears David dies soon after birth, as Nathan had predicted. The Egyptian pharaoh's ambassador brings news that the grain David wanted to buy from Egypt is not available. Nathan enters while Absalom watches from the sidelines, clutching the dagger David gave him. Nathan tells his famous parable of the ewe lamb (see 2 Sam. 12:1–15). After David says that such a man deserves to die, Nathan says, softly but firmly, "You are the man." Nathan says it is not God's will that David die, for God remembers all the good things David has done. Nonetheless, because he shed innocent blood, the sword will never depart from David's house. Nathan demands that the woman be stoned, but David says it was his fault, not hers. Nathan says the drought and famine are the punishment for Bathsheba's sin. The people in the palace seem about to revolt. David still lies and asks where the accusers who will say he knew Bathsheba before their marriage are. But Michal comes forward, and so does David's troublesome son Absalom. David goes to Bathsheba and tells her they will escape through the rear of the palace, but Abishai tells him the palace is surrounded. Bathsheba does not believe she is guiltless, though David says she is. She admits they are both sinners, for she wished Uriah dead, and says, "God sees into our hearts, David." Oddly, at this point she takes down David's harp from the wall and asks him to play something from his boyhood. He plays briefly, then recites Psalm 23 and says, "When I wrote those words, I believed in such a God." He says he learned about the love and glory of God from observing nature, and "Then I wandered from him. . . . His image paled in the lights of the cities . . . and now Nathan has found him for me, not the God of my boyhood days, but the God of justice." This scene, which could've been very corny, is actually the highlight of the movie, very well handled.

David is determined Bathsheba shall not die. He tells Nathan he does not believe God wants to punish the woman. Walking through a mob of people about to rebel, David goes to the ark to pray. He kneels and prays to "the God of my early youth." He calls himself a "worthless servant" and says, "I have been a faithless shepherd. . . . Take not thy Holy Spirit from me" (see Ps. 51:11). David asks God not to punish Israel for his individual crimes. He asks God to let Bathsheba live, for David alone is guilty. He touches the ark with both hands, apparently believing he will die as Uzzah did. He has a flashback of his boyhood, with the prophet Samuel coming to Jesse's house. Samuel looks at Jesse's oldest sons and agrees that they are fine boys, but he tells Jesse that God does not see as man does. David enters, and Samuel tells David he is God's chosen one. Flashback to Saul's camp, where no one is willing to take on Goliath. David enters Saul's tent. He is Saul's armor-bearer. Saul allows him to face Goliath, thinking this will prove the boy is definitely not God's anointed. The hulking giant throws a spear at David, which pins his tunic to the ground, but David gets up and dispatches Goliath with one stone. Back in the present, David seems amazed that God has not punished him for touching the ark. Then he hears the sound of rain. He takes it as a sign that he is forgiven. Outside the city, people kneel in gratitude to God. A choir sings Psalm 23. David goes to Bathsheba. They clasp hands and watch the rain fall. The end.

David and Bathsheba is the only biblical film ever to be the top-grossing film in the year of its release.

The real David and Bathsheba story is told in 2 Samuel 11–12. No incident with Michal leads into the story. The Bible matter-of-factly says that one afternoon (not night, as in the movie) David awakened from his daily nap, walked on the palace roof, and saw Bathsheba bathing. He sent for her and made love to her, and later she told him she was pregnant. The Bible makes no attempt to "explain" or justify their behavior, much less condone it. It is related that Uriah would not go home to sleep with Bathsheba while on leave. The movie's incident of the drought and famine in the land are pure fabrication, as is David's touching the ark. The incident of Uzzah touching the ark is, however, related in 2 Samuel 6:6–11. The chronology of the movie is all wrong, since the incident of Uzzah and the ark occur before David ever sees Bathsheba. The festive bringing of the ark to the city and David's dancing are omitted. The incident of the stoning of the adulteress is pure fabrication, as is the matter of Michal standing up as accuser of Bathsheba and the threat of a violent revolt when David's adultery is revealed. Regarding the rivalry between sons Amnon and Absalom, 2 Samuel 3:2 does say that Amnon was David's firstborn son, though not that he was ever designated heir. Perhaps audiences were expected to see in the boyhood rivalry an omen of the later deadly battle between the two sons. Mention of a long famine appears in 2 Samuel 21, but it has nothing whatsoever to do with the affair with Bathsheba. In 2 Samuel, Abishai is a warrior, like his brother Joab, not a court advisor for David.

But none of these departures from 2 Samuel seemed to bother audiences in 1951, nor did the movie's lax attitude toward adultery. The film premiered in New York on August 14, 1951. The *New York Times* critic Andrew Weiler called Peck's role "an authoritative performance," one that kept the film from being "merely a two-hour dissertation."[8] Some reviewers were not so kind, considering it a failed attempt to do a Cecil B. DeMille epic, and certainly it lacked the spectacle of *Samson and Delilah* and the later *Ten Commandments*. But the public loved it. It was the hit of the year, outgrossing even *An American in Paris*, *Born Yesterday*, *Father's Little Dividend*, *A Place in the Sun*, Disney's *Alice in Wonderland*, and the religious epic *Quo Vadis*. Earlier in the year Peck had been voted World Film Favorite by a poll of over a million moviegoers in various countries. The success of *David and Bathsheba* was largely a result of his box-office appeal, not of the public's affection for the Old Testament. But his appeal was more than visual: he did convey something of the depth of the complex David. It is a pity that this religious element is reserved till almost the end of the movie. The studio knew it was more profitable to keep religion to the end and focus on two attractive stars acting out a dangerous adulterous affair. The story even downplayed the role of David as warrior, and there are no actual battle scenes in the movie, though at one point David does revisit Mount Gilboa, the site where King Saul and his son Jonathan perished after fighting the Philistines. The studio apparently believed that David the handsome lover was a bigger draw than David the fighter or David the man of spiritual depth.

> Regarding Peck's performance as David, director Martin Scorsese stated that "in the last fifteen minutes of the picture, from the moments starting with his recitation of the Twenty-third Psalm to his supplication before the Ark of the Covenant, we experienced his truly remarkable ability to convey the darkest struggles of the human soul."[9]

It's worth noting that in Peck's boyhood, he was fond of the Bible stories his mother read to him. Though he was not religious as an adult, he still found the stories appealing. Early in his career he had acted in a play called *Family Portrait*, which set the Jesus story in rural America. Peck played the Judas role. His breakthrough role in film was playing the gentle Catholic priest-missionary, Father Francis Chisholm, in *The Keys of the Kingdom*. Though not a religious man, Peck seemed to have great success playing religious figures. In the 1970s a much older Peck would have the dubious honor of playing the lead in a new type of semi-biblical movie, the apocalyptic thriller *The Omen*.

A word about the ark of the covenant seen in the movie: it was built of actual acacia wood and was made (as best as could be determined) to the measurements described in Exodus 25. Years later Susan Hayward, who had played Bathsheba, purchased it when it was auctioned off by the studio. Aside from this fidelity to the Bible's description of the ark, the movie did not make an effort to show the real Israel of 1000 BC. The Jerusalem in the movie is squeaky clean, with wide streets and enormous palace rooms. People in 1951 did not want to see realism; they wanted a color film that was a feast for the eyes, and they got one. The movie received four Academy Award nominations: best costume design, best color cinematography, best story and screenplay, and best art direction—in other words, three out of four honoring the movie's visual impact.

To sum up, *David and Bathsheba* is an entertaining and visually appealing movie but lacking in spiritual depth, not to mention departing seriously from the Bible in its story line.

Let's pause here to mention an "almost biblical" film that was the top-grossing film of 1952, *Quo Vadis*. Released by MGM late in 1951, it was the third version of a popular novel by Nobel Prize-winning Polish author Henryk Sienkiewicz, telling the story of a Roman aristocrat's pursuit of a pure Christian girl. Eventually he becomes a Christian himself, of course. The story involves several historical characters, including the apostles Paul and Peter, both of whom are martyred under the despicable Roman emperor Nero, who sets Rome afire and blames the Christians, leading to horrible persecutions. The original 1913 version, made in Italy, awed moviegoers worldwide and broke new ground in its day, costing a fortune but earning back several more fortunes and proving that audiences would sit through a long film if the story was engaging enough. The three-hour MGM film starred Robert Taylor, Deborah Kerr, and Peter Ustinov (as Nero), and its mix of ancient pageantry, religion, violence, a love story, and a near-psychotic villain certainly drew the audiences in. It was nominated for several

Academy Awards, including best picture. It was not included in this book because its story covers events that take place several years after the time covered by the Bible. Nonetheless, its great success sent Hollywood the message that religious pictures were moneymakers. It was filmed in Italy's Cinecitta studios over a two-year period, setting a precedent for ancient film epics to be shot in that country. And incidentally, the film's producer, Sam Zimbalist, would go on to produce an even more profitable religious film at the end of the decade: *Ben-Hur.*

Salome: *Sweetened and Sanitized*

Released February 1953	**Salome:** Rita Hayworth
Columbia	**Claudius:** Stewart Granger
103 minutes	**Herod:** Charles Laughton
	Herodias: Judith Anderson
Director: William Dieterle	**Tiberius:** Cedric Hardwicke
Producer: Buddy Adler	**John the Baptist:** Alan Badel
Screenplay: Harry Kleiner	**Pilate:** Basil Sydney
Photography: Charles Lang	**Ezra:** Maurice Schwartz
Music: George Duning	**Marcellus:** Rex Reason

For a character who is not even named in the Bible, Salome has been the subject of many movies. The earliest was produced in Germany in 1902 and has the distinction of being the first film about a New Testament character other than Jesus himself. At least ten different versions of the story were produced in the silent era, and Salome has appeared in several movies about the life of Christ. This 1953 spectacular with Rita Hayworth as the title character has the distinction of being the first color—and sound—film centered around her, but not the last. So just what is the appeal of Salome?

First of all, the Bible does not name her. She is simply "the daughter of Herodias," Herodias being the second wife of Herod Antipas. She had divorced her first husband, Philip, to marry his brother Herod, and this immoral marriage brought the condemnation of the prophet John the Baptist. Mark 6:19–20 states that Herodias nursed a grudge against John because of this. Herod finally threw John in prison but was afraid to execute him because the people thought John was a true prophet of God. According to Matthew 14:1–12 and Mark 6:14–29, at Herod's birthday party the daughter of Herodias danced so enchantingly that Herod rashly promised to give her whatever she wanted. Prompted by her mother, she asked Herod for the head of John on a platter. The unwilling Herod had John beheaded. That is all the Bible says of the unnamed woman. We know nothing about her age or character. We know her name only from the Jewish historian Josephus. But the biblical story was used by Oscar Wilde as the basis of his popular play *Salome* (1893), which in turn served as the basis of a Richard Strauss opera (1905). In these versions Salome has a perverse crush on the prophet John, who spurns her, and after his beheading, she kisses his decapitated head, leading the outraged Herod to have her executed. In the Strauss opera, she dances the famous "Dance of the Seven Veils" (again, not mentioned in the Bible), which is presumably very erotic. Aside from the Wilde play and Strauss opera, Salome has been a popular subject for artists, who have delighted in painting the decadents at Herod's birthday party, not to mention Salome gazing at the head of poor John. So thanks to the artists and writers, this very minor (and nameless) woman has gained great fame, which explains why filmmakers were drawn to her story.

The amazing thing about this 1953 film is that it follows neither the Bible nor the Wilde/Strauss embellishing of the story but goes off in its own strange direction. The story didn't really matter much, for the whole point of the film was to showcase Miss Hayworth's physical charms and dancing ability. Yet, oddly, the film ended up being more inspiring than the real story told in the Bible. Columbia Studios didn't particularly care if it was inspiring or not, of course. The studio knew Paramount had a huge hit with *Samson and Delilah*, as did Twentieth Century-Fox with *David and Bathsheba*. Obviously it was time for Columbia to get on the biblical bandwagon.

The movie opens with a red screen and these words: "King Herod and Queen Herodias held the throne. So wanton was Herod's court, the Queen sent the young Princess Salome to Rome. . . . And it came to pass that a man appeared in Galilee who many thought was the Messiah. This was the prophet known as John the Baptist . . ." In the first scene is John announcing the day of judgment and denouncing the sin of Herod marrying his brother's wife. As John, actor Alan Badel simply does not seem fiery enough. A spy of the court goes running off to tell Herodias of John's rants.

She is told that more than just the rabble is listening to John. In Herod's palace, it is obvious enough that Herod and his wife are well tired of each other. Herod thinks John is harmless and doesn't particularly care if Herodias is called an adulteress. Ezra, Herod's spiritual advisor, reminds him of the prophecy of a Messiah during his father's reign. For all Herod knows, John may be the Messiah. Does Herod want to die an agonizing death like his father (Herod the Great) did? If not, he certainly can't engage in the bloodshed of his father. This is not in the Bible, but it's a good explanation of why Herod held off from harming John. (Worth noting here: Judith Anderson is perfect as the haughty Herodias and Charles Laughton perfect as the pudgy, effete, but tortured Herod.)

Roman emperor Tiberius sends Pilate to govern Judea. (The movie has some details wrong: Caesarea, not Jerusalem, was the governor's capital. Also the chronology is wrong, since Pilate had been in Palestine several years already when the events in the Gospels take place.) In Rome, Salome dances at a party. She and Marcellus, a handsome young Roman, are in love but cannot marry by order of Tiberius, who is Marcellus's uncle. Worse, she is sent back to Galilee to be with her mother and stepfather. Hayworth is stunningly beautiful, of course, but hardly looks like a Middle Eastern woman of the first century. On the ship from Rome to Galilee, Salome snubs the Roman soldier Claudius, but he is smitten with her. Claudius is decent, giving water to a beaten galley slave. We later learn that Claudius is a follower of John the Baptist, whom he urges to keep a low profile while Pilate is around. This is not too far-fetched, since Luke 3:14 indicates that John did have some admirers among the soldiers.

Herod is enchanted with the new woman at his court, then is told she is his stepdaughter. It occurs to Herodias right away that Herod's lust can serve a purpose, i.e., getting rid of John. We learn her whole purpose in sending Salome abroad was to keep her from Herod's clutches.

John preaches, denouncing Herod as an alien, not a true Jew (which was true). Salome sneaks from the palace to hear him and takes him to task for denouncing the family. She is shocked when he identifies her as Herodias's daughter, yet he says that she need not be held responsible for her mother's sins.

To Herodias's delight and surprise, Herod has John arrested and brought before his council. John admits he would glady serve an-

other king, one greater than either Herod or Caesar. He would serve
this Messiah and denies he himself is the Messiah. The councilors
condemn John, and Herod tries to make them responsible for John's
death. Ezra protests and walks out. John shows not a trace of fear,
calling them a "generation of vipers." Herod clears the room and
talks alone with John. He promises to leave John alone, but only
if he will stop denouncing Herod on his home turf. John tells him
to repent. Herod has John thrown into prison but with no plans to
ever kill him. Claudius tries to persuade him to release John, but
Herod will not. He rattles Salome when he tells her that Claudius
is on John's side. His imprisonment of John pleases Salome, but
not as much as he hopes. (According to the historian Josephus,
John was in fact imprisoned at the fortress of Machaerus on the
Dead Sea shore, not in any "city," as the movie has it.)

Claudius visits John in prison and tells him he has seen the
Messiah, Jesus of Nazareth, raise a man from the dead. John is
pleased, for he remembers Jesus. John realizes he can now die
peacefully, since the true Messiah is made known. Salome over-
hears John and Claudius. She laments that her whole life she has
been surrounded by wickedness but that she now desires to find
good in life. She has just heard her own mother suggest to her
that she offer herself to Herod, hoping she can cajole him into
having John killed. She has her own plan: dance to please Herod,
then ask for John's release.

At his feast, Herod's blood is already up after watching two
voluptuous Oriental dancers. Salome does her famous Dance of
the Seven Veils, gradually revealing more and more flesh, as much
as could be shown in 1953. (Hayworth started her show-business
career as a professional dancer, incidentally.) Then comes the
greatest distortion in the story: Watching Salome dance, Herod
says, "I would give half my kingdom . . ." at which Herodias says,
"No, give me the head of the Baptist"—and Herod nods his assent.
(In the Bible, it is Salome herself who asks for John's head.) Her
dance ended, Salome screams in horror as the head is brought in
on a platter. Salome is disgusted with her mother. Claudius enters,
and Salome rushes to him. Herodias seems triumphant (hardly the
reaction to be expected when her beloved daughter has renounced
her), but Herod is rattled, rushing off to his advisor Ezra.

From a distance and from behind, we hear Jesus preaching his
Sermon on the Mount. In the crowd are Claudius and Salome. We

see a screen with clouds and the words "This was The Beginning." Presumably both Claudius and Salome become Christians. Somehow the biblical story of the daughter of Herodias, brief as it is, is turned into a Christian tale of inspiration, with an innocent young woman choosing the way of Christ over the decadence and malice of her family. A worthy message in any age, even if it contorts the little information that Matthew and Mark give us.

German-born director William Dieterle had a long career of historical epics with lavish costumes—*The Hunchback of Notre Dame*, *The Life of Emile Zola*, *A Midsummer Night's Dream*, *Juarez*, *Omar Khayyam*. For him Salome was not a religious picture but just another historical epic. Yet for all the inaccuracies in the story, some of the exterior shots were actually done in the Holy Land, rare at that time.

Years earlier, Cecil B. DeMille had hoped to star Hayworth in an epic about Salome. Columbia studio head Harry Cohn hired Jesse Lasky to come up with a story line (in two days) that Hayworth would agree to star in.

In the spirit of Hollywood in those days, Salome had to be a good character, at least at the end—thus the shocking change in the true story of Salome.

New York Times movie critic Bosley Crowther referred to the film as a "flamboyant, Technicolored romance based vaguely on a Biblical tale," full of "pseudo-ostentation and just plain insinuated sex."[10] Crowther perceived, correctly, that despite the pious ending and the virtuous character of this Salome, the movie had more to do with Rita Hayworth dancing and wearing lavish costumes than it did with religion. It continued the popular formula of *David and Bathsheba*: find some attractive stars, titillate the audience with suggestions of sex, but tack on a moral ending.

Still, the film was popular (as the studio intended), and despite its straying far afield from the Gospels, no believers were offended that in this version of the story, Salome was a good girl, not a vil-

> Columbia made a nice profit from *Salome* and planned to star Rita Hayworth in a film about Joseph and his brothers. Considering that the only female role in that story is that of Potiphar's randy wife, the world probably did not miss much by that project going unproduced.

lainess. It is still watchable and entertaining today, so long as one does not take it too seriously.

The top-grossing movie of 1953, *The Robe*, fits into the same general category of semibiblical films as *Ben-Hur*; that is, films in which the main characters' lives intertwine with characters from the Bible. Like *Ben-Hur*, *The Robe* was based on a phenomenally popular novel, in this case one by Lloyd Douglas, a Lutheran minister who cranked out several inspiring bestsellers. *The Robe*, published in 1943, was the nation's top-selling novel for over a year, its story of faith triumphing over a corrupt empire appealing to a nation at war with Hitler. Somehow the creative Douglas had spun an entire novel out of the brief mention in John's Gospel that the Roman soldiers at Jesus's crucifixion cast lots to see which of them would get the crucified man's seamless garment. One of those soldiers, Marcellus Gallio, is eventually converted to Christianity (along with his lady love) and at the end is martyred. We see Jesus's crucifixion, see the gambling for the robe, and meet Judas and Peter. We see Peter perform a miracle of healing, which is in keeping with the book of Acts. Jesus's face is not seen up close, which was also true years later in *Ben-Hur*. Both movies preferred to show people's reaction to Christ rather than trying to find an actor who looked right for the part (since that was a difficult task, as every movie about Jesus has proven). *The Robe* seems a bit slow and pompous by today's standards, but it is certainly more inspiring and reverent (and even believable) than *Salome*, released earlier the same year. Its success prompted Hollywood to crank out several more biblical and semibiblical epics.

The Prodigal: *The Bible, Swimsuit Issue*

Released May 1955
MGM
114 minutes

Director: Richard Thorpe
Producer: Charles Schnee
Screenplay: Maurice Zimm, Joe Breen
   Jr., Samuel Adams Larsen, "adaptation
   from the Bible story"
Photography: Joseph Ruttenberg
Music: Bronislau Kaper

Samarra: Lana Turner
Micah: Edmund Purdom
Nahreeb: Louis Calhern
Ruth: Audrey Dalton
Asham: James Mitchell
Rhakim: Neville Brand
Eli: Walter Hampden

One of the world's best-known stories, found in Luke 15:11–32, is known as the parable of the prodigal son. Though it is one of Jesus's longest parables, it consists of a mere five hundred words in the King James Version. That doesn't sound like the makings of a full-length film. But in fact the story does have great possibilities, telling of a young man who asks his father for his share of the inheritance and goes to a "far country" and wastes it all in riotous living. He ends up as a keeper of pigs until he "comes to himself" and returns home, repentant, to his father, who accepts him mercifully and orders a celebration. Obviously Jesus intended the father to represent God and the son to represent any human soul that wastes itself in "riotous living." It could make a great film, but so far that great film has not been made.

This was not the first film based on the parable of the prodigal son. *The Wanderer*, released in 1925, was the first. It was silent and black and white, of course. For this 1955 version, MGM pulled out all the stops in terms of costumes, scenery, and all the other "gloss" that was MGM's trademark. In fact, MGM had been amazingly slow about venturing into biblical (or semibiblical) films, while Twentieth Century-Fox had huge success with *The Robe* and *David and Bathsheba* and Paramount with *Samson and Delilah*. MGM was Hollywood's biggest and most prestigious studio, so it intended to cash in on the public's taste for glossy epics with a moral veneer. Production of *The Prodigal* occupied four huge sound stages and supposedly employed four thousand extras. It had the proverbial "cast of thousands" and one of MGM's glamour ladies, Lana Turner, as a selling point. It resulted in a very pretty but rather silly wide-screen movie that is barely connected to the Bible.

Like so many biblical films of this era, it opens with narration: "In the times before Christianity, only a few people believed in one God . . ." The narrator goes on to say that two of the chief gods were Baal and Astarte, fertility deities that sometimes demanded human sacrifice, which is true. The story is, the narrator says, adapted from the parable in Luke, and the setting is the port of Joppa in 70 BC. (Joppa is remembered as the port where the prophet Jonah tried to sail away from God and also a locale where the apostle Peter ministered and converted some Gentiles.)

Young Micah (the title character) learns his father has arranged a marriage for him, to Ruth, a virtuous neighbor girl. In the city,

Micah is scandalized at seeing some people worshiping an idol inside a tent. Micah mocks the "priestesses," telling the priest, Nahreeb, that they are no better than harlots. Then Samarra, the high priestess of Astarte, walks in, and Micah is enchanted. She is the scantily clad Lana Turner. Micah says he must have her, "one way or another." Back home, Micah tells his father he cannot marry Ruth. His father slaps him and says he is disinherited, but he relents and lets Micah do as he intends. His elder brother gives him a ring, a family heirloom that was always handed down from eldest to eldest. (It is interesting to hear father and son exchange the words "I love you" in a movie made in the 1950s.) Micah takes his sad leave of Ruth.

> The Old Testament contains page after page telling of how the Israelites were constantly forsaking their true God and worshiping Baal and Astarte.

In Damascus, Micah really does not engage in the "riotous living" mentioned in the parable. He tries to be admitted to the temple of Baal and Astarte but is turned away because his beard (which all Jewish men wore) marked him as an "infidel." But then a servant girl arrives and says Samarra has summoned him. Samarra shows him all the jewels and other riches that people have given to the temple of Astarte. Micah makes it clear that it is Samarra he seeks, not Astarte. He is, he assures her, no idol-worshiper.

Back in Joppa, Micah's father prays in the synagogue, quoting the words of Proverbs about the dangers of evil women who lead men astray. The priests of Baal and Astarte are shown living richly off the gifts given to the gods. They gamble and trade slaves like toys. Nahreeb makes it clear to his cronies that he intends to get Micah's fortune and make him abandon his god Jehovah.

Micah's shaving off his beard is a sign he is slipping, spiritually speaking. We see a gaudy ritual in which a muscular man jumps as a human sacrifice into a pit of fire. Micah woos Samarra and says he wants to marry her, but she says as high priestess she belongs to all men. As she passes through the temple, he sees that all the people are in awe of her.

She is horrified to learn that Micah has lost everything and is to be sold as a slave—to Nahreeb. She knows how Nahreeb abuses his slaves. In the slave quarters, the men fight over food that is set out in troughs. Injured men are thrown into pits to be devoured by vultures. Nahreeb tells Samarra that Micah can be freed—but only if he renounces his god. Samarra goes to the prison and tells Micah to renounce his god, though he needn't mean it. He asks her if she could renounce Astarte, and she says no. Micah tells her that the worship of Baal and Astarte has made her people brutal. (As in *Salome* and *Samson and Delilah*, the evil woman has been somehow made noble. Apparently audiences did not want to see a film with the star playing a genuinely *bad* woman.) She departs, and Micah looks down on a dying slave and recites the traditional Jewish statement of faith, the Shema: "Hear O Israel: the LORD our God, the LORD is one" (Deut. 6:4). The next morning he resolves to break out. He feigns death, and the guards abandon him to the pits, where he is tossed among the dried bones and has a battle with a very fake-looking vulture. Once outside, friends of his fellow prisoners aid him. He organizes them into a slave revolt. Samarra finds him and asks that they flee away together, but he says his revolt is also directed at the gods she serves. The priests flee but Samarra stays on, dressed to kill (literally) in front of her idol in the temple. When the mob enters, she throws herself into the pit of fire. The men tear down the huge idol, which also falls into the pit.

Micah makes his way home, saying he would rather be a servant in his father's house than a king in Damascus. He and his father embrace. He throws himself at his father's feet. Only at the very end does the story use the actual words of the parable. "I have sinned against heaven and in your sight. I am not worthy to be called your son." His father says, "This my son was lost and is found." He calls for killing the fatted calf. Ruth, of course, is pleased to have him back. The elder brother is sullen, as in the parable. The two sons shake hands; all is well.

As this synopsis should make clear, the film was "suggested by" the parable, not a faithful telling of the parable itself. Still, Micah makes a good hero, and he struggles with moral temptations, which in a biblical film is an admirable thing. One interesting aspect of the film is that Micah, the believer in God, is constantly referred to as the "infidel." Christians are usually portrayed as the intolerant persecutors of unbelievers, but here it is the pagans who are intolerant, which is probably the truth.

Years after the film was released, Lana Turner referred to it as "a costume stinker." Perhaps "stinker" is in the nose of the beholder, but certainly the costumes (especially hers) were eye-catching. (Some critics noted that her diaphonous gowns resembled swimsuits more than the garb of ancient Damascus.) Whatever its faults may be, this is a very beautifully photographed film, with rich colors in rich settings. The city of Damascus, where most of the action takes place, is a feast for the eyes. Sadly, the costumes and scenery stick in the mind much more than the morality in the story.

MGM spent a fortune on the film and promoted it heavily. Audiences were willing to turn out to see Lana Turner in slinky costumes, as usual, but it was certainly not the blockbuster MGM hoped for. The studio would have to wait four more years and find its biblical gold mine in *Ben-Hur*.

The Ten Commandments: *The Gold Standard*

Released November 1956
Paramount
219 minutes
Filmed in Hollywood and Egypt

Producer-Director: Cecil B. DeMille
Screenplay: Aeneas MacKenzie, Jesse L. Lasky Jr., Jack Gariss, Fredric M. Frank
Photography: Loyal Griggs
Music: Elmer Bernstein
The credits also list as "authors": Dorothy Clarke Wilson (from *Prince of Egypt*), Rev. J. H. Ingraham (from *Pillar of Fire*), Rev. A. E. Southern (from *On Eagle's Wings*)

Moses: Charlton Heston
Rameses: Yul Brynner
Nefretiri: Anne Baxter
Dathan: Edward G. Robinson
Sephora: Yvonne De Carlo
Lilia: Debra Paget
Joshua: John Derek
Sethi: Cedric Hardwicke
Bithiah: Nina Foch
Yochabel: Martha Scott
Memnet: Judith Anderson
Baka: Vincent Price
Aaron: John Carradine
Narrator: Cecil B. DeMille

Not many films can still attract a network TV audience after fifty years, but one still can: *The Ten Commandments*. In March 2006, a fiftieth anniversary DVD of the film was released, which included DeMille's 1923 version of the same story, plus a documentary about the making of the 1956 film. ABC ran the film on April 14, 2006—in the same week that it ran a new four-hour miniseries with the same title. Not surprisingly, the 1956 epic achieved higher ratings than the new one.

In his autobiography, producer-director Cecil B. DeMille stated: "I make my pictures for people rather than critics."[11] In fact, he never pleased the critics, who only gave him grudging credit for being able to handle crowd scenes very well. DeMille has been

One of the most memorable confrontations in the Bible—and in the history of film too: Moses (Charlton Heston) versus Pharaoh Rameses II (Yul Brynner) in director Cecil B. DeMille's second version of *The Ten Commandments*—this time (1956) with glorious color, sound, a wide screen, and a splendid cast. It is the only biblical film ever nominated for a best picture Oscar.

ridiculed as a director of actors, with critics claiming he made even capable actors look hammy, a holdover from his days directing silent films. Perhaps so, but not many old films draw people the way *The Ten Commandments* does. Part of that is due to the DeMille touch, but part of it is due to the story of Moses itself.

As already noted in chapter 2, DeMille had directed *The Ten Commandments* in 1923. It was silent and in black and white. After the huge success of his 1949 *Samson and Delilah*, followed by his circus epic *The Greatest Show on Earth*, which made a killing and won a best picture Oscar, DeMille had no trouble getting the Paramount studio to agree to a new film of *The Ten Commandments*, this time in glorious color, wide screen, and stereophonic sound. He told the Paramount bosses that the film would need a budget of $8 million—or more. It ended up at more than $13 million.

Part of the huge budget went to research. In fact, one man credited as a costume designer had no previous experience in costume or makeup. He was Arnold Friberg, an artist of biblical scenes. The clothing in the film may look "Hollywood," but in fact most of the costumes were authentic. Nefretiri's gowns were painstaking reproductions from Egyptian wall paintings. One actress who had a small part in the film stated years later that DeMille obsessed over details, such as having Jethro's daughters tint their fingernails with henna—even though the color wasn't even visible in the final film. Other details were visible, though, such as the pharaoh playing a board game called hounds and jackals.

Film composer Elmer Bernstein was tapped to do the film's score. DeMille told him to produce music that would have the solemn, brass-laden quality of Richard Wagner's operas. DeMille got what he asked for, and the music contributes greatly to the film's epic feel.

For the role of Pharaoh Rameses, DeMille was obsessed with finding an actor who would look right with his head shaved and wearing eye makeup. When he saw Yul Brynner (head already shaved) in the musical *The King and I*, he was certain that Brynner had the perfect face and build for Pharaoh—and (obviously) would look fine with his head shaved. Brynner was born in the Asian part of Russia, and his facial resemblance to some of the pharaohs' mummies is amazing.

The research done for the film was actually published as a book, *Moses and Egypt*, by the University of Southern California.

Finding the right actor for the part of Moses was even more important. DeMille had directed Charlton Heston in the award-winning *Greatest Show on Earth*. Heston thinks his getting the role of Moses was partly due to his own resemblance to Michelangelo's famous statue of Moses in Rome. DeMille had a sketch done of Heston in a white beard. DeMille claimed that "the resemblance was amazing, and it was not merely an external likeness."[12] He seemed to think that Heston had the soul of a man who would lead his people to freedom. Heston prepped for the films by reading Exodus and Deuteronomy, as well as a history of ancient Egypt.

The combination of Heston and Brynner was perfect. DeMille understood that to have a truly dramatic story, both villain and hero must be charismatic. Corny and pompous as some of the dialogue may be, the two men deliver it with conviction. We believe for the duration of the film that Brynner really *is* Rameses and Heston *is* Moses—a sure measure of a film weaving its magic spell.

The film actually has a second villain, the wicked Dathan, a Hebrew who serves as a spy for the Egyptians and is later made governor of the Hebrew slaves. He grudgingly leaves Egypt with the other Israelites, but we sense he is going to make trouble. Dathan is an actual character in the book of Numbers, where he leads a rebellion against Moses and dies with the other rebels. The film expands his role considerably, and he is well played by an old Hollywood stalwart, Edward G. Robinson. Once the Hebrews are out of Pharaoh's reach, it is Dathan who serves as Moses's nemesis, which is true to the Bible, since the chief danger to Moses in the wilderness was the Hebrews constantly threatening to rebel against him.

One other "role" in the film required some thought: the voice of God speaking to Moses. Though DeMille and Heston agreed to let Heston's own deep, resonant voice be the voice of God, it was deepened and otherwise "tweaked" by the technicians so that it was distinct from Heston's natural voice. And for the scene of God giving the actual commandments to Moses, DeMille hired an actor to speak the lines. The name of that actor has never been divulged. DeMille himself did the narration for the film, his paternal voice conveying the seriousness of the story.

Aside from the lead actors, the film had the proverbial cast of thousands. The exodus scene used eight thousand extras and five thousand head of livestock. The extras were poor Egyptians, many of them dressed in centuries-old styles. Most of them had never seen a film before. As Muslims, they honored *Musa* (Moses) and seemed in awe of Heston when he was in costume.

Although the film has been accused of "looking Hollywood," much of it was actually filmed in Egypt, including on Mount Sinai itself. DeMille's crew built a veritable city in the Egyptian desert, with walls 120 feet high and a half mile wide and with a double avenue of two dozen sphinxes, each fifteen feet high. These were the famous Per-Rameses walls and gates in the scene of the Hebrews leaving for Canaan (and, a few minutes later, Pharaoh's chariots in hot pursuit). DeMille's claim that he "paints on a large canvas" was never more true than in this film. He got full cooperation from the Egyptian government, partly due to some of the officials having seen his 1930s film *The Crusades*, which presented Muslims with some degree of sympathy.

The first scenes were shot in the Sinai Desert. The crew spent time at St. Catherine's Monastery, founded in the year AD 339 at the supposed site of the burning bush. Mount Sinai is visible from the monastery. The Muslims call it *Jebel Musa*, "Mount of Moses."

The earliest shots were at the summit, which Heston walked to, since Moses himself walked it. The first shot was him coming back down the mountain after the burning bush encounter. He told DeMille he should be barefoot, since "If you just heard God tell you to free the Jews, you don't stop to put your shoes back on." DeMille agreed.

DeMille had a mild heart attack during the filming in Egypt—after climbing a hundred steps and another twenty feet up a ladder to check a camera position. He would not go to a hospital but merely took three days off, then went back to work—against his doctor's orders. He was past seventy already.

As noted in the material dealing with the 1923 film, DeMille thought of himself as a Christian and thought of his biblical films as more than just profit-makers. In the 1950s, many Americans were deeply concerned about the global spread of communism, and DeMille was among them. So while he saw his film as conveying the spiritual message of Exodus, it was also a timeless story about freedom versus tyranny. In his memoirs Heston wrote that DeMille "believed deeply in the message of the film and the power of the man, Moses, to reach across the millennia and move people of every faith, kind, and condition. . . . Over the centuries, Moses and the Exodus he led have inspired those who search for liberty."[13]

Heston's Moses has become the most recognized biblical character ever on film, with Heston outshining the many men who have played Jesus on film. Oddly, Heston has been extremely evasive when asked about his own religious convictions, always refusing point-blank to discuss the matter. Yet he has written affectionately about playing Moses, Ben-Hur, and John the Baptist, and he has lent his voice and presence to the video series *Charlton Heston Presents the Bible*. If he is not a Christian, he seems to have become a "fellow traveler" of sorts.

As with his *Samson and Delilah*, DeMille opens the film with grand orchestral music, with the word "Overture" in gold over a rich red background. DeMille knew how to let an audience know it was about to see not a *movie* but an *event*. Following the brief overture, DeMille himself appears onstage in front of a rich damask curtain. He tells the audience that the film is about the "birth of freedom" and also observes that the book of Exodus omits many details about Moses's young manhood. "The theme of this picture is whether men are to be ruled by God's law or ruled by the whims of a dictator like Rameses. Are men the property of the state, or are they free souls under God?" He refers to the Moses saga as "divinely inspired."

The credits roll in gold on red. Unlike DeMille's earlier biblical film, this one takes its time in listing the cast members and other crew. The credits also list the various "authorities" involved, including the Metropolitan Museum of Art and the University of Chicago's Oriental Institute. The credits also note that "those who see this motion picture produced and directed by Cecil B. DeMille will make a pilgrimage over the very ground that Moses trod more than 3,000 years ago." The credits refer to the "ancient texts" of Philo, Josephus, and Eusebius and, in rich lettering, "The Holy Scriptures."

The actual film opens with the biblical words "God said, 'Let there be light.'" But then we see that man learned to conquer and enslave other men, the strong dominating the weak. We see the infant Moses at the home of Jochebed and Amram. Pharaoh's astrologers prophesy that a deliverer will arise from the Hebrew slaves. The pharaoh orders the death of every newborn Hebrew child. Soldiers go from house to house, but Jochebed and her daughter hide the baby in a basket floating in the river. (The baby was actually Charlton Heston's infant son, Fraser.) Pharaoh's daughter Bithiah and her maids frolic in the river. She finds the floating basket. Memnet, her servant, recognizes the cloth around the baby as Hebrew and knows why the baby is floating in the river. Bithiah scolds her and says her newfound son will grow up to be the prince "of the two lands"—the ancient Egyptians' name for their country. She names him Moses because she drew him from the water (see Exod. 2:10). (Many people miss the irony in the story: Moses was raised at the same court that had condemned him and all other Hebrew children to death.)

In the next scene Moses is a handsome and popular adult prince. The film makes the same leap in time as Exodus, which jumps from Moses in the basket to "after Moses had grown up" (Exod. 2:11). The ruling pharaoh is Sethi I, and his son is Rameses II—which, according to most scholars, are probably the correct names for the men called simply "Pharaoh" in Exodus. Rameses II ruled from 1290 to 1224 BC, and the exodus probably took place around the year 1280. Regarding Moses being raised as a "prince of Egypt": the book of Exodus tells us nothing about this, but apparently the Hebrews held an old tradition that Moses was indeed a rising star in the Egyptian court. DeMille was right in listing the ancient authors Philo and Josephus as sources for the script, because both those authors give details about Moses's youth and young manhood that Exodus does not cover. In Acts 7:22 the martyr Stephen states that "Moses was instructed in all the wisdom of the Egyptians, and he was mighty in his words and deeds" (ESV). Apparently Stephen was aware of the same traditions as Philo and Josephus, who claimed that Moses was both handsome and brilliant, the inventor of the alphabet and wise in all fields of learning.

DeMille couldn't resist loading the film with two romantic triangle subplots—Moses and Nefretiri and Rameses, and Joshua and Lilia and Dathan. The princess Nefretiri is destined to be Rameses's wife, but she obviously prefers Moses. (Some people pooh-poohed the princess being named Nefretiri, knowing there was an Egyptian queen named Nefretiti, but that woman was from a different time period.) Lilia, not mentioned in the Bible, is a beautiful Hebrew girl who loves Joshua but is pursued by the lecherous Dathan, the unscrupulous Hebrew who collaborates with the Egyptians. Rameses asks Dathan to scope out the Hebrew "deliverer." The slaves toil away, Moses's own mother applying grease under a huge stone and almost being crushed by it. Joshua saves her by striking an overseer, and Lilia begs Moses to show mercy to Joshua. Moses cuts Jochebed loose from the stone, not knowing she is his mother. Moses admires Joshua's spunk and has him released. Moses tells Rameses the slaves need adequate food and rest. He orders the temple granaries opened. Back at court, Rameses warns Sethi that Moses may be the slaves' deliverer.

Sethi visits Moses on the building site. The slaves use ropes to lift a huge monument to Pharaoh. Moses assures Sethi that the better-fed slaves are working harder. Sethi is impressed with the building project and vows that Moses will be the next pharaoh. Nefretiri looks forward to being Moses's wife, but the servant Memnet tells her that Moses is actually a Hebrew. She tells her a Hebrew slave had been Moses's wet nurse (see Exod. 2:9). Nefretiri is so angry she pushes Memnet off a balcony. She tells Moses the truth and he confronts his "mother," Bithiah, who admits Moses is a Hebrew. Moses finds his true mother, along with his sister Miriam and brother Aaron. Moses makes the radical choice: he gives up being the future pharaoh to be a slave.

We next see Moses making clay bricks with the other slaves, smeared with mud. Nefretiri has Moses brought to the palace to be her personal slave. Moses kills Baka, the Egyptian master builder, for whipping Joshua (a loose version of Exod. 2:11–12). Dathan sees and reports to Rameses that Moses is the hoped-for deliverer and is actually a Hebrew. Rameses has Moses brought before Sethi. Moses is driven into the desert at 105 minutes into the film. After much wandering he finds his way to the well in Midian, where he rescues Jethro's seven daughters from some surly shepherds (see Exod. 2:16–22). Exodus calls the one when Moses marries Zipporah; here she is called Sephora. Jethro tells him the Midianites are descendants of Abraham just as the Hebrews are (see Gen. 25:2), though the script errs in saying they were descended from Ishmael.

Sethi dies and Rameses becomes Pharaoh. On Sinai, Moses sees the burning bush and utters the exact words of Exodus: "I will turn aside and see this great sight" (3:3). The voice from the bush tells him to take off his shoes. He is the God of Abraham, Isaac, and Jacob. He has seen the Hebrews' affliction and is sending Moses to lead the people to freedom. Moses asks his name, and he says "I am that I am." The events of Exodus 4, with Moses protesting that he is "slow of speech," are omitted, and rightly so, since Moses has proved to be quite eloquent. Also omitted are the signs God gives Moses, such as his staff turning into a snake. An intermission occurs when Moses decides to return to Egypt, at 135 minutes into the film. In keeping with the solemnity of the film, an orchestral *entr'acte* plays during intermission.

The incident of Moses and Aaron meeting in the wilderness is omitted. Moses and Aaron go to Pharaoh and demand he release the slaves. Heston is impressive when he utters the fateful words "Let my people go!" Moses's staff turns into a snake, and Pharaoh's magicians duplicate the trick—but Moses's snake devours the others' (see Exod. 7:12). (One of the magicians is called Jannes—a name not found in Exodus but mentioned in 2 Timothy 3:8.) Pharaoh responds by telling Moses the slaves must meet their quota of bricks but must make the bricks without straw. The people are furious and on the verge of lynching Moses and Aaron.

As described in Exodus 7, Rameses goes down to the river, where Moses causes the first plague, turning the Nile waters to blood—a slap at the god of the Nile. Some of the plagues are referred to but not shown: frogs, lice, flies. Rameses says all the plagues had a natural explanation and were not the will of Moses's God. Moses says that hail and three days of darkness will follow. As in Exodus, this is no ordinary hail, for it is "like fire upon the ground." The plague of locusts is not shown. Rameses's counselors urge him to free the Hebrews, but as in Exodus, his heart is continually hardened. He threatens another massacre of the Hebrew infants—which is not in Exodus but is an interesting touch. Moses warns that God is about to strike down every firstborn son in Egypt. The Hebrews mark their doorposts with blood so that the angel of death will pass them by but strike down the Egyptians. The "angel" takes shape in the sky as a kind of sinister green hand. In the Hebrews' homes they celebrate the first Passover meal. The sound of the Egyptians wailing over their dead is heard. The death angel is like a low green fog moving through the streets. Rameses's son dies. Rameses summons Moses and tells him to take the Hebrews and go. He lays his son's body in the lap of a statue of one of his gods, praying for life to return. (The same scene occurred in the 1923 version.) The crowd scene that follows—the Hebrews readying for the exodus—is truly impressive, the kind of thing DeMille handled so well, showing the crowd but also giving little snippets of chatter between individuals to humanize the mob. The thousands passing through the boulevard of huge sphinxes, with the four colossal statues of the pharaohs behind them, has the effect DeMille intended. As in Exodus 13:19, the bones of the patriarch Joseph are carried forth. The Hebrews pack up not only their own belongings but treasures taken from the Egyptians, who are eager to see them go (see Exod. 12:35).

Goaded by Nefretiri and by the sight of his dead son, Rameses changes his mind and decides to pursue the slaves. Again we have an epic DeMille scene, the chariots thundering forth from the gates. Camped out by the sea, the Hebrews hear the thunder of the chariots. Dathan urges the people to stone Moses, who has led them into certain death. Moses reminds them that they know God can work miracles, having seen all the plagues. All the while, dark clouds have been gathering. A pillar of fire, rather like an orange tornado, holds the chariots back for a while (see Exod. 14:19–20). Then follows one of the most famous scenes in the history of film: the clouds form into hands that part the raging sea. The waters roil like living walls as the Hebrews pass through. (Huge water tanks at the Paramount studio were used for this, but DeMille did not like the way the waters moved, so gelatin had to be added to get the right look. The scene of the parting was made by releasing the waters

> DeMille was such a stickler for details that the tablets carried by Heston were carved from granite taken from the actual Mount Sinai.

and running the film in reverse.) The pillar of fire disappears, and Rameses orders the troops to pursue the Hebrews, though he himself does not go. The Hebrews panic, but then the waters close in on the Egyptians. As in the 1923 version, we see horses and men under the waters. Rameses returns to Nefretiri and sits on his throne, his final words in the film being "His God is God."

The next few chapters of Exodus are omitted, and the story moves immediately to Sinai (see Exodus 19). Moses is on the mountain so long that the people (led by Dathan) grow restless. Dathan wants to lead them back to Egypt, promising them that the Egyptians will welcome them back if they bear an Egyptian idol before them. The people force Aaron, who "knows the art of the temple," to fashion a gold calf idol (see Exodus 32). The scene cuts from the Hebrews making their golden idol just as God, appearing to Moses on the mountain, gives the commandment prohibiting idols. A finger of fire engraves stone on the mountainside as Moses hears God speaking the commandments. Down in the camp, the people rally around their idol. In his memoirs Heston noted that "movies couldn't be very specific with orgies in 1956, but DeMille knew how to suggest a great deal."[14] Much pagan "worship" was simply an excuse for a drunken orgy, and the worship of the calf in the movie hints at sex without showing any. Most of the words God speaks to Moses on the mountain are taken directly from Exodus. As in Exodus, the loyal Joshua awaits Moses when he comes down. Moses is horrified at this idolatrous party taking place in the camp. He throws down the tablets on the golden calf idol, which sets it on fire.

The rest of the Moses saga is compressed into a few minutes, as the narrator relates that God kept the people in the wilderness for forty years to test them and that all the generation that had left Egypt had died off, except Moses himself and Joshua. At this point Moses's hair is snow-white, his beard long; he looks like the famous Michelangelo statue. We learn that Moses will not enter the Promised Land himself because he had once angered the Lord in the wilderness. Moses appoints Joshua to be his successor to lead the people to Canaan. Joshua speaks the biblical words, "As for me and my house, we will serve the Lord" (Josh. 24:15 ESV). Moses gives to the priest Eleazar the "five books" (that is, the first five books of the Old Testament, known as the "books of Moses"). Moses's final words are the words from Leviticus 25:10—the words inscribed on the Liberty Bell in Philadelphia: "proclaim liberty throughout all the land unto all the inhabitants thereof" (KJV). He wanders off to the mountain. (Deuteronomy 34 relates that Moses died and that God himself buried him, no human knowing the site.) The final shot shows the tablets of the law and the burning bush, with the words "So it was written, so it shall be done" on the screen. In keeping with the solemnity of the film, the words "Exit Music" appear in gold on a red background.

The Ten Commandments premiered November 8, 1956, at the Criterion Theatre in New York. It more than recouped its huge budget, making $83.6 million on its initial release. The public loved it, but, as usual for DeMille, critics praised the movie's epic quality while mocking the acting and dialogue. Some of the dialogue is over the top, particularly Nefretiri's, such as "Oh, Moses, Moses, you stubborn, splendid, adorable fool." Yet it remains one of the few classic films that is still shown annually on network television, usually around Passover and Easter. The rich color of the film still dazzles the eye, and some fans of old movies admit that it is more eye-pleasing than *Gone with the Wind*.

The Ten Commandments has been the only biblical film ever nominated for a best picture Oscar, though it did not win. It was nominated but did not win in the categories of art direction, cinematography, costumes, editing, and sound. It did win one award, for special effects, not surprisingly. Perhaps the most glaring omission: DeMille was not nominated for best director. But, adjusted for inflation, *The Ten Commandments* is the fifth-highest-grossing film of all time.

It is easy to criticize the film for taking some liberties with the Old Testament. Certainly it plays up some fictional elements while omitting such biblical incidents as the sending of manna and quail in the wilderness, the rebellion of Aaron and Miriam, the installation of Aaron as the first high priest, the encounter with the Moabite prophet Balaam, the rebellion of Korah, and the battle with the Amalekites. The film, at almost four hours, could have done justice to the full story in the Bible but chose instead to waste time on such folderol as Moses and Rameses vying for the affections of the vixenish Nefretiri and the vile Dathan leering lecherously at the innocent Lilia. But DeMille's showman instincts might have been right. He did "ginger up" (his phrase) the biblical stories to make them more interesting on-screen, but in doing so he drew a larger audience, exposing more people to the moral and spiritual elements of the story. And the script is almost saturated with direct quotations from the King James Bible.

> The Ten Commandments is one of the three biblical films honored by being listed in the Library of Congress's National Film Registry, the others being *Intolerance* and *From the Manger to the Cross.*

As he did with *The King of Kings*, DeMille donated his profits from the film to a trust fund for religious and charitable purposes. Partly to publicize the film and partly because he really believed the Ten Commandments were important, DeMille donated funds to the Fraternal Order of Eagles so that parks, courthouses, and other locales could post images of the Ten Commandments. It might surprise him that fifty years after the film, the U.S. was still seeing legal battles over whether such images in public locations were unconstitutional.

The Ten Commandments was DeMille's last film. He died in 1959. Though he had spent a huge chunk of his long life in Hollywood, he stated in his autobiography, "I am very glad that I know the America between the coasts."[15]

Charlton Heston would star in an even more profitable film, *Ben-Hur*, subtitled *A Tale of the Christ. Ben-Hur* has been a true success story, highly profitable as a novel, then a play, then three different film versions. The 1880 novel by Lew Wallace, a Civil War veteran, became a huge bestseller; for fifty years it was the top-selling book in America after the Bible itself. An 1899 stage version ran for twenty-one years. Inevitably it was filmed, first in 1907, then in 1925, and finally and most famous, the epic

1959 version that was for many years the top-grossing film of all time.

Despite the novel's subtitle, it is not truly a tale of the Christ. It is a tale of two boyhood friends—a Jew and a Roman—who find themselves on opposite political sides. They become mortal enemies, until the Jew beats the Roman in a spectacular show-down and sees him die—but even then he cannot find spiritual peace. That, of course, is where Christ comes in. In fact, spiritu-ally speaking, the movie *is* a tale of the Christ—he is not at the center of the story, but he seems always present on the side, as if the audience knows that only Christ will bring peace to the tor-mented main character. Throughout the story, people from the Gospels appear—one of the three magi, Pontius Pilate, even Jesus himself. Near the film's end, Ben-Hur and Christ come together at the cross, and the final shot shows an empty cross. Christ is risen, and Ben-Hur has a new life. That, more than the famous chariot race, is really at the heart of the film and is why audiences were willing to sit through a movie running more than three hours.

The movie premiered on November 18, 1959, and the public turned out in droves to see the epic. They were not disappointed, since the film has everything: adventure, deep friendship turned to hate, glorious costumes and settings, a man seeking his lost mother and sister, a climactic battle between hero and villain, even the joy of seeing a stalwart masculine hero transformed by faith. While the film is not biblical in the full sense that some of the other films in this book are, it does have the distinction of being the most profitable religious movie ever made—and the most profitable film showing the crucifixion of Jesus. In time, Mel Gibson's *Passion of the Christ* may surpass it, however.

Solomon and Sheba: *So Much from So Little*

Released December 1959
United Artists
139 minutes
Filmed in Spain

Director: King Vidor
Producer: Ted Richmond
Screenplay: Anthony Veiler, Paul Dudley, George Bruce
Photography: Fred A. Young

Solomon: Yul Brynner
Sheba: Gina Lollobrigida
Adonijah: George Sanders
Pharaoh: David Farrar
Abishag: Marisa Pavan
Joab: John Crawford
Baltor: Harry Andrews
David: Finlay Currie

The posters advertising this movie had the following taglines: "The mightiest motion picture ever created!" and "Only once in 3000 years—anything like it!" Well, like in all advertising, there was some exaggeration involved—quite a lot, in fact. But the movie was the seventh-highest-grossing film of 1960 (it was released late in 1959), and audiences apparently loved it, even if it did play fast and loose with the Bible.

In fact, the movie bears more than a passing resemblance to the 1953 *Salome*. Both films were centered on very minor biblical characters—Salome in one case, the queen of Sheba in the other—but characters that had caught the imaginations of artists, writers, and musicians over the centuries so that despite their relative unimportance in the Bible, their impact on the culture at large was considerable.

Here is the main part of what 1 Kings tells us about the queen:

> When the queen of Sheba heard about the fame of Solomon and his relation to the name of the LORD, she came to test him with hard questions. Arriving at Jerusalem with a very great caravan— with camels carrying spices, large quantities of gold, and precious stones—she came to Solomon and talked with him about all that she had on her mind. Solomon answered all her questions; nothing was too hard for the king to explain to her. When the queen of Sheba saw all the wisdom of Solomon and the palace he had built, the food on his table, the seating of his officials, the attending servants in their robes, his cupbearers, and the burnt offerings he made at the temple of the LORD, she was overwhelmed. She said to the king, "The report I heard in my own country about your achievements and your wisdom is true. But I did not believe these things until I came and saw with my own eyes. Indeed, not even half was told me; in wisdom and wealth you have far exceeded the report I heard."
>
> 1 Kings 10:1–7

The chapter goes on to say that the queen praised Solomon's God, she and Solomon exchanged expensive gifts, and then "she left and returned with her retinue to her own country" (1 Kings 10:13). (Sheba, incidentally, is generally assumed to have been somewhere in the southern Arabian Peninsula.)

Out of these few sentences, storytellers and artists have spun many fancies, including the legend that Solomon and the queen conceived a child together and that this child is the ancestor of the kings of Ethiopia. In some legends the queen has a name—Balkis, Belkis, or Melkis. Her gift-laden visit to Solomon was a favorite subject for artists, and Handel based one of his oratorios on it. Inevitably a movie had to be made on the famous meeting, slender though the original material was. Surely it would be a hit, especially if it starred the newest "find" from Europe, Italian actress Gina Lollobrigida, and the old Hollywood standby, Tyrone Power. Unfortunately, while filming the movie in Spain, Power died of a heart attack. He was replaced with Yul Brynner, who had been so dynamic as the pharaoh in *The Ten Commandments*. As Solomon, however, he was not allowed to sport his famous shaved head.

The film opens with Solomon and Adonijah, two sons of Israel's King David, meeting each other on the Egyptian frontier, both spying out the Egyptians. Characters are established right away—Adonijah the tough warrior, Solomon more intellectual but not shying from war. A battle ensues with the Egyptians. The Israelites win. Adonijah clearly glories in war. He does not like David's policy of "defend but do not attack." A captive from the battle is a servant of the queen of Sheba, and he shows contempt for the "barbarian" Israelites. None of this is in the Bible, of course.

A messenger brings word that David is on the point of death. Some of the soldiers already proclaim Adonijah as king. Solomon says this is irreverent while David still lives. (Neither Adonijah nor Solomon has a beard, which is very unbiblical.)

Solomon hurries to David's side. David manages to get out of bed and address the tribal leaders. David speaks of Adonijah and Solomon as his two "halves"—the soldier and the poet. Solomon says he is willing to serve Adonijah as his king, but David says it is the Lord's will that Solomon, a man of peace, will rule. Adonijah is furious. David dies, making Solomon promise to build the Lord's temple.

Solomon prays the prayer of 1 Kings 3, almost word for word. God's answer comes: Solomon will have more than the wisdom Solomon asked for—he will have wealth as well.

Solomon asks Adonijah to command Israel's armies—a risky gesture, as Adonijah reminds him. This is not in the Bible.

Israel's prosperity under Solomon is shown by scenes of lush fields and happy farmers. Overlooked is the Bible's revelation that the people were horribly taxed to fund Solomon's lavish building projects. At the dedication of the magnificent temple, Solomon offers almost word for word the prayer of 1 Kings 8.

Out on Israel's frontier, Adonijah encounters the queen of Sheba, who is scantily and clingingly clad throughout. She and her troops are in league with the Egyptians. Adonijah tells her she should ally herself with Israel, not Egypt. She answers by striking him with a whip. Sheba is an exotic sybarite and plays with a parrot (a macaw, which is impossible, since they are native to the tropical Americas). She sneers at Israel's God, before whom all men are equal. She is a femme fatale, going to visit Solomon so as to learn his weakness and destroy him, though the Bible claims she was only curious to learn of Solomon's fabled wisdom (see 1 Kings 10). Her exotic caravan to Israel fascinates the locals. Her first meeting with Solomon is a riot of color, with Sheba in gold, Solomon in red. Rich gifts and treasure are brought. Sheba hypocritically praises the "glories" she sees in Israel.

With the queen present (although according to the Bible she had not traveled there yet), Solomon delivers his famous judgment on the two women claiming the same child (see 1 Kings 3). Later she tries to seduce him in her enormous, luxurious tent, but Solomon insists on her remaining an ally, nothing else. But clearly he is smitten with this exotic creature.

Though we see a glimpse of Solomon's large harem, no actual mention is made of his numerous wives or concubines. Abishag, the bed-warming servant of his father, David, is always nearby, but seemingly in the role of baby sister. She is also the sweet-faced foil to the exotic Sheba. Solomon finally caves in to Sheba's charms. While canoodling in a multicolored boat, he quotes to her poetic lines from his own Song of Solomon.

Two courtiers complain to Adonijah that Sheba is living in the palace. Adonijah sends them away but is gleeful for this pretext to snatch the throne. Meanwhile the queen realizes she really is in love. Solomon offers to marry her, uniting the kingdoms. She points out that their gods are different. She says she must return home to celebrate one of her gods' feasts—unless Solomon will let her celebrate it in Israel, but he cannot (which surely contradicts what the Bible says about his being so accommodating to his women's gods).

Joab and another man attempt to assassinate Solomon but fail. (This is definitely not in the Bible.) Solomon confronts Adonijah, who claims that Solomon's dalliance with the "Sheban slut" has brought shame on the nation (hardly the case). Solomon has given in and allowed Sheba to celebrate her rites. His courtiers reproach him for this. Sheba presides at the festival honoring her god of love (or fertility, more precisely). She dances as erotically as could be done in a 1959 movie, barely covered. Solomon hears the drums and is drawn to the rite, even though Abishag begs him not to go. He is enchanted. In the temple Abishag prays to God to preserve Solomon from divine wrath. Lightning strikes the image of the fertility god, burning it. But it also strikes the temple, killing Abishag. (This is absurd, and her role in the plot of Adonijah is totally ignored.) Solomon is heartbroken but realizes he has been punished for his dalliance with Sheba. She herself begins to wonder if Israel's God is real.

> Rahman, the god of love and fertility mentioned often in the movie, really was a god of Sheba.

The idea that Israel was about to break apart over Solomon's affair is absurd (just as it was absurd in the 1951 movie *David and Bathsheba*). Solomon's council deserts him, leaving Solomon alone on the throne, saying, "Vanity of vanities," words attributed to him in the book of Ecclesiastes.

Adonijah visits Pharaoh, telling him to strike at Solomon. Pharaoh is angry that Sheba has not reported back to him, so he tells Adonijah to make sure Sheba is punished. Adonijah leads an army of Egyptians and disgruntled Israelites against Solomon. There is a huge battle scene. Correctly, Joab is shown as Adonijah's ally and chief supporter.

Fearing Solomon's defeat in battle, Sheba makes her way to the temple to pray for forgiveness and for Solomon's safety. She promises that if God spares Solomon, she will return to her land and worship only the true God.

Israelite troops make their way to Solomon's side. But in the meantime, an overly optimistic Adonijah sits on the throne in Jerusalem, crowning himself without ritual. Solomon faces off with Pharaoh's army. Israel's battle strategy is to literally blind the Egyptians by turning their shields to reflect the rising sun, causing a tumult of horses running amuck, tumbling into a canyon. It is a great scene but utter nonsense, with hundreds of dead bodies piling up (although 1 Kings 10:16–17 does mention Solomon possessing hundreds of gold shields).

Solomon returns to Jerusalem while the locals are stoning Sheba as she comes from the temple. He and Adonijah have a sword fight on the temple steps. Solomon kills Joab, then turns to the unconscious Sheba. He carries her body into the temple (which is still a wreck from the lightning). The prophet Nathan tells Solomon that Sheba alone had prayed for his safety. Before dying Sheba revives and turns to the ark to thank God. God's voice is heard, telling Sheba to return home and keep her promise to worship him. Miraculously, her wounds disappear. She tells Solomon that she is bearing his child but she must return home, and Solomon's child will rule Sheba and worship the true God. This perpetuates the old legend of descendants of Solomon and Sheba. Solomon ends it by repeating the words of Psalm 30:5: "his anger endureth but a moment; in his favour is life: weeping may endure for a night, but joy cometh in the morning" (KJV)—words the Bible attributes to his father, David.

Yul Brynner's son, in his biography of his father, said that *The Ten Commandments* was the high point of biblical epics but *Solomon and Sheba* was its low point.

For all its faults, the movie is never boring, and the idea of the pagan queen being so taken with Solomon that she converts to his religion is not so far-fetched, given the queen's words in 1 Kings 10. The script can also be commended for actually quoting the Bible many times, including Solomon's famous prayer for wisdom and his prayer at the dedication of the temple, plus lines from the Song of Solomon and Ecclesiastes, two books attributed to the king.

As Solomon, Brynner had his limitations. Though he exudes charisma, he hardly seems like the wise man that Solomon was supposed to be. In his book *King Vidor on Film Making*, the director lamented that Brynner was not up to the task of playing a man torn between two sides of his character. Gina Lollobrigida was certainly watchable as the queen, but we can doubt her clingy outfits were what a woman of ancient Arabia would have worn. George Sanders did well enough in the role of Adonijah, though the movie seriously distorts what the Bible tells us about his attempt to seize the throne from Solomon. (See the first two chapters of 1 Kings for the details of Adonijah's plot, a story that ended with Solomon ordering Adonijah's and Joab's executions—events that happened long before the queen of Sheba's visit.)

In reviewing the film, *Time* referred to it as "two hours of full-color, wide-screen lust, in which all of Solomon's affairs are lumped into one." The review mentioned this was a "large lump," given the hundreds of wives and concubines attributed to the king.[16] But the review actually caught one aspect of the movie that is very significant: in the Bible, the division of the kingdom after Solomon's death is a result of Solomon building pagan temples for his wives and concubines (see 1 Kings 11—which, as it happens, immediately follows the story of the visit of the queen of Sheba). The Bible takes Solomon's dalliance with false gods very seriously, giving it as the reason Israel was split in two under his son Rehoboam. Though the movie is historically wrong in showing that a split was threatened due to Solomon's liaison with Sheba, it is correct (spiritually speaking) in linking political disaster with the worship of false gods—an idea seen in page after page of the Old Testament. So this lavish epic, for all its liberties with the story of Solomon, does present a key spiritual truth of the Bible, one not often dealt with in biblical movies.

Like *Ben-Hur*, *Solomon and Sheba* made most of its profits in 1960, *Ben-Hur* being the top-grosser of that year and *Solomon and Sheba* in seventh place.

In concluding this chapter on the golden decade of biblical films, it should be noted that it was also a busy decade for Christian film companies, which were producing some high-quality (though often low-budget) films based on the Bible, mainly about the life of Jesus.

5

THE SILVER AGE

The 1960s

The 1960s began as a promising decade for biblical films, with two religious films released late in 1959—*Ben-Hur* and *Solomon and Sheba*—being among the top-grossing films of 1960, *Ben-Hur* holding the number one spot. But the culture was about to undergo some serious changes.

We think of the 1960s as the era of "flower power," with long-haired youth hating authority and losing themselves in sex, drugs, and rock 'n' roll. That was part of the picture but definitely not the whole picture. When the decade began, the fatherly Dwight Eisenhower was still president, but the next man in that office would be much younger. Having John and Jackie Kennedy in the White House seemed to inaugurate a new age of youth, vigor, and optimism. There was nothing hippie-ish about the Kennedys (other than John's "free love" lifestyle), but as the decade progressed, hair got longer, clothes got more casual, and youth became more inclined to pessimism and apathy than to optimism. For 1966

Time magazine gave its Man of the Year honor not to an individual but to "Twenty-five and Under U.S. Youth," making this observation: "No adult can tell the young what earlier generations were told: this is God, that is Good, this is Art, that is Not Done. He has signaled his determination to live according to his own lights and rights."[1] Three years later *Time* gave its Man and Woman of the Year distinction to another broad group, "The Middle Americans, U.S. Adults," saying, "No one celebrated them. Pornography, dissent, and drugs seemed to wash over them in waves, bearing some of their children away. But in 1969 they sought to reclaim their culture."[2] They did not totally succeed in reclaiming it, and in some ways today we are living more by the standards of the youth of that decade than by their parents' standards.

The 1950s saw America turn into a nation of TV-watchers, but that didn't keep a big batch of biblical movies from finding success. The 1960s would see another batch of such films, but they would be not nearly as successful. Part of the reason was that fewer people were going to the movie theaters. By 1968 only 20 million Americans, about 10 percent of the population, were going to the movies every week. The number of new films had shrunk from over 500 in 1946 to less than 175 in 1968. The films of the 1960s were not only fewer in number but also progressively less G-rated with every year. It's true that some of the biggest successes were squeaky-clean: Walt Disney fare (*Mary Poppins*, *The Swiss Family Robinson*, *The Love Bug*, *The Absent-Minded Professor*), musicals (*My Fair Lady*, *The Sound of Music*, *West Side Story*, *Oliver!*), and historical epics (*Lawrence of Arabia*, *The Alamo*, *El Cid*). But some of the top-grossers were definitely not family-friendly: *Bonnie and Clyde*, *The Carpetbaggers*, *The Graduate*, *Who's Afraid of Virginia Woolf?* The old Hays Code was finally dropped, and in 1965 the once formidable Catholic Legion of Decency got a new name, the National Catholic Office for Motion Pictures. It continued to review films, but clearly its influence was weakening. Profanity and sex came rushing in. The year 1969 reveals how divided the culture was, with two of the top-grossers of the year being *Easy Rider* and *Midnight Cowboy*, another two *The Love Bug* and *Hello, Dolly*. *Midnight Cowboy* was actually rated X (though it would barely qualify as an R today), and it went on to become the first X-rated film to win a best picture Oscar. Everything on television was still G-rated, but things were changing, as seen in the most

popular variety program, Sunday night's *Ed Sullivan Show*, with
Sullivan—suit, tie, and slicked-back hair—looking a little odd
standing shoulder to shoulder with rock groups like the Rolling
Stones and the Doors. (Sullivan famously made the Stones change
their song lyrics from "Let's spend the night together" to "Let's
spend some time together.")

What had changed? Perhaps *Playboy* and rock 'n' roll, both making their debuts in the 1950s, were having an effect. The Vietnam
War certainly did. Though most Americans, including youth, supported the intervention in Vietnam in its early years, they gradually
came to oppose the war (which implied they had lost interest in
fighting communism). A war they didn't support led many youth
to thumb their noses at the U.S. government—and at authority in
general, as *Time* recognized. The young also thumbed their noses
at traditional sexual morals—made easier by the introduction of
the birth control pill in May 1960.

Another disturbing trend was seen in the April 8, 1966, *Time*
magazine cover that asked in bold red letters, "Is God dead?" There
was a brief flowering of "death of God theology" among a few
liberal professors who thought that God was literally dead—or at
least that the traditional language used in talking about God was
no longer valid. In reaction to this, many people bought bumper
stickers saying "If your God is dead, try mine" and "God is not
dead, I talked to him this morning." Not too many people bought
into the "death of God theology," but it was another sign that the
religiousness of the 1950s had declined. Or perhaps the religiousness of the decade had been shallower than anyone realized.

The multitude of 1950s children who were dutifully taken to
church by their parents did not turn into churchgoing teens in the
1960s. Church attendance declined, and, unlike during the 1950s,
few religious books made the bestseller lists. Billy Graham's *World
Aflame* and Catherine Marshall's *Christy* were exceptions, but they
shared space on the lists with *Sex and the Single Girl*, *Valley of the
Dolls*, *Human Sexual Response*, and *Myra Breckinridge*. Two new
versions of the New Testament did sell well: the New English
Bible and the American Bible Society's *Good News for Modern
Man*—both of them showing a break from the King James English that people had associated with churchgoing. Ironically, the
one biblical movie of the decade that was a great success was *The
Bible . . . In the Beginning*, which drew most of its dialogue and

narration word for word from the King James Bible. Perhaps in this authority-bashing era, audiences took some comfort in hearing the familiar old words.

The Story of Ruth: *Wide Screen, Small Story*

Released June 1960	**Ruth:** Elana Eden
Twentieth Century-Fox, Cinemascope	**Naomi:** Peggy Wood
132 minutes	**Boaz:** Stuart Whitman
Filmed in Hollywood	**Tob:** Jeff Morrow
	Mahlon: Tom Tryon
Director: Henry Koster	**Priestess:** Viveca Lindfors
Producer: Samuel G. Engel	
Screenplay: Norman Corwin	
Music: Franz Waxman	

The tiny book of Ruth is wedged in between Judges and 1 Samuel in the Old Testament. Its four chapters can easily be read in fifteen minutes or so. The book has no miracles, no battles, no confrontations between charismatic characters. Its main characters are two women, a widow and her daughter-in-law who live on the edge of poverty until the younger woman finally finds a husband and bears a child. The book is included in the Bible because Ruth was the grandmother of the great King David and because it showed that God would accept foreigners who turned to him. Its story of loyalty between two destitute women is also very touching. Still, it seems like a very odd choice for a full-length theatrical movie. But Twentieth Century-Fox had had a huge hit with *The Robe* in 1953 (the first movie released in wide-screen Cinemascope) and had followed it up with successful sequels, and, as already noted in this book, throughout the 1950s the other studios cranked out wide-screen movies set in ancient times with religious themes that seemed to strike a chord with the public. So the studio assigned a new religious film to the director of *The Robe*, hoping for the best. The studio was disappointed, as the film was a flop at the box office. Still, it has some good things in it.

The film opens with the words "Across the centuries, many legends have grown up around the biblical story of Ruth." A mysterious gray-haired "narrator" who will appear later comments on the importance of the town of Bethlehem. Obviously this is intended as a hook to the audience, since they would know that Bethlehem was the birthplace of Jesus (and some would also recall it as the hometown of David). The scene moves immediately to nearby Moab, and we see an iron image of the bug-eyed god Chemosh, constructed as a grisly furnace for the sacrifice of children. Ruth's poverty-stricken father tearfully sells her to the Chemosh temple to be raised as a priestess. She is a "daughter of Chemosh." The voluptuous priestesses prepare to sacrifice the children, who naively believe it is an honor to die for Chemosh. A Hebrew artisan, Mahlon, who is making a crown for the sacrifice, lets the chief priestess know his views on child sacrifice and idol worship.

After Ruth expresses an interest in Israel's mysterious invisible God, Mahlon tells her that their God is known by many names— Jehovah, Elohim, Adonai. Mahlon is arrested for corrupting Ruth, and his father, Elimelech, and brother Chilion are both murdered. He is dragged before the king (who plans to make Ruth part of his harem) and sentenced to work in the quarries. Ruth has to do penance for her apostasy, but afterward she helps Mahlon escape the quarries, providing the one scene of real adventure. He is injured in the escape and literally marries her on his deathbed, though the Bible suggests they were married longer and that Elimelech died before his two sons did.

Orpah, Chilion's wife, who barely even appears on-screen, departs as in the Bible. Sticking with her widowed mother-in-law, Naomi, Ruth repeats almost word for word the King James Version text of Ruth 1:16–17, a famous pledge of loyalty and of turning from her false god to the God of Israel. They trek through the wilderness, evading the Moabite soldiers sent to capture Ruth.

The two women encounter Boaz at an oasis, where he makes his anti-Moabite feelings clear. Naomi finds the family homestead gone to ruin. Ruth, gleaning in the fields, is mocked by the men as a "loose" Moabite woman, alluding to the Moabites' orgiastic worship. She meets Boaz and feels an attraction. Boaz explains the long enmity between her people and his. Some of the locals go on a "witch hunt" because of the "idolater" among them. Ruth asks for Boaz's aid, and he defends her at a meeting of the elders.

Naomi prays for Ruth's safety. The mysterious narrator from the movie's beginning appears, drinking water from Naomi's long-dry well, assuring her that Ruth will be the ancestor of a great king (David) and of "a prophet who many will worship as the Messiah." (Note the choice of words: he is not actually called the Messiah.)

He disappears mysteriously, suggesting he is an angel. Obviously this is not from the Bible.

Dragged before the elders, Ruth admits she was a priestess of Chemosh. But her two accusers are not Hebrews but Moabites in disguise, and she catches them when they cannot name the tribes of Israel nor the Ten Commandments. Ruth is exonerated.

Henry Koster, German born, had directed *The Robe* and another popular religious film, *A Man Called Peter*. His other religiously themed films included *The Singing Nun*, *The Bishop's Wife*, and *Come to the Stable*. He was Twentieth Century-Fox's resident "religious director."

Tob, a kinsman, is infatuated with Ruth and claims his right to wed her. He gets embarrassingly drunk at the harvest festival, and Ruth and Naomi realize he would make a poor husband. This Tob is the unnamed "redeemer" of Ruth 4 who relinquished his right to Ruth. But in the movie, Ruth is dressed in her bridal garb but says at the wedding she does not love Tob but loves Boaz. Tob and Boaz go through the sandal ceremony mentioned in Ruth 4:7–8. The film ends with the mention of Ruth being the ancestor of King David.

Ruth is played by Elana Eden, an attractive but unknown actress whom this movie was supposed to make a star. It did not happen, and she largely vanished from Hollywood. She does well enough in the role of Ruth, her dark complexion and vaguely "foreign" accent being effective, since Ruth is a foreigner living in Israel.

Naomi, though well acted by Peggy Wood, never seems appropriately bitter enough over being left widowed and poor, as Naomi is in the Bible. Her bonding with Ruth doesn't quite ring true, since she barely knows Ruth at the time they leave Moab. The Bible suggests Ruth was her daughter-in-law for much longer when Mahlon died. Still, the two actresses do well together in their roles.

Norman Corwin, the scriptwriter, was noted for radio scripts, including having been commissioned by President Roosevelt to do some radio programs on the Bill of Rights. But he also wrote the screenplay for *Lust for Life* and a biblical opera, *The Warrior* (1947), based on the story of Samson and Delilah.

The advertising tagline for the film touted "All the spectacle of heathen idolatry, human sacrifice, pagan revelry—all the beauty of one of the Bible's timeless love stories." The film doesn't offer that much spectacle, though there is a certain amount of female dancing at the harvest festival. The child sacrifice scene is shocking because Ruth has gotten attached to the little girl Tibbah, and though Ruth's scream interrupts the proceedings, the audience is shocked that the child is sacrificed anyway. One plus of the movie is that it is the rare film to dwell on paganism's practice of human sacrifice, something that is condemned frequently in the Old Testament. The book of Ruth itself doesn't dwell much on the human sacrifices offered to the god Chemosh because its ancient readers already would have been aware that when Ruth turned from Moab's god to Israel's God, she was exchanging a cruel religion for a better one. One of the moral tragedies of the Old Testament is that the wise King Solomon, builder of the Lord's temple in Jerusalem, later built a place of worship for the Moabite god Chemosh (see 1 Kings 11:7)—Solomon, son of David and thus the great-grandson of Ruth, the Moabite woman who turned away from Chemosh to worship the true God.

To the movie's credit, it repeats many biblical phrases "Peace be with you," "the Lord be with you," and the like. Also, the very opening of the film lets the audience know that the story is based not just on the Bible but on the "many legends" that have grown up around the life of Ruth.

This is a quiet film, and the public largely ignored it in theaters, despite the studio's efforts to promote it as another grand biblical epic, which it is not. It is still watchable today, and its story of a woman turning from a cruel pagan religion to a better one still has some appeal.

Esther and the King: *Saint Joan*

Released November 1960
Twentieth Century-Fox
109 minutes
Filmed in Italy

Producer-Director: Raoul Walsh
Screenplay: Raoul Walsh, Michael Elkins
Photography: Mario Bava
Music: Francesco Lavagnino, Robert Nicolosi

Esther: Joan Collins
King Ahasuerus: Richard Egan
Mordecai: Denis O'Dea
Haman: Sergio Fantoni
Simon: Rick Battaglia
Klydrathes: Renato Baldini
Vashti: Daniella Rocca
Hegai: Robert Buchanan

Bible characters as pinups: villainous Persian official Haman (Sergio Fantoni) and virtuous Jewish girl Esther (Joan Collins) in the 1960 *Esther and the King*. It wasn't overly faithful to the Bible, and the fair-skinned, beardless men in the cast didn't remotely resemble men of ancient Persia.

The book of Esther is neglected by many Christians, partly because the book does not mention the name of God or even mention prayer. Its story of Jewish exiles in Persia facing the threat of persecution is interesting, yet somehow it seems a little cold because God himself is never named. Jews are fond of the book because of its connection with their joyous (even rowdy) festival of Purim. But its lack of familiarity to Christians kept filmmakers from taking much interest in it.

Yet in another sense the book of Esther seems a natural for the movies, with its Persian setting, palace intrigues, and violence against an innocent group of people. However, only one film had ever been made of the book, a French film of 1910. This 1960 curio does not do the book full justice, but it remains available because its star was a future TV star, Joan Collins, the vampish middle-aged vixen of the soap opera *Dynasty*. In 1960 she was young and beautiful and, amazingly, able to play a virtuous character.

The movie opens with martial music as credits roll over illuminated parchment (a standard look for many biblical films of the 1950s and 1960s). In the first scene the Persian army is on the march, and a narrator says it is 2,500 years ago. The Persians have conquered a wide empire from Egypt to Ethiopia. The uniforms and weapons seem to be authentically Persian. King Ahasuerus (the pronunciation of it in the film sounds like "Asirus"), the short-haired, beardless Richard Egan, does not look remotely Persian. (Here, as in all ancient epics, the men show a lot of leg.) The king greets Simon, one of his Jewish aides, and gives him a pearl necklace as a bridal praise for the aide's betrothed. The king says, "May the gods bless you," and the aide says, "May my God bless you, sire." In the next scene we see his betrothed is Esther (no mention of her original name being Hadassah). She laments the injustice of the evil Haman. She longs to return to Judea, but he reminds her that she is longing for a homeland she has never seen, since she was born in Persia.

News of the king's approach startles Queen Vashti, who is having an extramarital affair with Haman, an official who has designs on the throne. (Haman is blond and beardless.) He gloats that he served the king "politically and domestically" in his absence. He notes that the queen has many lovers. He also observes that queens are not necessarily permanent.

Haman greets the king on his return, showering him with his many titles. We see the king has some slight doubts about Haman's loyalty. Haman bewails the absence of the councilor Mordecai, who foolishly wastes time on his "invisible Hebrew God." However, Mordecai's joy on seeing the king again seems genuine. He says he prays for the king, and the king says the prayers seem to work. The king asks him about Vashti's behavior, and Mordecai is evasive.

Vashti's maids (who appear to be Oriental) are dressing her hair when the king enters. He denounces her as a "harlot" and says that from then on she is "dead" to him. She begs him not to believe palace gossip, but he literally shoves her aside.

Mordecai goes to visit Simon and his niece Esther. (In the Bible, she is Mordecai's orphaned cousin, raised by him like a daughter.) Mordecai laments that the king is powerful but unhappy, saddled with evil counselors and an unfaithful wife.

In the palace, scantily clad dancers gyrate while an African woman sings lustfully. The scene is about as bawdy as could be filmed in 1960. Vashti decides she will attend the king's feast even though she knows she is not wanted.

The king asks Mordecai if his troops are adequate to defeat "that young upstart" Alexander of Macedon. (The chronology is ridiculous. The actions in Esther take place at least a hundred years before Alexander lived.) Mordecai says he pines for a time when humans will use their resources for building, not for making war. Haman lashes out against the Hebrews and their invisible God. Mordecai warns him not to push God too far. (Why exactly was this three-man war council held in the middle of a feast? The movie is full of absurdities.)

When the king leaves the war council and returns to the feast, Vashti is dancing lewdly in front of everyone, tossing veils aside as she goes. The king is disgusted, Haman highly amused. She appears to be bare-breasted (seen from the rear). He orders her out; she spits as she leaves. Haman tells him the punishment for shaming the king is death or banishment. The king orders banishment. Haman says he will send her back to her own tribe and also find the king a new wife. Mordecai reminds Haman that the old Persian law stipulates that the entire empire must be canvassed for a suitable queen, so the choice does not depend on Haman's discretion. The entire Vashti incident is absurd, since the Bible says it was Vashti's refusal to "display her beauty" before the drunken feast that led the king to put her aside. However, in the movie she is made vixenish to contrast her with the virtuous Esther.

Klydrathes, one of the generals, drinks wine with Haman. They are both corrupt—Haman stealing from the treasury, Klydrathes selling military secrets to the Greeks. Haman tells him he plans to make Mordecai and all the Jews the scapegoats if their treacherous dealings are ever found out. In the meantime, Haman has one of the palace servants murder the queen by smothering her with a pillow.

Persian soldiers carry out the law's orders: they raid the villages for women, carrying off the prettier ones. (Some are shown in a cornfield. What was corn, native to America, doing growing in ancient Persia?) Esther is carried off literally seconds before her wedding to Simon. After Simon scuffles with a Persian soldier, the soldier orders the village burned.

Taken to the harem, Esther prays to God to let Mordecai know of her plight. Mordecai does learn of what happens and also of the persecution of Jews in her village. He fears persecution spreading across the empire.

Mordecai goes to Esther. He tells her Simon is a hunted man. He tells her she can help save all the Jews by becoming the queen. She pines for Simon but says she will do as Mordecai asks. He tells her to act "undercover," not revealing to the king she is a Jew.

Hegai, the chief eunuch, enters and sees the ten finalists for the queenship being beautified. He gives them lessons in court etiquette. He commends Esther's choice of a plain white dress. In the reception hall, the women individually bow before the bored king. Esther bows before the king, who sends her away, then tells her to wait. She tells him his soldiers had taken her from the man she was about to marry. The king says the law of his grandfather Cyrus has turned out to be a good law, since it has brought her to him. (Ahasuerus was not actually the grandson of Cyrus the Great.)

Mordecai on the other hand is pleased that the king has chosen Esther. She confides to him that she feels genuinely attracted to the king. Later Haman enters Esther's quarters. She realizes she has a very dangerous enemy in him.

> The movie almost never uses the word "Jews," instead always using "Judeans," which was also true of the same studio's *Story of Ruth*. However, in a key scene, Esther tells the king, "I am a Jew."

Esther tells the king that she hated him at first for taking her away from her fiancé and her home but that she has learned to admire and even love him. She thinks he has the makings of a man of integrity and that the evils of the empire are largely due to Haman. Esther is formally crowned queen, and the king praises her good influence on the administration of the empire. Spoiling the moment, alas, is Haman, who brings up an old law of Cyrus that all people of the empire must all bow down to the god Mithra—or be destroyed. (Mithra is not mentioned in the Bible, but he was indeed the chief god of Persia.) Esther protests, and Haman remembers another law that a woman interrupting the king must be put to death. The king reminds Haman that the law does not apply if the king holds out the golden scepter to the woman—which he does. (The custom of holding out the golden scepter is mentioned in Esther 4:11; 5:2; and 8:4.) The king orders Haman to a distant outpost. Later Haman determines it is time to put his plot into action.

In the royal court, Haman presents forged tables showing that Mordecai had planned to pass on Persian military secrets to the Greeks. The king begins to think he has trusted these alien people too much, especially Mordecai. Haman says Mordecai and Esther are conspiring together. He does not say she is a Jew, but Esther readily admits it herself, saying she is not afraid to die with her people. The king asks her politely to renounce her faith, but she says her God will live on when the Persian gods are long forgotten.

The story becomes incomprehensible toward the end. Haman's plot to have the king assassinated is put into action. Klydrathes, the chief assassin, is killed by Simon, who then fights with his former king for depriving him of Esther. Before dying, Klydrathes admits that Haman was behind the plot. The king then beheads him. The king realizes that the Judeans are about to be exterminated by Haman's order, so he sends Simon off with his signet ring, giving the order to arm all the Judeans. The soldiers in the palace say that the time has come to exterminate, since the Judeans are gathering for the Sabbath "in their temples," which is inaccurate, since the Jews gathered in synagogues.

A high gallows (mentioned in Esther 5) is built to hang Mordecai. Haman sends his thug to kill Esther, but she escapes. In prison awaiting execution, Mordecai recites Psalm 23.

Sitting on the king's throne (and presuming him dead), Haman is horrified when one of his henchmen brings him the head of Klydrathes. His plot has been discovered.

While Mordecai waits with a noose around his neck, the Judeans rise up to face their exterminators. Haman tries to flee the city gates but comes face-to-face with the king, who gives the order, "Hang him—hang him high!" Mordecai is freed and Haman hanged on the gallows. The wounded Simon is brought to Esther at the Sabbath service. Esther has her head covered, as do the other Jewish women. Mordecai recalls that Haman cast *pur* (lots) to decide the Jews' doom, so the day should be remembered as the day of Purim, a day of celebration and gladness—as is explained in the book of Esther. The camera focuses on a stone star of David. Simon dies, and Esther chooses to remain with the king.

"The laws of the Persians and the Medes" are mentioned in Esther 1:19 (KJV). In fact, a similar phrase, used several times in the book of Daniel, passed from the King James Version into the English language as a symbol of old, irrevocable, and stupid laws. The phrase in Daniel is "the law of the Medes and Persians, which altereth not" (6:8, 12 KJV). The same chapter has the Persian king's counselors saying to him, "Know, O king, that the law of the Medes and Persians is, that no decree nor statute which the king establisheth may be changed" (v. 15 KJV). The script for this movie follows this idea of the Persian court being bound by both law and precedent, often binding the king's hands legally.

This was director Raoul Walsh's last film. He had played John Wilkes Booth in *Birth of a Nation* and directed his first film back in 1915. In 1925 he had directed *The Wanderer*, based on the parable of the prodigal son.

Esther and the King is not a great movie by any means. *New York Times* critic Bosley Crowther lamented that "the beautiful Bible story of Esther has been thumped into a crude costume charade."[3] Its dialogue is stilted, acting rather stiff, chronology very confused, and no attempt was made to make the men look even remotely Persian. As already noted, the film departs from the Bible at numerous points. Still, in reflecting the overall aim of the book of Esther—showing how the Jews in Persia were saved from the plotting of the wicked Persian vizier Haman and how the events led to the institution of the festival of Purim—it is biblical enough. Esther and Mordecai are the virtuous heroes of the story, as in the Bible.

One final note: years earlier, the great Cecil B. DeMille had commissioned Pulitzer Prize–winning novelist Mackinlay Kantor to write the script for *The Story of Esther*, but DeMille never made the film. It is interesting to speculate how DeMille, with his flair for gaudy historical epics, would have handled the story.

David and Goliath: *Obese Orson*

Released in the U.S. October 1961	**Saul:** Orson Welles
Embassy Pictures	**David:** Ivo Payer
92 minutes	**Samuel:** Edward Hilton
Filmed in Israel, Italy, and Yugoslavia	**Abner:** Massimo Serato
	Merab: Eleonore Tossi Drago
Director: Richard Potter, Ferdinando Baldi	**Michal:** Guilia Rubini
Screenplay: Umberto Scarpelli, Gino	**Jonathan:** Pierre Cressoy
Mangini, Ambrogio Molteni, Emimmo	**Goliath:** Kronos
Salvi	**Ashdod:** Furio Meniconi
Photography: Carlo Fiore	
Music: Carlo Innocenzi	

In viewing and reviewing films for this book, I saw one trend that is rather sad: stars who were past their prime performing in low-budget biblical movies. It's true that the really popular biblical epics boasted stars who were at the peak of their popularity—Gregory Peck in *David and Bathsheba*, Charlton Heston and Yul Brynner in *The Ten Commandments*, Richard Gere in *King David*, for example—and that other films were launching pads for rising stars—Richard Burton and Jean Simmons in *The Robe*, Gina Lollobrigida in *Solomon and Sheba*. But sadly, the lesser of the biblical films often had to rely on has-been stars (or directors) to draw the public in. This was certainly the case with *David and Goliath*, where most of the cast were Italian unknowns (or, in the case of David, a Croatian unknown) but where the one big name was Hollywood's former boy wonder, actor-director-writer Orson Welles, who had lost prestige steadily since his 1941 *Citizen Kane*. Welles was overweight and unreliable at this stage of his career, yet the producers of *David and Goliath* put enough stock in his name to put "Orson Welles as King Saul" above the movie title itself.

As noted elsewhere in this book, David's story is a fascinating one, his biography being the longest in the Bible. As yet no theatrical movie has quite done it justice, though a TV movie of the 1990s came close. This low-budget Italian sub-epic did not come anywhere near succeeding, nor did it even do justice to the interesting relationship between rising king (David) and falling king (Saul).

The movie opens with a bit of honesty: as the credits roll, we see the words "Screenplay freely adapted from the Bible by" above the names of the four writers involved. "Freely," indeed! All biblical movies take liberties with the Bible text, but this script is so "free" that "loose" would be more accurate. The "free" quality is evident in the still images over which the credits roll, which instead of being Hebrew are generic "ancient Near East," showing winged Assyrian bulls and so on. Nothing is specifically Hebrew about the images. And what is one of these winged bulls doing in Saul's throne room? And why is there a statue of a muscular, bearded man there when the Israelites would not allow such images?

The story opens with the white-bearded judge-prophet Samuel making his way, a cane-crutch in each hand, to Saul's palace. Saul's costume seems to be modeled on the kings in a deck of playing cards rather than on ancient Hebrew fashions. Abner's and Saul's sons are pointed out to Samuel, who recalls how badly his own bribe-taking sons turned out. He explains this as the reason the Israelites had made him anoint them a king to rule them (see 1 Samuel 8). The speeches are King James English, peppered with "thee," "thou," "spake," and so forth. Samuel recalls his warning to the people of how a king would oppress them, that their desire for a king so they could be like other nations would backfire on them. So far the script has stuck pretty close to the Bible, in words if not in costumes and scenery.

As Saul, Orson Welles is bloated and repulsive. It is hard to believe he is the Saul that the Bible describes as strikingly handsome. Surely a man of hard fighting would not be so obese. (Then again, the hard-fighting king William the Conqueror of England was grossly fat in his later years, so "fat warrior" is a possibility.) Saul is not pleased to see Samuel but tries to greet him warmly. Samuel laments that the ark of the covenant has been taken by the Philistines (which is incorrect—the ark had been back in Israelite possession for a long time). Samuel tells him privately that Saul has broken the Lord's commandments. The words in this section are taken almost word for word from the King James Version of 1 Samuel 15. There is no mention of the incident with the Amalekites and their king that is the center of that chapter. As Samuel walks away, Saul wants to know who the replacement king will be. Samuel tells him the Lord told him that the Lord does not see things as man does (see 1 Sam. 16:7). Samuel tells him the king-to-be is in Bethlehem, but he will not say his name. Samuel has a superb, resonant speaking voice but is a bit hammy.

The young, muscular, bare-chested David is tending his sheep and practicing with his sling. He chats with his young sweetheart, and the "thou" and "smite" language continues. Abner is courting Saul's daughter Merab, who doubts his love is genuine. The Bible makes no mention of her having an affair with Abner. Her sound dubbing is very bad.

In the Philistine court, their king gloats over capturing the ark but says he wants Saul's blood also. No Philistine king is named in the Bible, but this one is named Ashdod—which in fact was the name of a Philistine city. An advisor tells the king of the usefulness of the "Persian chariots," though the Persian Empire did not exist at this time. He also tells the king of a gigantic warrior named Goliath who could prove useful to the army. Goliath is hairy and muscled and does not actually speak through the course of the movie (though he does growl).

A feast is held in front of a huge iron image of the Philistine god Dagon. Goliath is brought in, and the king is impressed. Scantily clad dancing girls entertain him. The king has his men bring in the "rock of Samson," something no man has lifted but Samson himself. Goliath is able to lift it. There is no "rock of Samson" in the Bible, but the incident does call to mind how Samson was a major foe of the Philistines—one they would have remembered.

Old Samuel makes his way to the home of Jesse in Bethlehem, where he meets all Jesse's handsome sons. Samuel passes over them all, but David enters. He is "ruddy," as the Bible says (1 Sam. 16:12 KJV). Oddly, Samuel quotes several passages from Proverbs and Ecclesiastes (supposed to have been written decades later by David's son Solomon). The actual anointing with oil does not take place. David sets off through the wilderness for Jerusalem. In the crowded city, David takes pity on some slaves, whom he buys and then frees. The city is an immoral place, full of slave dealing and gyrating dancing girls. Men beat their wives and children. Men are shown being punished for rebelling against Saul. David calls out to the Jerusalemites and denounces their wickedness. He tells them they are full of evil and their ruler Saul is full of corruption. Saul walks out and hears him. He is standing on the temple steps, even though there was no temple at the time, nor was Jerusalem Saul's capital. The priests give David refuge in the temple. Saul knows David is the one Samuel chose to be king, which is not biblical. Abner offers to get rid of David, but Saul orders David brought to him.

Abner questions David, who assures him he respects Israel's laws and king but must denounce corruption. Michal, Saul's daughter, says they should give David a fair hearing, but Merab is scornful. Saul enters and orders the others out. Saul tells David he has heard David is not only courageous but also a skillful musician. He asks David to live in the palace and play for him. David as Saul's "musician-therapist" is biblical. Alone, David prays for Saul, recalling what a valiant man he once was. He asks God to delay the day when Saul will no longer be king.

Saul tells David that Samuel has died and that all Israel mourns for him, though this does not occur till later (see 1 Samuel 25). Saul tells David about the Philistines' giant, Goliath, describing him in almost the exact words of 1 Samuel 17:4–7. David takes to the road, meeting people who are fleeing before the rampaging Philistines.

Goliath was played by an Italian circus muscleman named Kronos.

David rides out to meet Ashdod, who says he has heard of David's "wisdom." David demands that they return the ark and leave Israel alone. Ashdod makes an offer: defeat Goliath in battle and the Philistines will retreat. David rides out to meet the giant and dismounts while Goliath laughs. Couldn't they have had him taunt David, as in the Bible? Goliath hurls a huge spear at David, then some more, but David dodges. David dispatches Goliath with one stone, then beheads him with his own sword. (The Bible says he fell facedown, but all movies show him faceup, for some reason.) Instead of the Philistines fleeing in panic, as in the Bible, they rush in to battle the Israelites, with David in the thick of it. Ashdod is killed, and the Philistines surrender.

David returns in triumph to the palace, and with Saul's connivance, Abner plans to kill him with a spear. But just before Abner hurls the spear, Saul kills Abner with an arrow. Jonathan says he has gotten rid of his evil spirit, but the grief-stricken Merab says the evil spirit will not die until Saul does. David calls out, "Long live Saul!" Saul is guilt-stricken and gives David his daughter Michal as wife, saying, "Blessed be thou, my son David, for thou shalt do great things." The people rejoice outside the palace.

This last scene is ridiculous, but it does have some loose ties to the Bible, where (much later in the story) Saul himself tries to kill David with a spear. But the movie's story of Abner plotting to seize Saul's throne (with the conniving of Saul's daugher Merab) is plain silly, and Saul definitely did not kill Abner at this stage or any other time.

Some of the film was "authentic" in the sense of being filmed in Israel (as few biblical movies are), but the acting is generally bad (many of the Italian actors had their voices dubbed for the English version). The young man who plays David is handsome but not a good actor at all, and the script certainly failed in not showing some of the Bible's examples of David's early courage (killing a lion, for example). Welles was good at playing melancholy characters (apparently he really *was* melancholy at this stage of his life), but he badly overacts as Saul.

One closing note: in the opening credits, the name of Saul's daughter is spelled "Michael" instead of the correct "Michal." That error rather sets the tone for this low-budget, badly scripted Italian-into-English film.

Let's pause here to mention a handful of other Italian-made biblical films of the 1960s, none of them as yet available on home video (though based on what we know of them, this is no great loss). As already noted in this book, Italy has long been the cradle of movies set in ancient times, and one of the first feature-length films was the Italian-made epic *Quo Vadis*. The highly profitable *Ben-Hur*, released in 1959, was a Hollywood production but did most of its shooting in Italy to take advantage of cheaper labor. Most of the Italian-made films set in ancient times were not up to the *Ben-Hur* standard by any means, and that includes the two films just discussed, *Esther and the King* and *David and Goliath*. Fans of movie westerns know that the 1960s saw the beginning of the "spaghetti western," which generally featured two or three English-speaking leads (usually Clint Eastwood) with the rest of the cast being Italian, their voices usually dubbed. But the 1960s was also the golden age of "spaghetti ancient epics," some of these based (often loosely) on the Bible. Like the spaghetti westerns, they kept costs low by hiring only a handful of English-speaking actors, usually former stars (like Orson Welles) or rising stars (like Joan Collins). Unlike *Ben-Hur*, these low-budget items could not spend a fortune on historical research—or on writers who could provide good dialogue.

One of these not-yet-on-video films was *I Grandi Condottieri*, released in 1965 in English as *Samson and Gideon*, two of the heroes
of the book of Judges. The film included sequences of Samson's
angelically announced birth and his carrying off the gates of Gaza,
slaying Philistines with the jawbone of a donkey, and destroying
the Philistines' temple. It was all rather cheap looking compared
to Cecil B. DeMille's 1949 *Samson and Delilah*, though the new
Samson was more muscled up. On the positive side, it is the only
film ever made of the heroic Gideon.

Another Italian film was the 1962 *Giuseppe venduto dai fratelli*,
released in English as both *Joseph and His Brethren* and *Sold into
Egypt*, with English and American actors in the leading roles but
mostly an Italian cast. The movie was very silly, with Potiphar
and Joseph hunting for lions and elephants in "the jungles of
Egypt" (Egypt has no jungles). The beasts were obviously stuffed,
and the sets abounded with very fake-looking palm trees. Bosley
Crowther of the *New York Times* called it "the clumsiest, the sil-
liest, the worst of the quasi-biblical pictures to come along since
the wide screen was born."[4] *Ponzio Pilato* was released in English
as *Pontius Pilate* and starred former leading lady Jeanne Crain as
Pilate's wife, who, in Matthew's Gospel, tells her husband she had
a dream about the innocent Jesus.

The Italian-made "sword and sandal" epics of the 1950s continued. In the 1964 *Hercules, Samson, and Ulysses*, the two wandering
Greek heroes aid Samson in fighting the Philistines in Israel—not
exactly the Samson story told in Judges. A very nonbiblical Samson
also was featured in the 1968 rubbish *Samson and the Lost Treasure
of the Aztecs*. The Italians seemed comfortable using "Samson"
as a name for any muscleman of an earlier time. There were also
several "Goliath" movies made in Italy in the 1960s with Gordon
Scott, Rock Stevens, and Steve Reeves; none of the films were even
remotely connected with the Goliath of the Bible.

King of Kings: *Jesus Handsome and Peaceful*

Released October 1961
MGM
163 minutes
Filmed in Spain

Director: Nicholas Ray
Screenplay: Philip Yordan
Music: Miklos Rozsa
Producer: Samuel Bronston

Jesus: Jeffrey Hunter
Mary: Siobhan McKenna
Pilate: Hurd Hatfield
Lucius: Ron Randell

Claudia: Viveca Lindfors
Salome: Brigid Bazlen
Herodias: Rita Gam
Mary Magdalene: Carmen Savila
Barabbas: Harry Guardino
Judas: Rip Torn
Herod: Frank Thring
Caiaphas: Guy Rolfe
John the Baptist: Robert Ryan
Peter: Royal Dano

Narrator: Orson Welles (uncredited)
Narration script: Ray Bradbury (uncredited)

Amazing as it may sound, a film about Jesus Christ had not been released since Cecil B. DeMille's 1927 *The King of Kings*. Jesus had been on the sidelines in several popular films, notably *The Robe* and *Ben-Hur*. After MGM's smashing success with *Ben-Hur*, it seemed time to return to the Jesus saga once again. Released late in 1961, *King of Kings* was a smashing success, becoming the sixth-highest-grossing film of 1962. Not until Mel Gibson's *Passion of the Christ* in 2004 would a film about Jesus be such a crowd-pleaser.

In DeMille's film, Jesus had been played by H. B. Warner, who was past fifty. Jeffrey Hunter, the actor chosen for MGM's *King of Kings*, was in his early thirties—about the same age as Jesus was when he began his ministry, according to Luke's Gospel (3:23). Critics joked then and now about how youthful Hunter was, dubbing the film *I Was a Teenage Jesus*, apparently not aware that Hunter was just the right age.

Director Nicholas Ray noted that Hunter's eyes "have the luminous quality needed to convey the spirit of Christ," a statement with which many people would agree. Some people were skeptical about the casting, since Hunter was divorced from his first wife and had played nothing but cowboys and loverboys. At the time of the film's release, Hunter did a lot of interviews, basically saying, as in one interview, that he thought of God as "infinite love and understanding and forgiveness" and saying (depending on the interviewer) that he was either Episcopalian or Presbyterian.

Director Nicholas Ray had long identified with outsiders, particularly those at the mercy of the mob or establishment. His most famous film was the youth drama *Rebel Without a Cause* starring James Dean. Ray had no real religious motive for directing *King of Kings*, but rather he hoped that high-profit epics like it would enable him to make money, save it, and become independent of Hollywood—which did not happen. Producer Sam Bronston had tapped Ray to direct the film, also enlisting the aid of experts in Hebrew music, advisors from the Vatican, and composer Miklos Rosza, who had created the stirring music for *Ben-Hur* and *Quo Vadis*. Many people who saw the film when it was released remembered the music vividly, and rightly so, since the 163-minute film has 130 minutes of music. Miklos Rozsa's music is sometimes overpowering and obtrusive, but it does help to suggest the power of Rome.

Jeffrey Hunter was told by producer Samuel Bronston to keep his life squeaky clean during production time, making sure not to even get a traffic ticket. Hunter even chose to give up smoking.

The film departs in many ways from people's expectations. Instead of opening with the nativity—which had been the opening of *Ben-Hur* two years earlier—it opens in 63 BC, setting up the political conflict of Jew versus Roman, which is a major feature of the movie. Martial music plays, Roman soldiers march, and the narrator (Orson Welles, lending his distinctive voice) tells of the Roman conquest of Jerusalem by Pompey. On the very steps of the temple, Pompey has his soldiers kill the chief priests. The narrator speaks of the Roman's rule of blood. Caesar appoints the slimy, effete Herod as "king of the Jews." Herod and the Romans are pleased to see crucified bodies. The Jews long for their promised Messiah. While the Bible says nothing about Pompey and his exploits, this is useful background for understanding the political situation of the New Testament world.

The narrator then reads almost word for word from Luke regarding the census under Augustus. The wise men arrive on camels. The shepherds are present also. Cut to Herod, muttering about this "king" who has been born in Bethlehem. He orders his captain to murder the infants of Bethlehem. For effect, Herod's equally vile son, who will later meet the adult Jesus, is present, egging his father on. Joseph awakens Mary, telling her of his dream telling them to flee to Egypt. We see the soldiers running amuck in

Bethlehem, slaughtering children. Cut to Herod, falling down in agonizing pain, while the younger Herod shows not a trace of pity. He seats himself on the throne while his father crawls on the floor. He even pushes his father away from the throne. We see just how dysfunctional this loathsome family really is. Historically speaking, Herod did die not long after the slaughter in Bethlehem. (In the film Joseph, departing from tradition, is the same age as Mary, not older. Siobham McKenna, though she hardly looks Jewish, is an appealing Mary.)

Pilate arrives as the new governor. As his entourage enters, he is watched by the Jewish rebel Barabbas and his fellow Zealots. They attack, using slings and spears against the better-armed Romans. This is a well-staged action scene, with Barabbas and a Roman fighting hand to hand at the edge of a precipice. The scene serves as a reminder to the audience that the Zealots pursued a path radically different from the path chosen by Jesus. The movie refers to them as "patriots" (a wise choice) instead of Zealots.

As John the Baptist, Robert Ryan is rugged looking enough, but he doesn't project the charisma of a prophet. He badly needs some volume. Our first glimpse of the adult Jesus is when he is standing before John in the Jordan River—both men blue-eyed. Oddly, Jesus does not hear the voice of God at the Jordan but afterward in the wilderness. We hear Satan's voice but do not see him. The scene does show that Jesus was fasting and very weak after forty days.

Jesus calls his apostles. As Peter, Royal Dano is very scrawny. Oddly, Jesus calls him "Peter, the rock" from the very beginning. He certainly does not play any kind of leadership role among the disciples. He does have big, soulful eyes, however.

Pilate is irked that there are no imperial statues or banners in Jerusalem—which is historically correct. He orders his lieutenant to place plaques of the emperor on the columns of the temple. A riot ensues, with the people egged on by John the Baptist. Pilate is dining with Herod and Caiaphas, which is absurd but good drama. Herod, Herodias, and Salome go to the balcony, where John calls Herod on the carpet for taking his brother's wife. John is brought in before Herod, utterly fascinating the bratty Salome. John bluntly reminds Herodias that she not only bedded her brother-in-law but has been promiscuous elsewhere.

A fine healing scene follows: a blind beggar taps his cane along a plaster wall, and we see the shadow of Jesus on the wall.

Judas starts out as the right-hand man of Barabbas but is drawn to the new prophet, Jesus. While Jesus and his disciples are in Jerusalem, a group rushes through, following a woman caught in adultery. Judas is impressed with Jesus's handling of the situation. So is the woman. Jesus does say, "Go and sin no more." The narrator says that Judas had to choose between Barabbas, the "messiah of war," and Jesus, the "messiah of peace."

Unbiblically, Jesus goes to visit John in prison. Their hands touch through the bars.

Herodias is jealous, because Herod obviously lusts for his bratty step daughter. After much begging from Herod, Salome finally agrees to dance, after extracting his promise for "anything." Salome's dance is about as sensual as could be done in a film in 1961. She demands John's head on a platter, but Herod tries to talk her out of it. He caves in. John is beheaded with a huge curved sword. (Interestingly, Frank Thring, who plays Herod, had played Pilate two years earlier in *Ben-Hur*.)

The crowd for the Sermon on the Mount is huge. (The extras were people from the Spanish village near where the film was shot.) Obviously making this section of the Bible come alive on-screen is difficult. It is done through the reaction shots of the listeners. Judas is impressed with the sermon, but Barabbas walks away in disgust, sputtering, "Words!" At this point Judas leaves him and follows Jesus. (The narrator pronounces the "t" in *apostles*. Didn't someone involved with the film know this wasn't correct?)

The narrator notes that these men were not learned but were "pure in heart" and willing to learn. They, like the people in general, wanted to throw off the power of Rome, but Jesus taught a new way. Cut to Barabbas and his men forging weapons in their caves. Judas tells Barabbas that Jesus and the disciples will soon be in Jerusalem and that Barabbas and his men should show up, concealing their weapons, and make Jesus king, hopefully convincing the Romans to throw down their weapons without loss of blood. But when Judas leaves, Barabbas tells his men that this is their chance for the battle they have longed for. Meanwhile, Pilate and Lucius discuss the possibility of Jesus's and Barabbas's followers joining forces and staging a rebellion.

On Palm Sunday, Jesus draws one crowd, Barabbas another. The Zealots go to battle with their makeshift weapons, but the Romans are better organized and armed. Barabbas is wounded and captured. Judas assures the remnants of Barabbas's band that Jesus will aid them, as he can do miracles. Judas says that Jesus will only unleash his power against the Romans when he himself is captured by them. Two of the Gospels record that Barabbas was in prison for murder and his part in an insurrection in Jerusalem (see Luke 23:17–19; John 18:40).

The Last Supper is, as usual, shown with the disciples seated at conventional high tables. But the feast, following the Passover ritual, is handled well. Judas goes to Caiaphas's house, hoping his betrayal will force Jesus's hand.

In Gethsemane, Jesus finally does turn loose some emotion, showing agony and doubt. Rip Torn does a good job as Judas—intense and humorless. The camera lingers a moment before the kiss in the garden, allowing for tension to build.

The trial before the priests is not shown. Apparently producer Bronston and director Ray remembered how DeMille's 1927 film was charged with being anti-Semitic, so they simply chose not to include the crucial scene of Jesus being condemned by the religious leaders of his own people. Jesus is brought before Pilate, who says he has been charged with blasphemy. The priests are not present when Pilate sees him. And, oddly, Pilate appoints his man Lucius as a kind of "public defender" at the trial. Lucius reminds Pilate that Jesus has said nothing directly against the power of Rome. Following Luke's Gospel, Jesus is sent by Pilate to Herod, who, with Herodias and Salome present, wonders if Jesus is John come back to life. He asks Jesus to turn a clay vase into gold or to produce thunder. As in the Bible, "Jesus gave him no answer" (Luke 23:9). (How odd to include the scene with Herod, which is found only in one Gospel, and to omit the trial before the Jewish leaders, which is found in all four Gospels.)

Judas, witnessing the scourging of Jesus, is in agony. We hear the strokes but do not see the actual beating. Judas swoons when he sees carpenters making crosses. Barabbas is freed, told by Lucius that Pilate gave the mob a choice and that Barabbas's followers yelled louder. Lucius tells him, "Go, look at the man who is dying for you."

Judas and Barabbas watch the crucifixion. Judas finally sees that no miracle is going to happen. For someone hanging on a cross, Jesus does not seem to be in great pain. Also, we don't witness the mocking by the Jewish rulers and the soldiers—a missed opportunity for some real drama. Lucius says, "He is truly the Christ"—not quite the same as the Gospel's words "Truly this was the Son of God" (Matt. 27:54 KJV). Later Barabbas finds the dead Judas with the noose around his neck.

Mary Magdalene finds the tomb empty. She asks a man where the body has been taken. He turns to her and she sees it is Jesus. Later, by the Sea of Galilee, Jesus (offscreen) delivers the Great Commission to the disciples. The last face we see is Peter's, though we do see Jesus's shadow on the shore. The film ends.

Jeffrey Hunter does have a great face—compassionate but also intense. What a shame he doesn't cleanse the temple, which would have been a great scene. We don't get to hear him denounce the Pharisees and scribes either. He always seems very much in control, never doubting. Obviously the 1970s would introduce a different kind of Jesus, but it was not one that pleased audiences much. Reviewing films about Jesus in 2004, after the release of Mel Gibson's *Passion*, *Time* film critic Richard Corliss stated that Jeffrey Hunter was "a Jesus with star quality to spare—which the original must also have had." He notes that the crucifixion, especially compared to Gibson's, "lacks wallop."[5]

MGM released *King of Kings* with the ad line "The Power, The Passion, The Glory." Like most advertising copy, it was a bit inflated. Yet, all things considered, this is a good film, sticking reasonably closely to the Gospels, plus filling in some historical and political details that help audiences understand the life of Jesus better. It is regrettable that scriptwriter Philip Yordan was so determined to fend off charges of being anti-Semitic that he didn't include the episode of Jesus being condemned by Caiaphas and the other Jewish leaders. It is also regrettable that the film shows very few miracles and omits the driving of the money changers from the temple. The Roman Catholic Legion of Decency, which

> For the crucifixion scene, Jeffrey Hunter had to shave his chest and armpits. Supposedly a preview audience had been offended by the hair, even though the two crucified thieves had armpit hair.

still had some clout in 1961, criticized the film as "theologically, historically, and scripturally inaccurate," and the Catholic magazine *America* claimed that the producer and writer saw the film as a chance to make a profit, nothing more. But many Christians, including some Catholics, loved the film. Its Jesus is an appealing one, and a more appealing one would not be seen in films or television until the 1977 TV miniseries *Jesus of Nazareth*.

Let's pause here for a brief look at a film released by Columbia in October 1962. *Barabbas* is, like *Ben-Hur* and *The Robe*, a "semibiblical" movie, one in which key events of the Bible are an important part of the story but in which the main plot is not drawn from the Bible. In the cases of *Ben-Hur* and *The Robe*, the main characters are not found in the Bible. This is not true of Barabbas, who is mentioned briefly in the Gospels as the criminal whom Pontius Pilate releases to the crowd instead of Jesus Christ. Barabbas is described as a "notorious prisoner" (Matt. 27:16) and also as a murderer and one who led an insurrection in Jerusalem (see Luke 23:19). We know nothing else about him, but these few words in the Gospels imply he was a Zealot, a Jew who stirred up trouble against the Roman government, often resorting to violence. Despite being mentioned only briefly in the Gospels, he has often been an important character in biblical movies, since scriptwriters assumed he was a Zealot and that his way, the way of violence, was a contrast to Jesus's way, the way of peace and mercy. Thus Barabbas was a key character in the 1961 *King of Kings* and also in the 1977 TV miniseries *Jesus of Nazareth*.

Swedish novelist Par Lagerkvist published his novel *Barabbas* in 1950, and it was translated into English in 1951, the same year the author won the Nobel Prize for Literature. A 1953 Swedish film version of the novel was released but went largely unnoticed. The choice to make the novel into an English-language film was based not on the author's fame (he was barely known in America) but on the assumptions that ancient epics were highly profitable and that people might turn out to see a color extravaganza about this notorious figure from the Bible. (*Give Us Barabbas*, a TV version of Barabbas's life—but not based on the novel—had been broadcast in 1961 and was well received.) The movie's ad tagline was "The man of violence in whose place Christ died," and posters featured Barabbas in his gladiator scene, playing up the movie's violent angle.

Sodom and Gomorrah: *Not the Sin We Expected*

Released January 1963	**Lot:** Stewart Granger
Twentieth Century-Fox	**Ildith:** Pier Angeli
154 minutes	**Queen:** Anouk Aimee
Filmod in Morocco	**Astaroth:** Stanley Baker
	Shuah: Rossana Podesta

Director: Robert Aldrich
Producer: Goffredo Lombardo
Screenplay: Hugo Butler, Giorgio Prosperi
Music: Miklos Rozsa

The ancient city of Sodom's name lives on in *sodomy*, referring to homosexuality in general, male homosexuality in particular. The story of the wicked city (and its equally wicked sister city, Gomorrah) is told in Genesis 18 and 19, where we learn that the patriarch Abraham's nephew, Lot, had gone to dwell in Sodom, even though "the men of Sodom were wicked and were sinning greatly against the LORD" (Gen. 13:13). The Lord, in the form of three angels, pays a visit to Abraham and tells him he intends to destroy the wicked cities, and Abraham engages in a haggling episode with God, asking if God will spare the cities if there are fifty righteous people there. And what about twenty? Or ten? There aren't enough, as it turns out, so the Lord rescues Lot and his wife and daughters, and after they flee the city, God rains down fire and brimstone on the evil place. Disobeying God's command not to look back, Lot's wife does and is turned into a pillar of salt. The word *sodomy* is rooted in the fact that the men of Sodom surrounded Lot's house and told him to bring out the angelic visitors "that we may know them"—meaning have sex with them, as the New International Version has it (Gen. 19:5 KJV). Sodom is mentioned numerous times in the Bible as an example of a wicked place that received God's just punishment (see Isa. 1:9; Zeph. 2:9; Matt. 10:15; 2 Peter 2:6; Jude 7). For centuries the names Sodom and Gomorrah conjured up images of great wickedness, even if people were barely aware of the story in Genesis.

The story has great potential for a film, what with the angelic visitors, the rescue of Lot, the flight from the city, and the destruction. In fact, it was told very well in the 1966 film *The Bible . . . In the Beginning*, where the episode takes up about a half hour. This 1963 film plays so fast and loose with the story from Genesis that it is almost unrecognizable.

The opening shot shows several scantily clad people collapsed at a banquet in Sodom. A narrator speaks of Sodom and Gomorrah as cities of wealth and terrible vice, while the Hebrews live as peaceful nomads in the wilderness. Abraham and his nephew Lot, the narrator says, divide up their grazing lands, and Lot settles near Sodom (see Gen. 13:7–12). Lot is first shown carrying a child on his shoulders, indicating he is a decent man. Lot and the Hebrews encounter a servant of the queen of Sodom, carried in a litter by slaves. Lot tells her it is wrong to keep slaves, but the woman says, "Everything that gives pleasure is good." At the gate in Sodom, an old prophet speaks out against the city's sin, but the people mock him. Slaves are shown at hard labor, used like machines. (According to Genesis, the Hebrews *did* keep slaves, for Abraham, who is held up as a role model of faith, had slaves and fathered a child by his slave woman Hagar.)

In the court of Sodom, dancing girls gyrate lewdly. The queen has slave girls branded and is happy when they scream with pain. The queen's brother, equally depraved, warns her that the wandering Hebrews are trying to "propagate their faith." The queen is concerned about a threat from the "Helamites," a totally fictional name. It is implied that the queen is a lesbian, choosing a "favorite" from among the girl slaves, which is the closest this movie comes to touching on homosexuality.

Lot and his band arrive at the land they sought. Lot thanks God for letting them find water and warns the people not to go near the cities of Sodom and Gomorrah. In a rocky canyon, Lot finds a "disposal site" where the Sodomites deposit their dead or dying slaves. The old prophet is lying there still alive, and Lot gives him water.

At the Jordan River, Lot goes to meet with the queen of Sodom. The queen gives Lot her favorite female slave, Ildith, who is reluctant to live among herdsmen. She is peeved at wearing the simple clothing of the Hebrews and doing household labor. One of the Hebrews refers to the "tabernacle," even though there was no tabernacle until the time of Moses. Lot's daughter puts on Ildith's slinky dress, and Lot is scandalized. Obviously Ildith is going to corrupt the daughters. The queen's lecherous brother stays for a while in Lot's camp and tries to corrupt one daughter. It is implied that the queen and her brother have had an incestuous relationship in the past.

All the men in the film have beards except Lot, who explains to the queen that it is the Hebrew custom to shave the beard after being widowed. As in all biblical movies made in this period, there is a great deal of "beefcake," with men shirtless and showing a lot of leg, and the queen and many other women wearing seductive costumes.

The plot is, frankly, very confusing, with the queen's brother plotting against her and the queen attempting to use the Hebrews as soldiers against the Helamites. The key point is that Ildith, the slave girl from Sodom whom Lot liberated, falls in love with him and he with her, though she warns him she was made for pleasure, not love.

Lot and Ildith marry, but their wedding is interrupted by a battle with the Helamites. The battle is exciting, with the Hebrews and Sodomites using pitch and fire to scorch the huge, mounted Helamite horde. Reluctantly, Lot has to order the breaking of the dam the Hebrews had built to irrigate their land. Letting the waters loose defeats the Helamites and also provides a watery scene that must have reminded viewers of *The Ten Commandments*. (The battle episode was, incidentally, directed by Sergio Leone, who would later gain fame as director of the "spaghetti westerns" that made a huge star of Clint Eastwood.)

With the dam gone and the land infertile, Lot takes it as a sign from God that the Hebrews should live in Sodom and become merchants of salt—supposedly living separately from the sinful Sodomites. The Hebrews become wealthy, and Lot wears a rich red gown and lives in a marble palace. At a grand banquet (with more dancing girls, of course), the queen announces that Lot is now her chief minister, which peeves the queen's brother, naturally. While the banquet goes on, some of the Hebrews free the Sodomites' slaves, but none of the Sodomites—not even the Hebrews—will give them refuge, so the soldiers hunt them down. Except for Lot, the Hebrews at the banquet show no concern for the captured slaves. The queen's brother boasts of having seduced both Lot's daughters, so he and Lot have a duel with swords. Lot wins and kills him, and his daughters grieve.

The queen shows no emotion over her brother and gloats that Lot and his people have become just like the Sodomites. He allows himself to be imprisoned. Later the slaves are coated with oil and and turned on a kind of spit to amuse the Sodomites. Lot prays, sorry that he let his people dwell in such a horrible place and for being so foolish as to think they could convert these wicked people. Two angels—white-bearded men—appear and tell him to leave because God is about to destroy the place. Lot asks if God will destroy the innocent along with the guilty— the "bargaining" scene that in Genesis takes place between God and Abraham. The angels say that even for ten innocent, God would not destroy the place. Lot's chains miraculously fall off, and his cell door opens. The Hebrew elders come to him, and he tells them they must flee, but the Hebrews don't want to. The queen's soldiers appear to take Lot, but lightning blinds the soldiers. Out of prison, Lot warns all the Hebrews to leave the city before sundown, while the people laugh. The queen laughs, telling him that his God is impotent and that what he calls "sin," she calls "virtue."

> If a person had seen the movie but never read Genesis, he would have no idea why the word *sodomy* is connected with homosexuality.

Many more than ten people go with him (so the bargaining episode makes no sense at all). In fact, the slaves manage to escape their pens, and hundreds flee the place. His daughters both go, but grudgingly, for they hate him for killing the queen's brother. A wind begins to blow; it is followed by an earthquake, and buildings begin to crumble. Oddly, fire comes forth from the cracks in the ground. The queen is buried under falling pillars. The people are so wicked that they rob each other while trying to flee. Ildith looks back at the city and is turned into a pillar of salt. Lot grieves.

The movie's advertising tagline was "The cities that mocked the very name of God!" Obviously the scriptwriters succeeded in showing that Sodom really was a wicked place in not only keeping slaves but also abusing them horribly. The people delight in cruelty, and they know much about lust but nothing about love. So in one sense the script succeeds in presenting us with a place that seems to deserve destruction, even if it does omit the Genesis episode of the men of Sodom wanting to rape Lot's angelic visitors. And, alas, the earthquake that destroys the city is dramatic, but the "fire and brimstone" of Genesis would have been equally dramatic.

New York Times film critic Bosley Crowther was right in calling it "one of those mammoth costume splurges,"[6] and quite a few of them were made in this era. *Newsweek* reviewed the film and noted that after two and a half hours, the Lord finally got around to destroying Sodom: "His patience is divine indeed."[7] Audiences were generally unimpressed with the film also, and it was not the huge moneymaker that its producers—American, Italian, and French—had hoped. Film producers were beginning to wonder if the age of profitable biblical epics was passing.

Incidentally, the full title of the film was *The Last Days of Sodom and Gomorrah*.

The Greatest Story Ever Told: *A "Wonderful Failure"*

Released February 1965
United Artists
Original running time 260 minutes
 (MGM/UA Home Video running time:
 197 minutes)
Filmed in Utah, Nevada, Arizona, and
 Hollywood

Producer-Director: George Stevens
Screenplay: James Lee Barrett, George
 Stevens, "in creative association with
 Carl Sandburg"
Music: Alfred Newman
Photography: William Mellor, Loyal Griggs

Jesus: Max Von Sydow
John the Baptist: Charlton Heston

Peter: Gary Raymond
Judas Iscariot: David McCallum
Pilate: Telly Savalas
Caiaphas: Martin Landau
Herod Antipas: Jose Ferrer
Mary Magdalene: Joanna Dunham
Lazarus: Michael Tolan
Martha: Ina Balin
Mary of Bethany: Janet Margolin
Mary: Dorothy McGuire
Joseph: Robert Loggia
Simon the Zealot: Robert Blake
Matthew: Roddy McDowall
Thomas: Tom Reese
Simon of Cyrene: Sidney Poitier
Herod the Great: Claude Rains

Years after the release of this film, actor Max Von Sydow, who had played Jesus, reflected that the movie, like any telling of the Jesus story, had to be a failure in some way because no one version of the story could please everyone. The movie was a failure but, in his words, a "wonderful failure."

The movie's director and producer, George Stevens, did not intend to make a failure, of course. He had been an extraordinarily successful director in Hollywood, winning Oscars for his direction of *A Place in the Sun* and *Giant* and also directing *Shane*, *Woman of the Year*, *I Remember Mama*, *Penny Serenade*, and *The More the Merrier*. He had directed a very serious film, *The Diary of Anne Frank*. He wanted his next film to be a subject even more serious than the Anne Frank story. Stevens, like Cecil B. DeMille, didn't just want to make a biblical epic that would earn money. He approached the project with the belief that the world was headed in the wrong direction, godless communism was wrong, and Hollywood needed to promote religious values.

Stevens claimed he wanted simply to do the story of Jesus with no interruption for theatrical embroideries. In one sense he succeeded, for this has to be the most biblical movie Hollywood ever made, in the sense that it is totally saturated with Bible verses throughout—spoken, chanted, and sung (it used Handel's "Hallelujah Chorus," which is based on a verse from Revelation). It quotes more sayings of Jesus than any other Jesus movie, plus tons of lines from the Old Testament prophets.

During filming, director George Stevens would not allow photographs to be taken of Max Von Sydow, since he wanted his Jesus to be a fresh face for audiences.

In his 1995 autobiography *In the Arena*, actor Charlton Heston, who played John the Baptist in the film, had much to say about the film and its director: "The life of Christ has often been explored by filmmakers, from DeMille in the silent era onward, because it probably *is* the greatest story ever told. Directors of various persuasions have tried different versions, including rock opera. None of them has quite brought it off. None was better equipped for the task than George, I think. Aside from the firm backing of United Artists, he had his own talents and reputation, as well as a deep Christian conviction."[8]

Stevens also had a man he thought would make the perfect Christ, Swedish actor Max Von Sydow, well known in his native land but a new face to America. He was associated with noted Swedish director Ingmar Bergman and had appeared in several of his films (including one in which he was shown naked). Stevens "borrowed" him from Bergman for almost two years. Von Sydow is six foot four, certainly the tallest Jesus ever on film. His slight accent helped in making him seem not so ordinary. The actor was thirty-six when the movie was being filmed, thus not far off Luke's statement that Jesus was "about thirty" when he began his public ministry (3:23).

Finding the right locale was not easy. Stevens had scoped out locales in the Holy Land itself but decided that locales in the U.S. Southwest probably looked more like the Holy Land that Jesus actually walked. So the epic was filmed in Arizona, Utah, and Nevada, with the western landscapes very striking—not surprising, given that Stevens had directed the classic western *Shane*.

The film opens with credits on a parchment background. After naming Max Von Sydow, the other cast members are listed alphabetically. The credits are small, suggesting the subject is greater than the individuals involved. A narrator reads from John 1: "In the beginning was the Word, and the Word was with God, and the Word was God . . ." We see what appears to be a fresco of Jesus (in Von Sydow's guise), then hear the words "the light shines in the darkness, and the darkness grasped it not." We see first a bright star in the sky, which then fades to a flickering of an oil lamp and a dim view of the baby in the stable. The narrator says, "The greatest story ever told." (The title, incidentally, was borrowed from the very popular book by Fulton Oursler.)

A camel caravan crosses the wilderness. Three luxuriously dressed visitors call on King Herod in Jerusalem. A paranoid Herod learns from his councilors of a Messiah to be born in Bethlehem. The obviously ailing Herod admits he's not a Jew but an Idumean, and though he lavished his attention on the temple, he is despised by the Jews. As in Matthew's Gospel, Herod tells them to find the child and bring him word so he too may worship him—then has an aide follow them secretly.

The wise men arrive in Bethlehem by camels, the shepherds on foot. Mary, gazing on the baby, recalls the angel's prophecy of Jesus's greatness (see Luke 1:30–33). The men present their gifts and speak of their symbolism—gold for sovereignty, frankincense for the worship of God, myrrh for preservation until time everlasting. The wise men spy Herod's men in the distance. In a dream Joseph hears a voice saying, "Take the child and flee" (see Matt. 2:13).

Herod is disturbed to hear that the wise men did indeed go to Bethlehem, as the prophecy said. Herod himself recalls the prophecy of Rachel weeping for her children. He brings it to pass, ordering the slaughter of every boy infant in Bethlehem (see Matt. 2:16–18, quoting Jer. 31:15). The scene of Herod's soldiers in the village, as the women and older children shriek in terror, is horrifying.

At an oasis in Egypt, Joseph reads from the scroll of Isaiah the prediction of one who will be called "the prince of peace." A boy runs to the couple and tells them he heard Herod is dead. They will return to Nazareth, though it is never explained why they were in Bethlehem.

On the road back to Nazareth, Mary and Joseph pass crucified men on the road. Throughout this passage we hear people reading psalms in the background, including Psalm 22, "My God, my God, why has thou forsaken me?" (v. 1). They also continuously pray for a deliverer. Romans pass by the crosses with no reaction.

Over a shot of the temple and a sacrifice of a calf, we hear the strong voice of John the Baptist, who says (quoting the prophets) that it is not sacrifices that God desires but steadfast love and the knowledge of God. "Prepare ye the way of the Lord, make straight in the desert a highway" (Isa. 40:3 KJV). We see long aerial shots of people flocking to see John by the Jordan River. He looks as wild and shaggy as the Gospels say. John predicts the coming of One whose sandals he is not worthy to carry. Suddenly, out of nowhere, we see the face of Jesus, asking for baptism. "Is it not you who should baptize me?" John asks. Jesus is baptized; they embrace. There is no dove and no voice from heaven. As Jesus walks away, John quotes Psalm 24: "Lift up your heads, you gates . . . behold, your God!"

Jesus climbs into the forbidding, stony mountains. A hermit (Satan) welcomes him into a cave. The hermit tells him life need not be hard if a man knows the way to power and glory. He offers food, but Jesus says he is fasting. The hermit continues to eat and asks Jesus if he would like to rule the world. He can give Jesus this power—if Jesus will worship him, that is. As they gaze down a steep cliff, the hermit says, "If you are the Son of God, throw yourself down." The devil also tells him to turn stone into bread. The order is not the same as in the Gospels, but Jesus's replies are the same.

Jesus and the disciples near Jerusalem, and he speaks of it as the city that stones the prophets. They are welcomed at the home of Lazarus, Mary, and Martha.

Pontius Pilate calls on the high priest Caiaphas, wanting to know about the "revolutionary" John. He tells Caiaphas he has no interest in the Jews' "superstitions."

At Lazarus's house, Jesus says that the two greatest commandments are to love one's neighbor and to love God with all one's heart. Though Lazarus is presented as wealthy, Jesus speaks out against the worship of wealth. But they part warmly, obviously setting things up for Jesus's later miracle.

At Herod's palace, he hears of the troublesome John. He is obviously already lusting after his stepdaughter. He mocks all prophets but is disturbed to hear John's prophecy of a Messiah (given the fear that it put into his father). This is wrong, of course, since it was John's preaching against Herod's adultery that got him into trouble.

At a synagogue, Jesus heals a lame man. The scene is handled well— he is not cured instantaneously but rises slowly, taking very hesitant steps, while the others have their hands out, expecting him to fall. Anyone who has ever had a broken limb and worn a cast knows that a healed limb does not suddenly spring to vibrant life again once the cast is removed.

At sunset by the river, John is arrested. Herod has him brought from his cell. John has zero respect for this "king," for only God is his king. He prophesies Herod's damnation for taking his brother's wife.

Caiaphas hears of Jesus's miracles and scoffs. But he sends a spy to Galilee to find out more.

Back in Capernaum, Jesus is greeted warmly, notably by the cripple he healed. The old hermit (Satan) greets him: "Hail, son of David." We see the woman caught in adultery literally dragged out of bed and brought to Jesus (she is dressed in red). Jesus asks her if the accusations are true, and she won't deny them. Jesus holds a stone in his hand and tells the people, "Let him who is without sin cast the first stone." Dramatic pause. No one does, and he slams the stone down dramatically. She says she is Mary of Magdala. He says, "Go your way—and sin no more." The story in John 8 actually takes place in the temple at Jerusalem.

At a party in Herod's palace, several men report many miracles of Jesus. Herod goes to John's cell and tells him of this "messiah." Herod assures John that the child born in Bethlehem is long dead, but John tells him the child was taken to Egypt and still lives.

Herod tells John he will kill him before the night is over. While we see Salome dancing erotically, John is already brought from his cell with an axman on the ready. John's last word, shouted as the girl still dances, is "Repent!" Herod tells his men to go and arrest Jesus also. This is the one movie that shows that Herod meant to capture Jesus (see Luke 13:31). But it completely forgets the Gospels' story that Herod thought Jesus was John back from the dead.

Messengers tell Jesus that Lazarus is on the verge of death. Lazarus dies, and in a few days Jesus visits. Mary and Martha almost mock him—he has come too late, even though he had time to get there. Why had he not come earlier and healed him? This doubt and anger are not in the Gospels but seem appropriate. When Jesus looks into the camera and says, "I am the resurrection and the life," we take him seriously. Jesus does weep. He makes his way to Lazarus's tomb cut in a hillside and says, "Lazarus, come forth!" Before we ever see Lazarus himself, we see the faces of the people there. Handel's "Hallelujah Chorus" is sung. Witnesses spread the news quickly.

In the version released in theaters, an intermission occured at this point. This is the perfect pausing place, not only because of the running time but because the raising of Lazarus is the greatest miracle prior to Jesus's own resurrection at the end. Also, according to John's Gospel, the raising of Lazarus was the point at which his enemies, the Jewish priests in particular, decided for certain he had to be done away with.

At the beginning of part 2, Caiaphas mocks the story of Lazarus. Back in Bethany, Mary Magdalene anoints Jesus's feet with some expensive ointment and wipes them with her own hair. Judas, who seemed sour even during the raising of Lazarus, chastises her for "wasting" the expensive perfume, since the money could have been used for the poor. (In John's Gospel it is Mary of Bethany who anoints Jesus, and rightly so, following the raising of her own brother.) As Mary anoints his head with oil Jesus's face is truly angelic.

Seated on a white donkey, Jesus travels from Bethany to Jerusalem, and people begin their cries of "Hosanna!" In the temple courts, Jesus causes a ruckus when he overturns the tables of the money changers. (Regrettably, the audience not familiar with the Gospels may not grasp what the "money changers" are actually doing.) He drives them out with a whip made of cords. Judas watches disapprovingly. Appropriately, after this Jesus tells the crowd that he has not come to destroy the law but to fulfill it. Then he denounces the Pharisees and teachers of the law.

Herod meets with Pilate, who assures him he can handle the rabble of Jerusalem. He and Herod laugh at the teaching to love one's enemies. This movie's Pilate is much more unpleasant than any of the others.

Jesus seems to come to life in Jerusalem, becoming much louder and more forceful than before. He states that the three greatest things are faith, hope, and love—but the greatest is love. These are Paul's words from 1 Corinthians 13:13, but they are not inappropriate on Jesus's lips.

While the disciples prepare the Passover meal, Judas exits. In the streets he bumps into the old hermit (Satan), and briefly their eyes meet. He goes to Caiaphas. He introduces himself as a "friend of the Nazarene" for three years. Looking guilty and confused, he says he will give him over—if they promise no harm will come to him, for "Jesus is the purest and kindest man I have ever known." Caiaphas is puzzled but lies, saying that no harm will come to Jesus.

In the Last Supper scene, the disciples are seated in one long line, exactly as in Da Vinci's famous *Last Supper* painting. An interesting touch: when the disciples partake of the bread—Jesus's body—Judas never eats his piece of it. At the very point where Jesus says, "Love one another," his eyes meet Judas's. He tells him, "Do quickly what you must do." Judas exits.

Following Jesus's arrest in the Garden of Gethsemane, he is brought with his hands bound before Caiaphas. Outside, Satan, in his old man guise, asks Peter if he is a friend of Jesus. Peter denies it.

Pilate asks Jesus just which son of God he is—Mars? Hercules? Which god? Pilate is very sarcastic. Where is Jesus's kingdom? What is "truth"? Pilate's wife calls him aside, but we don't hear what she says.

Jesus is taken to Herod, who is hosting a party. The cynical Herod asks Jesus to work a miracle. (The time shown is wrong, of course—Jesus was tried before the Sanhedrin at night, Pilate and Herod the next morning.) Herod mocks Jesus by having a red robe put on him.

Pilate shows the thorn-crowned Jesus to the people and says, "Behold the man!" Showing no particular sympathy, Pilate says he will scourge him and release him. Satan, in the crowd, is first to cry, "Crucify him!" Pilate offers to release either Jesus or Barabbas. Pilate reminds them that Barabbas is charged with murder. The crowd asks for Barabbas. Pilate asks what shall he do with Jesus. Again Satan leads the call with "Crucify him!" also shouting, "We have no king but Caesar!" To avoid any accusations of anti-Semitism, *The Greatest Story Ever Told* deliberately did not show Caiaphas present at the trial before Pilate, nor Pilate's handwashing scene, nor the crowd of Jews shouting "his blood be upon us." A voice-over reads the words of the Apostles' Creed: "Suffered under Pontius Pilate, was crucified . . ." The film places the blame squarely on Pilate and on Satan, not on the Jews.

> As the centurion at the crucifixion, John Wayne utters his famous one line: "Truly this man was the Son of God." He actually had more lines in the original script.

We do not see the scourging, but as Jesus carries his cross, his face, hands, and back are bloody. Jesus tells the sympathetic women of Jerusalem not to weep for him. Jesus falls again, and Simon of Cyrene voluntarily carries the cross—not ordered by the Romans. In fact, the two carry it together. After Judas throws the silver back into the temple, he kills himself not by hanging but by throwing himself into the fire burning in the temple court.

When the nail is driven into Jesus's hand (not wrist), Jesus does not make a sound. For some odd reason Jesus on the cross is not shown in close-up until, finally, he says, "I thirst." After he dies, thunder, lightning, and rain occur.

Caiaphas asks Pilate to place a guard around the tomb, since Jesus's disciples might steal the body. Pilate's soldiers arrive at the tomb, where Joseph of Arimathea is present, and confirm that Jesus is there; then the tomb is sealed. The soldiers awake and, to their shock, the tomb is open. The "Hallelujah Chorus" is heard again. Mary Magdalene goes to the tomb. A young man (angel) in the tomb says, "He is risen. Why seek the living among the dead?" Peter and John enter the tomb and find it empty. Caiaphas learns the body is gone and the soldiers saw nothing. One of his advisors states, correctly, that the soldiers would naturally deny being asleep, since the Roman punishment for sleeping on duty is death. Caiaphas says it is no matter, the whole thing will be forgotten in a week.

The risen Jesus tells his disciples, "I am with you always, even to the end of the world," echoing the ending of Matthew's Gospel. Clouds suggest Jesus's ascension into heaven. The film ends.

At the time of the film's release, the star cameos throughout the film got a lot of attention. Some worth mentiong: Sal Mineo as the healed cripple, Ed Wynn as the old blind man, Angela Lansbury as Pilate's wife, Shelley Winters as the healed woman, Sidney Poitier as Simon of Cyrene, Roddy McDowall as Matthew, Pat Boone as the angel at the tomb, and John Wayne as the centurion. Some people at the time found the "star-hunting" distracting, and today, more than forty years after the film's release, people still find the cameos a small distraction.

> Cecil B. DeMille once said to Charlton Heston, "You can always get good actors to play bad men. Heroes are harder." This has certainly proved true for every movie about Jesus.

Von Sydow did a reasonably good job as Jesus, reminding many people of the faces of Christ seen in Renaissance paintings. On the other hand, he certainly doesn't seem to suffer much during his scourging and crucifixion. The review in *Newsweek* magazine noted that Von Sydow "hardly varies his expression, as if he had a pebble in his sandal."[9] Anyone who has seen *The Passion of the Christ* cannot help but think that the Jesuses in all earlier movies were barely in pain at all. Like any actor who ever played Jesus, Max Von Sydow didn't quite make it, yet he does project a dignity and seriousness that make it understandable that people would be drawn to him.

When the film was released, critics were not kind to it, dubbing it "The Longest Story Ever Told." It was indeed the longest movie made about Jesus up until that time. Von Sydow's performance as Jesus was respected, but critics thought the film moved at a snail's pace, which is true. New Testament parables and quotations, which work so well in print, cannot really develop a dramatically viable figure on film. Richard Corliss, movie critic for *Time*, called it "monumentally, genteelly, stupefyingly reverent."[10]

The film was nominated for several Academy Awards: art direction, cinematography, costumes, score, and special effects. It did not win any. It did not win the public either, for the $20 million project earned a mere $8 million. After the success of the 1961 Jesus film *King of Kings*, Stevens was certainly disappointed. Perhaps timing was part of the problem. Two Jesus epics in a five-year period was just too much, even if *The Greatest Story Ever Told* boasted an all-star cast and a respected director. Still, many people who saw the film at the time of its release remember it fondly, despite its length and pacing.

Regarding length: it was originally released at 260 minutes, then cut to 238 minutes, then 197 minutes, then 147 minutes, and finally 127 minutes. The video version available today is the version of 197.

Director George Stevens, reflecting on the movie years later, said he had viewed it again and could not think of anything, while watching it, that he would've done differently. Critics would probably suggest picking up the pace of the movie and eliminating some of the star cameos, but that is all speculation. The failure of the film pretty much soured Hollywood on making any Jesus movies for several years. The 1970s would see some "alternative" Jesuses, musical and politicized, but Stevens's film sent Hollywood the message that films sticking close to the Gospels would not draw an audience. In 1977 something more satisfying than Stevens's film would be released: a TV miniseries much longer than *The Greatest Story Ever Told*. In the comfort of their homes, and on more than one night, people would take *Jesus of Nazareth* into their hearts. Television did what perhaps no theatrical movie can do: present the life of Jesus at the right length and at the right pace. And, surprisingly, the year after the release of *The Greatest Story Ever Told*, a handful of Americans would see a very satisfying film about Jesus—cheaply made, in black and white, and directed by a communist homosexual.

The Gospel According to Matthew: *The Un-Hollywood Jesus*

Released in the U.S. in February 1966
135 minutes
Italian title: *Il Vangelo Secondo Matteo*
Black and white
Italian with English subtitles
Filmed in Italy

Director: Pier Paolo Pasolini
Producer: Alfredo Bini
Original Music: Luis Bacalov
  Music from Bach, Mozart, Prokofiev,
  Webern, American spirituals
Photography: Tonino Delli Colli

Jesus: Enrique Irazoqui
Young Mary: Margherita Caruso

Older Mary: Susanna Pasolini
Joseph: Marcello Morante
John the Baptist: Mario Socrate
Peter: Settimio Di Porto
Andrew: Alphonso Gatto
James: Luigi Barbini
John: Giacomo Morante
Judas: Otello Sestili
Caiaphas: Rodolfo Wilcock
Pilate: Alessandro Clerici
Herod the Great: Amerigo Bevilacqua
Herod Antipas: Francesco Leonetti
Herodias: Franca Cupane
Salome: Paola Tedesco
Angel: Rosanna Di Rocco

As proof that truth is stranger than fiction, consider this very reverent, straightforward telling of the life of Christ—directed by an avowed Marxist and homosexual, a man who built his career on movies about pimps, drug addicts, and other lowlifes. Doesn't sound possible, does it?

Pier Paolo Pasolini's background deserves a look. His father was a military man, and his brother died in World War II. Pasolini was attached to his poetry-loving mother. He became deeply involved in the Italian Communist Party but was expelled from the party after being accused of homosexual activity with some of his students. Moving with his mother to a shantytown outside Rome, he supported himself with odd jobs and became intrigued with the poor and the petty criminals. He began writing poetry and novels and occasionally ended up in court with his works accused of indecency. He enjoyed his role of *intelletuale scomodo*—intellectual provocateur. When he began to make films, he focused on the same sorts of people as populated his fiction: pimps, whores, petty thieves. His first movie, *Accatone* (pimp), scandalized the authorities. He nursed a desire to do a movie about Christ, whom he saw as a revolutionary like himself, and he wanted to do a Jesus movie that would differ radically from the biblical movies of the past. Ironically, though he succeeded, the movie was well received by the Catholic church and gained Pasolini an audience that had never heard of him before. After all his "low" films, it was a religious film that brought him fame. By contrast, many liberals attacked him for the film, regarding it as pietistic.

He made some truly salacious films, notably *The Canterbury Tales* and *The Decameron*, choosing some of the smuttiest stories from those famous collections. His last film was *Salo, or 120 Days of Sodom*, which is true to its title (and based on a novel by the infamous Marquis de Sade). It was released just after Pasolini's own murder by a young male prostitute, then withdrawn from release.

In a 1966 press conference, Pasolini was asked, "Why do you deal with religious themes, you yourself being an unbeliever?" Pasolini replied, "I may be an unbeliever, but I am an unbeliever who has a nostalgia for belief." He stated that when shooting *The Gospel According to Matthew*, he thought he was shooting it from the perspective of a believer, which most viewers would say is true. Pasolini, who was noted for saying "all is sacred," said that what was important was not belief or unbelief in religion but whether someone believed in and longed for a better world.

The movie, which is in black and white, opens with this dedication: "To the dear, familiar memory of Pope John XXIII." The atheist homosexual filmmaker felt some affection for the pope, who had died in 1963.

The Gospel According to Matthew is on the list of "Important Films" announced by the Vatican in 1995.

In the first scene we see a close-up of a young woman, then a man, who seem distressed. We see the young woman is pregnant. The man (Joseph) walks off into the field, looking back on his village. He naps and awakens to see an angel (female) telling him the precise words from Matthew: "Do not be afraid to take Mary for your wife." Joseph hurries back to Mary. He smiles, then she smiles. In short, the movie begins exactly where the biblical story begins in Matthew 1:18.

The wise men appear at Herod's court. Herod's advisors tell him the Christ child will be born in Bethlehem, according to the prophets. An oily, hypocritical Herod tells them to find the child so that he too may worship him.

One of the wise men takes the baby in his arms, clearly delighting in the bambino. This is not a scene we've seen in any other religious film. Mary seems pleased, Joseph pleased but puzzled.

Only after this dandling do the wise men present their gifts. The same angel who appeared to Joseph appears to the wise men, guiding them on a different route so they do not return to Herod. In Matthew they receive this warning in a dream. We see a close-up of Mary and the baby in bed together, which is kind of touching.

Joseph sees the angel again, and it tells him to flee to Egypt so Herod will not destroy the child. Here and elsewhere in the film, we hear a voice reading words from the prophets, which Matthew quotes so often.

A band of young men gather on a hillside. One whistles as a signal, and they descend on the town with swords and clubs, killing all the infants. We actually see some of the slaughtered infants.

The chubby, hirsute Herod dies, seemingly in great pain. His councilors, wearing huge headdresses, sit by idly. Few people regretted the passing of this wicked king. The angel appears to Joseph again, telling him Herod is dead and it is safe to return home. By this time Jesus is an adorable toddler, walking to greet his papa, who embraces him warmly.

John baptizes people in the wilderness. Interestingly, we hear the old spiritual "Sometimes I Feel Like a Motherless Child." John does not immerse (which he most cetainly did) but baptizes by sprinkling, as the people kneel. It resembles a Renaissance painting of John, not reality. John isn't really shaggy enough, but he does seem intense. Some of the Pharisees and Sadducees appear, and John calls them a "brood of vipers." The crowd is impressed with his attacking the establishment.

Jesus, who has more a five o'clock shadow than a true beard, has intense eyes. He appears at the river. John reacts with an awed, reverent stare. There is no dove, but the people hear the voice of God saying, "This is my beloved Son, in whom I am well pleased."

Alone in the wilderness, Jesus prays silently. Satan, a brutal-looking character, tempts Jesus to turn stones into bread. He takes Jesus to the tower of a large church, telling him to throw himself down. Satan walks away.

We see John in prison (see Matt. 4:12), and Jesus's ministry begins, with the screen showing Matthew's quotation of Isaiah. Passing some farmers with their winnowing forks, Jesus tells them, "Repent, for the kingdom of heaven is at hand." Finding Andrew and Peter at their work fishing, he calls them to be "fishers of men."

John and James, mending their nets, are also called. The others are called, including the rather thuggish looking Judas Iscariot.

Up until the calling of James and John, the movie had precisely followed the chronology of Matthew. In the movie, Jesus teaches his disciples before beginning the healing ministry described in Matthew 4:23–25. Some of the people who come to him are hideously deformed by leprosy. The first leper is healed instantly—i.e., we see him deformed, then Jesus's face, then the man's face perfectly normal. On the mountain, Jesus pronounces the Beatitudes, most of it done in close-up of his face. The entire Sermon on the Mount is not given. Left out, for example, are the sections on lust and divorce.

The feeding of the five thousand (Matthew 14) occurs. As with the other miracles, we do not see it taking place; just suddenly the camera shows us several baskets heaped with bread and fish.

Jesus is accused of driving out demons by the power of Beelzebub. He says that every sin can be forgiven except blasphemy against the Holy Spirit.

His mother (now an older actress) appears with some of his brothers. He tells them all that whoever does the will of his Father is his true family. Mary does not seem distressed at this, perhaps because in the next scene he visits Nazareth, though at first he passes by her and says nothing. He is not made welcome in his hometown, for a prophet finds no honor in his own country.

People bring their children for blessing. His disciples try to shoo them away, but Jesus says the kingdom of heaven belongs to such.

In the section about John the Baptist's beheading, Salome is much more girl than woman. At Herod's party her dance is more graceful than sensuous, though the leering Herod looks like the type that could be aroused by the sight of a girl doing anything. The movie does not explain why John is held in prison, nor do the subtitles even tell us the names of Herodias and the girl. When she asks for John's head, Herod does not hesitate a moment. The beheading is carried out immediately, though we do not see the head fall nor see it brought to Herod. Jesus sheds a tear, apparently in grief over John.

In the wilderness, Jesus asks his disciples who he is. The burly Peter says he is the Christ. Peter is open-mouthed and wide-eyed as Jesus tells Peter that he has the "keys of the kingdom" and that upon this rock he (Jesus) will build his church. But immediately he refers to Peter as "Satan" when Peter says that no harm will befall him.

The priests watch disapprovingly as Jesus enters the temple court and turns over the money changers' tables. Oddly, it is immediately after this that the people—mostly children—greet him with cries of "Hosanna!"

Jesus finds a fig tree with no fruit. He curses it, and in the next shot it is dry and leafless. He tells the disciples that if they have faith, they too can do miracles. This is one of the few Jesus movies ever made that shows this disturbing miracle.

The priests confront him, asking him who gives him his authority to teach. He confounds them by asking if John's authority was from God or from men, and they cannot answer. The common people seem pleased when he denounces the pious Pharisees. Pasolini, so anti-establishment, must have liked this, since he quotes almost the entirety of Matthew chapter 23.

Judas, looking very peevish, protests the "waste" of the woman anointing Jesus's head with expensive ointment. At this point Judas leaves and makes his way to the priests. (Note: Matthew 26:8 says "the disciples" protested the waste, not Judas specifically. But the story of Judas going to the priests does immediately follow the anointing story.)

Jesus and the disciples eat the Passover meal together. Jesus predicts Peter's betrayal. The Gethsemane scene is nicely played, with good close-ups of Jesus as he looks upon Jerusalem, then prays to be spared. As in the Gospel, more than once he returns to his disciples to find them sleeping.

The trial before Caiaphas is shown at a distance. We watch it over Peter's shoulder. Three different people accuse Peter of being a follower, but he denies all. Oddly, the third time he says, "In the name of the living Christ, I know nothing of this man"—a peculiar change in the Gospel wording. Peter does sob convincingly.

The trial before Pilate is seen at a distance. The incident of Pilate's wife is omitted. The audience sees the event, very briefly, through the perspective of John.

The Roman soldiers are a rowdy lot, but the crown of thorns draws no blood. The scourging (see Matt. 27:26) does not take place at all.

What *The Passion of the Christ* covers in over two hours, this movie does in about fifteen minutes. We do hear the agonized screams of the thieves as they are nailed to the cross. Jesus on the cross does not seem to have a mark on him, except one trickle of blood from the crown of thorns.

Oddly, while he hangs on the cross, the screen goes black, and Jesus's words appear: "Listen as you will, even without understanding! Watch all, but nothing perceive! Your office is to dull the hearts of these people of mine, deaden their ears, dazzle their eyes so they cannot see with those eyes, hear with those ears." He is paraphrasing Isaiah 6:9–10, quoted by Jesus in Matthew 13, where he is explaining why he speaks to people in parables. What does this have to do with the crucifixion? Is he saying the crucifixion itself is a parable?

> The movie, filmed in Sicily, uses Christian music from various periods—not only classics like Bach but also American spirituals. The music, though often beautiful, is distracting at times.

There are no "seven words from the cross," only "My God, my God, why have you forsaken me?" as in Matthew 27:46. He cries out with a loud voice (see 27:50). We see a stone building collapse, apparently the movie's version of the earthquake (see 27:51).

The servants of Joseph of Arimathea take Jesus's body and lay it in Joseph's own tomb. As in Matthew, there are guards at the tomb. The women come in the morning carrying flowers. The stone falls forward; the tomb is empty. The female angel appears again, saying that Jesus is risen.

On a mountainside, Jesus gives his disciples the Great Commission. Close-up of Jesus's face: "Behold, I am with you always." The end.

The film did not include everything from Matthew's Gospel (some of the omissions have been noted already). However, almost none of the dialogue in the movie is not found in the Gospel. The transfiguration, a key event (Matthew 17), is not shown. Also, the film omits most of the parables. And, oddly for a movie with this title, the calling of the tax collector Matthew (see Matthew 9) is omitted.

The director's mother played the older Mary. Since Mary does not actually speak in Matthew's Gospel, she does not speak in the movie either. Pasolini cast many of his friends in the film. In most of his films he used nonprofessionals.

Never was there a movie with more close-ups—of Jesus and of the many faces responding to his words in various ways. Pasolini was working with a small budget, and close-ups are cheap—and sometimes highly effective.

Some of the sets are obviously anachronistic—for example, Gothic and Renaissance architecture. The landscape of Sicily has a biblical look, but the buildings do not. The film also made no attempt at all to be historical in terms of hairstyle, facial hair, and so on. Almost none of the men has a beard. They are simply Italians of the 1960s, dressed (more or less) in "ancient garb."

In a way, having the actors speaking Italian with subtitles pro duces the same effect as in Mel Gibson's *Passion*: a "documentary" feeling, as if we are actually hearing the words of Jesus, with subtitles required. In a 2004 interview in which he discussed Jesus films in general, Gibson described Pasolini's film as a "yawner." While it doesn't pack the emotional wallop of Gibson's film, it is hardly a yawner. In an article on films about Jesus, the evangelical magazine *Christianity Today* noted that in Pasolini's film, "This Jesus is hard to take, and perhaps that is as it should be."[11] In fact, the magazine had much higher praise for the film than for the other two Jesus movies of the 1960s, *King of Kings* and *The Greatest Story Ever Told*.

Pasolini's film was released in his native Italy in 1964 and caused quite a stir at the Venice Film Festival. Americans had to wait until early 1966 to see it, but few did, for it did not get a wide release in the U.S., playing mostly the "art house" theaters and hardly heard of in the American heartland. Those who saw it couldn't resist contrasting its gritty realism and documentary feeling with the overlong Technicolor epic of 1965, *The Greatest Story Ever Told*. It has had a long shelf life, partly because it is an intriguing film and partly because of its connection with its director, the homosexual atheist with his "nostalgia for belief."

The Bible . . . In the Beginning: *Good Creation*

Released November 1966	**Adam:** Michael Parks
Twentieth Century-Fox	**Eve:** Ulla Bergryd
171 minutes	**Cain:** Richard Harris
Filmed in Italy and Egypt	**Abel:** Franco Nero
	Noah: John Huston
Director: John Huston	**Nimrod:** Stephen Boyd
Producer: Dino De Laurentiis	**Abraham:** George C. Scott
Screenplay: Christopher Fry, Vittorio	**Sarah:** Ava Gardner
Bonicelli	**The Angel:** Peter O'Toole
Photography: Guiseppe Rotunno	
Music: Toshio Mayuzumi	

The creation of the world seems like a fit subject for a movie, yet no one had done it before—not well, anyway, and not in a film marketed by a major Hollywood studio. Doing it well was left to Italian producer Dino De Laurentiis, whose modest goal was to film the entire Bible, or at least those parts of it that were in story form. He did not achieve that goal, getting only as far as Genesis 22. Yet it was an amazing achievement, one faithful to the Bible and highly profitable as well, being one of the five top money earners of 1966.

The movie opens with no credits except for the title and "Directed by John Huston." Huston narrates Genesis 1 almost word for word, using the King James Version, which was still acceptable in 1966 even if many people were reading more modern versions. The footage of the creation is a feast for the eye—waves crashing, birds and beasts from all over the world. The creation of Adam from the dust is beautifully filmed. A literal wind, God's breath (the Hebrew word *ruah* in Genesis can mean both "spirit" and "breath"), blows over a lump in the soil, and very slowly the lump begins to look more like a human body. Sculptor Giacomo Manzu did three different sculptures of Adam, agreeing to do so only if he was *not* paid and if the sculptures were destroyed, with no casts made, once the shooting was done. He actually made the sculptures from the clay on the spot it was filmed. He did one sculpture per day, each one progressively looking more human than the one before. Blowing past the sculptures using wind machines, the golden dust filled the screen like the breath of God. Adam was played by the handsome young actor Michael Parks, though the producer and director toyed with the idea of having Adam and Eve be somewhat dark and primitive looking.

Noah (John Huston) is pleased to see his dove returning with a green twig, the sign that the floodwaters have subsided. A notorious Hollywood bad boy, the hard-drinking, womanizing, atheist Huston not only made an appealing Noah but also was the narrator and the voice of God in the very popular 1966 *The Bible . . . In the Beginning*. Incidentally, he also directed it.

As it was, Parks and the actress playing Eve were fair-skinned, like the Adams and Eves of classical paintings. (Huston stated that Parks had "a sensitive yet primitive face.") The nudity was handled discretely, with Eve covered with her long mane of hair, Adam seen from behind (briefly) but not from the front. A thin coat of Vaseline was placed over the camera lens so that the Eden segment has a misty feel to it.

The Eden serpent calls to Eve in a kind of deep dreamlike whisper. It is lying in the tree, a very unearthly tree. Huston wrote that "our Tree of the Knowledge of Good and Evil was covered with blossoms not of this world but of a design that might have been found in the Garden before the Fall."[12] The serpent seems to have an almost human shape, including its face, but is also reptilian looking. Eve seems to experience almost a moment of sexual ecstasy as she bites the fruit. The serpent smiles with glee. When Adam finds her, she practically forces it to his face, saying,

"It will make you wise." The humanlike serpent is transformed into a literal snake as punishment. Producer and director toyed with the idea of using an actual python in this section but opted for an actor. God calls to Adam and Eve as Eden grows dark and a wind blows. They are expelled, though there is no flaming sword or cherubim as in Genesis.

In the next story, from Genesis 4, Cain is shown being stingy with his sacrifice, which answers the question that the Bible does not answer: Why does God accept Abel's sacrifice but not Cain's? Cain is so angry at God for rejecting him that he tears down the altar. It is Abel, not God, who asks Cain, "If thou doest well, shalt thou not be accepted?" Cain kills Abel. When God calls on Cain, he childishly tries to hide his bloody hands behind his back. Adam finds the dead Abel, weeps, and buries him while Eve watches sadly. Interestingly, the mark God puts on Cain's forehead looks like the tree in Eden.

The inventors Jabal, Jubal, and Tubal-cain are seen briefly. Civilization is advancing, but people are becoming more and more evil, leading into the Noah story. (The movie omits Lamech and the various ancestors of Noah.) Noah is a lovable white-bearded codger (played by the director, John Huston, after several actors, including Charlie Chaplin, turned the role down). The scene of Noah being puzzled while God calls him at his work is funny but touching. Noah obediently begins pacing off the measurements God gives him for the ark. The ark's exterior was three hundred cubits long and thirty cubits high—"as specified by the Lord and executed by *The Bible*'s art director," Huston wrote in his autobiography.[13] The locals, all bizarrely dressed, mock Noah loud and long, and even his sons grow doubtful and tired of their task. Then follows a delightful scene of Noah playing pipes while the animals follow him into the ark. One large raindrop hits Noah's hands. He picks up a slow-moving tortoise, and the ark door shuts. It is very dramatic when the flood finally comes and the ark is no longer on land. The family hears the wails of the people drowning. Scenes of the big cats lapping up milk and Noah and the family tending the various creatures are amusing. The birth of a baby goat on board reminds them all that life will go on. To everyone's relief, Noah awakes and realizes the rain has ceased. The family and beasts are joyful to see the sun again. They dance for joy but still have to await the waters subsiding. It is amusing when the dove returns and lights on the dozing Noah. The family is overjoyed to see the olive leaf. Noah literally waves the beasts good-bye as they exit.

The Noah segment lasts about forty-five minutes. It spends too much time on the brief story, but the zoo atmosphere makes it watchable, and the moral element of the story is not overlooked. At this point the long film had an intermission.

The Noah story has been popular for ages and has been filmed several times, notably in the 1929 *Noah's Ark* directed by Michael Curtiz. But the version in Huston's film is probably the best—certainly much better than the horrible TV movie that aired in 1999.

The film's second half begins with a quickie genealogy of the descendants of Noah's three sons, then jumps immediately to the tower of Babel (see Genesis 11), which somehow makes Nimrod (see Genesis 10:8–12) its main character, probably basing this on the fact that Nimrod's kingdom included Babel, even though Genesis 11 makes no mention of Nimrod. The tower was modeled on the spiraling ziggurat towers of the Babylonians, still standing today in Iraq. Climbing to the top of the tower, Nimrod shoots an arrow into heaven—meaning what, exactly? That he has come close to reaching heaven, or that he is aiming at God? A stiff wind from heaven begins to blow, tearing down the builders' scaffolds. Once it passes, the men no longer understand each other and can no longer obey Nimrod's commands. Confused, they scatter over the earth.

> The film omitted the sordid story of Noah getting drunk and lying naked in his tent. No movie dealing with Noah has ever included this unpleasant episode.

The movie concludes with a long segment about Abraham, Sarah, and Isaac, which includes the destruction of Sodom and Gomorrah. God calls out Abram from the pagan city of Ur, along with his nephew Lot. Abraham tells Lot (though not in the Bible), "The understanding of God is not our understanding." The story of Abram and Sarai in Egypt is omitted, but there is a nice romantic scene between the loving but childless Abram and Sarai. They quote lines from the Song of Solomon—an anachronism but appropriate in the context. It is interesting seeing two middle-aged people play a deeply romantic scene together without seeming silly. (George C. Scott, who played Abraham, did in fact fall in love with Ava Gardner, who played Sarah, but she did not return his ardor.)

When Abraham's and Lot's men quarrel, Abraham proposes they separate themselves peaceably (see Genesis 13). Lot chooses the region of Sodom and Gomorrah, despite Abraham's warning (not found in Genesis) that the region is extremely wicked. There follows the story of God's covenant with Abraham (see Genesis 15), including God's command to sacrifice several beasts, with God coming down as a flaming torch upon the sacrifice. This all occurs in a dream (or swoon), as suggested by the "deep sleep" mentioned in Genesis 15:12.

Then follows the story of Abraham fathering a son by Sarah's maid, Hagar, with Sarah's approval. Since God has promised to make him the father of many descendants, Abraham wonders if this plan is God's way of giving him the promised son. Once pregnant, Hagar becomes haughty, mocking her "dry" childless mistress.

Then follows the Genesis 18 story of the three divine visitors to Abraham. Two of them keep their faces hidden under their cloaks. The angel (or God) is Peter O'Toole, whose icy blue eyes do give him an unworldly look. Her hair streaked with gray, Sarah hears his prophecy that she will have a child within a year, and she laughs.

In the "intercession" scene, Abraham's haggling with God over the fate of Sodom is compressed—moving quickly from fifty righteous men to ten. The angel vanishes from Abraham's sight, but his voice promises that even for ten he would not destroy Sodom.

The angel/God meets Lot in Sodom, and the two walk its streets. The town is almost surrealistically ugly, with scenes suggesting all kinds of sexual depravity, including a woman being forced to mate with a goat (suggested but not seen). In a temple an orgy is taking place beneath a huge stone statue of a bull. Describing the set, Huston wrote that it was "a dark, labyrinthine place where unspeakable things took place. There were niches, alleyways, and dark courtyards. The figures in the niches were either bas-reliefs or human. If human, you couldn't quite see what they were doing to one another, but you sensed it was decadent, erotic, and sinful."[14] Some of the Sodomite men seem to be transvestites. As in Genesis 19, Lot refuses to give over the divine visitors to the Sodomites. In the movie Lot adds the detail that they were sent from the

Lord. When they try to force their way in, the angel strikes them with blindness. While they stumble, the angel tells them to leave immediately. (In Genesis 19 they do not leave immediately but leave the next morning, after Lot's daughters' fiancés refused to heed his warning.) The destruction of Sodom appears as a kind of mushroom cloud, and Lot's wife looks back, turning into a pillar of salt. The film omits the sordid story of Lot getting drunk and fathering children by his two daughters.

Sarah bears Isaac. At a feast for the young boy, Sarah is incensed that Ishmael and Hagar seem to be mocking, so she orders them sent away (see Gen. 21:8–10). The two wander in the desert and Ishmael faints with exhaustion. An angel (with no wings) appears and tells Hagar that Ishmael will survive and father a great nation. While Genesis says "God opened her eyes and she saw a well of water" (21:19), in the movie a spring miraculously bubbles up from the sand.

Abraham teaches Isaac the genealogy beginning with Shem, the son of Noah, assuring him that his own name and sons' names will follow someday. But then in the next scene, God orders Abraham to sacrifice Isaac. Genesis says nothing of Abraham's reaction, but in the movie he first refuses, pounds a boulder with his fist, and then gives in. Abraham watches sadly as Isaac tells Sarah that he and Abraham are going away on a six-day journey, and Sarah kisses him good-bye. In a departure from the Genesis story, father and son walk through the ghastly charred ruins of Sodom, where no green thing grows and skulls are everywhere. Abraham explains why the city was destroyed and is reminded that he had asked God, "Shall not the judge of all the earth do right?"—something he now questions. (Unlike in Genesis, there are no servants accompanying them.) On the mount Isaac realizes that since there is no ram, he is to be the sacrifice, but he submits without a word while Abraham binds him with a sash. After God stays Abraham's hand, Abraham tearfully hugs and kisses Isaac. The movie ends with no credits.

The Abraham episode ran almost 90 minutes. It is not a particularly interesting bit of filmmaking, although the story of Sodom adds some spice to it. The truth is that the story of Abraham, the literal and spiritual father of the Hebrews, is an important one to know but does not lend itself to movies, except perhaps the final story of the near-sacrifice of Isaac. A person who did not know that this story ends happily would probably be on the edge of his seat, wondering if God really did intend that the child would be sacrificed. Curiously, the video version of this film features Abraham and Isaac on the package, even though most people would say it is not the most appealing story in the film.

The movie had some fine acting in it, notably Huston as both Noah and narrator—and the voice of God. George C. Scott was a bit hammy as Abraham, but all in all he did well in the role. Peter O'Toole was an inspired choice for the Lord's angel who visits Abraham and then rescues Lot from Sodom. The review in *Time* magazine described the acting style in the film as "holier-than-thou," but that did not seem to keep audiences away.

Huston noted in his autobiography that the different stories in Genesis have different "tones," which is why each story in the film has a distinctive look and style about it. Producer Dino De Laurentiis originally hoped to film the entire book of Genesis over twelve hours and to have each segment directed by a different high-profile director, but eventually he settled on Huston to do the film of Genesis 1–22, which turned out to be a good choice. Huston wrote, "When I make a picture, it's simply because I believe the story is worth telling."[16] As an actor and writer as well as director, Huston definitely had an eye for a good story, directing films as diverse as *The African Queen*, *Moby Dick*, *The Man Who Would Be King*, *The Maltese Falcon*, and many others. Inevitably interviewers asked him about his own religious convictions, since, after all, he directed and acted in this film—and literally played God in it also. He described himself as either an atheist or an agnostic. "The truth is I don't profess any beliefs in an orthodox sense. It seems to me that the mystery of life is too great, too wide, too deep, to do more than wonder at. Anything further would be, as far as I'm concerned, an impertinence."[17] Devout believers in the Bible would not agree, yet the boozy, womanizing Huston—one of Hollywood's stereotypical "bad boys"—felt enough affection for his source that he directed one of the best films ever based on the Old Testament.

Time magazine's review of the film urged readers, "Better read the book" and avoid "three hours of empty illustrations from Scripture." Yet the film was one of the top-grossing films in the year of release.[15]

Huston had much praise for the movie's script, written by English playwright Christopher Fry, who had written the script for *Barabbas* (see page 164) and was also the main contributor to the script of *Ben-Hur*. Since he drew his dialogue mostly from the King James Version, the lines seem a little stilted today, but it pleased audiences in 1966. The film was among the top five highest-grossing films of 1966. Not until the year 2004—the year of Mel Gibson's *Passion of the Christ*—would another biblical film be so profitable. The 1970s, 1980s, and 1990s would prove to be dismal years for biblical films.

6

MUSICAL MISHAPS AND THE
LONGEST BIBLE MOVIE EVER

The 1970s

The 1970s were not productive years for biblical movies—
not in theaters, anyway. Only a handful were made, and
most of these failed at the box office. These were years of
experimenting with "alternative Jesuses," either musicalized or
politicized, sometimes controversial, but not particularly appealing
to moviegoers. In the previous three decades, many biblical (or at
least religious) movies had been among the most profitable: in the
1940s, *The Song of Bernadette, The Bells of St. Mary's, Samson and
Delilah*; in the 1950s, *The Ten Commandments, Ben-Hur, David
and Bathsheba, Quo Vadis, The Robe*; in the 1960s, *King of Kings*
and *The Bible . . . In the Beginning*. No biblical movie of the 1970s
would prove so profitable. Hollywood seemed unwilling (for the
time being) to try any repeats of the familiar all-star Bible-as-epic
formula, and certainly the failure of the 1965 film *The Greatest*

Story Ever Told stuck in producers' craws. But television *did* make that epic formula succeed, resulting in the longest biblical movie ever made, as well as one of the most watched and most satisfying. Indeed, the decade saw several well-crafted, faithful-to-the-source biblical movies made for television. And at the end of the decade, a modestly budgeted "church movie" about the life of Jesus actually made its way into regular theaters. The decade also saw a new type of movie: the apocalyptic horror movie based on—or, more accurately, *suggested by*—the book of Revelation.

In the field of religion, Christianity and the Bible seemed to be faring well. The year 1976 was dubbed the "Year of the Evangelical" by *Time* magazine, and that same year a professed born-again Christian was elected president. The decade also saw the publication of several popular new Bible translations—the New English Bible, the Good News Bible, the New International Version—and the phenomenally popular Bible paraphrase *The Living Bible*, which in 1972 and 1973 was the top-selling nonfiction book in America. Evangelist Billy Graham's biblically based *Angels: God's Secret Agents* was the top seller for 1975. Convicted Watergate felon Charles Colson's *Born Again*, the story of his conversion to Christianity, was one of the huge hits of 1976. Two biblical novels, *Great Lion of God* (about the apostle Paul) and *Two from Galilee* (about Mary and Joseph), were runaway bestsellers. *The Total Woman* by Marabel Morgan was a popular Christian guide to marriage.

These bits of data make it sound like the 1970s was a very Bible-obsessed decade. But many other things were going on culturally. In 1971 the best-selling nonfiction book in America was *Everything You Always Wanted to Know About Sex but Were Afraid to Ask*, and in 1972 it was *The Sensuous Man*. (A successful sequel, *The Sensuous Woman*, inevitably followed.) Other big sellers of the decade were *The Joy of Sex* and the adultery-condoning *Open Marriage*. Several "Love thyself" books were huge sellers, including *Looking Out for #1* and *Pulling Your Own Strings*. In 1973 the U.S. Supreme Court made its landmark *Roe v. Wade* decision, making abortion more accessible and convincing many Christian conservatives and others that the nation was in moral decline. A U.S. vice president (Spiro Agnew) resigned in disgrace; then, after a long scandal, so did a president (Richard Nixon), leading many people, especially the young, to question authority figures—and traditional sources of authority like the Bible and the church. (That questioning of authority was already well under way in the 1960s, of course.) When the decade began, the Vietnam War was still raging, and the longer it continued, the more young people felt alienated from the government, parents, and all traditional sources of authority. Films and TV became increasingly less G-rated, a situation applauded by some and bewailed by others. Movies had become "spicier" in the 1960s, and now television was playing catch-up. Some filmmakers from Hollywood's heyday of the 1930s and 1940s, like Frank Capra, who directed so many classic comedies, retired in disgust at how audiences seemed to want more sex, violence, and profanity.

There were signs that two Americas were coexisting—a traditional, religiously oriented America and a tradition-free, authority-snubbing America—and the two sorts of Americans often lived (uncomfortably) under the same roof, a situation presented comically in the popular TV series *All in the Family* (which was very much on the side of the tradition-haters). The series (and its many imitators) offended some people with its profanity and its disrespect of tradition, but it was hugely popular, proving to TV and movie producers that audiences had a high tolerance for profanity, obscenity, and formerly taboo subject matter, including the mocking of traditional religion. The concept of an unbridgeable "generation gap" took hold. Not surprisingly, several of the biblical movies of this period were pitched toward the younger side of the gap. For the most part, the young did not line up to see them. They did line up to see highly profitable fare like *Star Wars*, *Saturday Night Fever*, *American Graffiti*, *Grease*, *The Sting*, *The Way We Were*, *Blazing Saddles*, *Rocky*, *Superman*, *Jaws*, *Every Which Way but Loose*, *The Jerk*, *Silver Streak*, and *Smokey and the Bandit*. It was not a profitable decade for serious films, with a few exceptions like *Patton*, *Kramer vs. Kramer*, and *The Godfather*. The one runaway hit movie that dealt with spirituality was, ironically, *The Exorcist*, which showed that Satan had a great deal of power. One sign of the change that had occurred in audience taste was the absence of any Disney films on the list of hit movies. In the 1950s and 1960s, a Disney film almost always ranked among the top five in any given year. Walt Disney may have been turning over in his grave because of the new level of violence, profanity, and sex in popular films.

Those who lived through the 1970s would agree that they were certainly *interesting* years, and, mirroring the decade, the Bible movies of those years were all interesting in their different ways—not necessarily profitable or inspiring but certainly interesting. In fact, *controversy* seemed to be a key element of many of the biblical movies of the decade—controversy that proved profitable in one case, not so in others.

Godspell: *Jesus as Adorable Hippie Clown*

Released March 1973
Columbia
102 minutes
Filmed in New York City

Director: David Greene
Screenplay: David Greene, John-Michael Tebelak, from Tebelak's stage play
Music and new lyrics: Stephen Schwartz
Photography: Richard G. Heimann

Jesus: Victor Garber
John/Judas: David Haskell
Disciples:
Robin Lamont
Lynne Thigpen
Katie Hanley
Gilmer McCormick
Jeffrey Mylett
Joanne Jonas
Jerry Sroka

The musical play *Godspell* has become a favorite of little theater groups around the world, partly because it can be staged cheaply but mostly because the songs are delightful and the play exudes joy and sweetness, as its author intended. In fact, the play (and the movie based on it) had its origins in a genuine religious experience: John-Michael Tebelak, a graduate drama student in Pittsburgh, attended an Easter vigil service in the city's Episcopal cathedral. He recalled later that it was snowing outside—and, more importantly, that the service left him cold on the inside. He couldn't understand how a ceremony celebrating the resurrection of Jesus could be so empty and unsatisfying, so he resolved to write a play—his master's thesis, as it turned out—that would capture the joy of the Jesus of the Gospels. He chose the name *Godspell*—Anglo-Saxon ("old English") for "good news" or "good message" and the root of the word *gospel*. Both words translate the Greek word *euangelion*, used many times in the New Testament to refer to the "good news" about Jesus the Savior. (It is, of course, the root of *evangelist, evangelical*, and so on.) One of the play's cast members recalled that Tebelak, when he asked her to be in the play, told her he wished "to weave God's spell over the audience."

Jesus (Victor Garber) baptized by John (David Haskell) in the 1973 musical *Godspell*, based on the popular play that billed itself as "based on the Gospel According to St. Matthew." The songs were catchy, and the young cast seemed to enjoy romping around Manhattan, but this hippie Jesus ("crucified" on a chain-link fence) just didn't seem like the Son of God.

Tebelak's *Godspell* was staged at his college, the Carnegie Institute (now part of Carnegie-Mellon University). Tebelak billed it as "A Musical Based on the Gospel According to St. Matthew," and much of the play consists of Jesus's sayings and parables (sometimes word for word) from the Gospel, though Tebelak felt free to throw in the well-loved parable of the prodigal son from the

Gospel of Luke, on the assumption that a youth-oriented musical should certainly include the Gospels' classic story of bridging the "generation gap." (The play has the story of the woman caught in adultery, found in John's Gospel, but it was not included in the film version.) The parable of the rich man and the beggar, found in Luke's Gospel, was also included.

The songs in the play were mostly old hymns set to new music, hymns with words that fit in with the sayings from Matthew's Gospel. "Bless the Lord, My Soul," for example, praising God the Father for all his many gifts, was written in the 1800s by Scottish author James Montgomery, who was paraphrasing one of the psalms. Other songs in the play were taken almost word for word from the Gospels—"Prepare Ye the Way of the Lord," "Light of the World," and "Alas for You," in which Jesus lashes out at the self-righteous Pharisees. The lyrics to "Light of the World" are taken from the Sermon on the Mount (and in the movie, sung bouncily aboard a tugboat sailing through the Hudson River).

One scene in *Godspell* was set in a locale that no longer exists: the World Trade Center.

Tebelak's play at Carnegie was moved to a theater in New York's Greenwich Village, with new music and several new songs added by budding songwriter Stephen Schwartz. Though Schwartz, a Jew, has stated that he sees the play as more about "community building, not about religion," his infectious music for the play did indeed capture some of the joy Tebelak found in the Gospels. The Schwartz-Tebelak *Godspell* proved to be an audience-pleaser; in time it moved to a Broadway theater, and a popular cast album was recorded, making a hit of the song "Day by Day" (a simple medieval prayer set to some very bouncy music). A film version became inevitable.

The movie version was directed by British-born David Greene, who would gain fame a few years later as director of the TV mini-series *Roots*. Released by Columbia, *Godspell* was advertised with the original catchphrase ("A musical based on the Gospel according to St. Matthew") and a new one ("The gospel according to today!"). Tebelak and the director collaborated on the screenplay, setting the action mostly in New York's Central Park.

As the film opens, several young New Yorkers are shown going about their frustrating daily lives until they heed the call of a strangely dressed man standing in a fountain singing "Prepare Ye the Way of the Lord" (from Matthew 3:3, which is quoting the prophet Isaiah). He represents John the Baptist, a prophet of repentance, Jesus's kinsman and also forerunner. He splashily baptizes the young people in the fountain, then baptizes the Jesus character (played by frizzy-haired Victor Garber, who was twenty-four years old at the time). Here the play follows the Gospels closely, for John is hesitant to administer a baptism of repentance to the sinless Jesus. The newly baptized Jesus emerges from the water in striped clown pants with suspenders, a Superman T-shirt, and clownish makeup. The other cast members also put on makeup and don gaudy clothing. Obviously they, like the original disciples of Jesus, have been "called out" from their workaday lives to live with and learn from their new teacher. While the group's "baptism" in the fountain seems a bit flippant (after all, to Christians, baptism is a very serious thing), it does remind the viewer that the first Christians actually found *joy* in beginning their new life of faith.

The young cast has a great deal of fun acting out Jesus's sayings and parables in various Manhattan locales—Central Park, an empty brownstone house, atop a skyscraper. The self-righteous Pharisees whom Jesus denounces are represented by a kind of robotic machine made of junk—funny but also somehow threatening. And every Jesus film has to have the passion, and in this version Jesus is tied to a chain-link fence with red ribbons. (One thing that bothers many viewers is that the same actor who plays the John the Baptist role also plays Judas the betrayer, which makes no sense.) Jesus "dies," and his disciples (including John the Baptist/Judas) take him down from the fence and carry his body off into the New York streets, all the while singing "long live God!"

Tebelak's original intention of showing the joyful, positive side of the New Testament was a noble one and a biblical one as well, for the words *joy* and *rejoice* are found often in the New Testament (something that would surprise many who have never read the Bible and see it as a book of joy-killing "thou shalt nots"). His Jesus is shown as a serious yet loving and often humorous character, thoroughly human in all the right ways. Likewise, the disciples are presented as eager learners, not the grumbling bores depicted in other biblical movies. But the *Godspell* Jesus is very much a lightweight character, someone we could hardly imagine being thought of as Savior or Son of God, to use just two of the titles the Bible applies to Jesus. Although he manages some depth and passion when lashing out at the Pharisees in the song "Alas for You," he somehow doesn't convince us he is the Son of God. And of course, he works no miracles at all, which for anything based on Matthew's Gospel is a major omission.

Perhaps the most frustrating thing about the movie is its ending. This Jesus doesn't rise from the dead. His body is simply carried away (meaning what, exactly?) by his disciples, who presumably will continue his teachings about love and compassion. It is ironic that the movie's Jesus isn't resurrected, considering that what moved Tebelak to write his play was the desire to recapture some of the joy of Easter—the annual celebration of Jesus's resurrection. Peggy Gordon, one of the play's original cast members, even stated that while *Jesus Christ Superstar* was about Jesus's humanity, *Godspell* was about his divinity—a nice sentiment but not one borne out by the play's ending. (Worth noting here: when Christian groups stage the play, they usually do have Jesus coming to life again.) Basically the movie gives us a Jesus who is a saintly and compassionate teacher who, alas, ends up crucified. Since he worked no miracles, it isn't too surprising that he doesn't rise from the dead either. This is a Jesus the secular world can accept (which explains why the play is so easily accepted by audiences with no particular religious interests), but it is not the same Jesus the New Testament describes as Savior, Lord, and Son of God.

But of course, this leads to another problem with the movie. it doesn't seem to take the gospel very seriously, and the Bible is *very* serious, even if it does allow for joy. People who love *Godspell* say it is a nice corrective to the oh-so-reverent Jesus movies of an earlier time. But the clownish Jesus of *Godspell* still seems a far cry from the Jesus of the Bible. Sharing the wine of the Last Supper in Dixie cups is amusing but certainly not inspiring. The fact is that the movie simply gives us some energetic, likeable young people, singing and dancing and having a wonderful time but certainly not taking the story of Jesus to heart. Even secular reviewers sensed the movie's lightness. *Newsweek* noted that the director "seems to have little confidence in the inherent interest of the text as entertainment—so he decorates every moment with slapstick."[1] Perhaps Tebelak neglected a key idea: in the New Testament, a reason the first Christians felt joy was that they had been forgiven for their sins. In fact, the good news—the *Godspell* of the title—is that people are freed from sin. The idea of human beings needing a Savior is barely present in *Godspell*, and sadly, the two songs from the play that were about sin—"We Beseech Thee" and "Learn Your Lessons Well"—were not included in the movie.

Columbia must have hoped that the movie would appeal to young audiences who (typical of the early 1970s) wanted something vaguely "spiritual" that was also fun. Presumably the target audience consisted of the many young people who saw themselves as joyous and fun-loving (and musical) and full of good intentions. In fact, the *Newsweek* review was perceptive in noting that "enough of Tebelak's contemporaries share his flattering view of themselves as pilloried idealists in a world of corruption to have made *Godspell* a runaway international stage success."[2] But that self-admiration did not make the movie succeed. It boasted no big stars, and the phenomenal popularity of the play did not make people to rush to see the movie version. (It's a general rule that "little" plays, such as the ever-popular *Fantasticks*, do not succeed as films.) Unlike *Jesus Christ Superstar* of the same year, *Godspell* caused little or no controversy among religious folks, even though, like *Superstar*, it had no resurrection scene. Christians who saw the *Godspell* movie were not terribly offended but not very inspired either. A few months after the movie opened, another hippie-ish Jesus would hit the screen.

Jesus Christ Superstar: *Rice's Rockin' Jesus*

Released August 1973	**Lyrics:** Tim Rice
Universal	**Conductor:** Andre Previn
108 minutes	
Filmed in Israel	**Jesus:** Ted Neeley
	Judas: Carl Anderson
Director: Norman Jewison	**Mary Magdalene:** Yvonne Elliman
Screenplay: Melvyn Bragg, Norman Jewison	**Pilate:** Barry Dennen
	Caiaphas: Bob Bingham
Music: Andrew Lloyd Webber	**Herod:** Joshua Mostel

Jesus Christ Superstar began not as a stage play but as a recorded (but as yet unstaged) "rock opera" by composer Andrew Lloyd Webber and lyricist Tim Rice, both of them English. The *Superstar* album sold well, and the play was staged in London, then on Broadway. Movie director Norman Jewison (who, despite his name, is not Jewish) found the original album appealing and agreed to direct the film version. (He had just finished *Fiddler on the Roof*. This next "Jewish musical" would be radically different from that one!) He chose to film it in Israel—not the prettier parts of Israel but the bleakest, rockiest regions, including the arid region around the Dead Sea. These probably were places that Jesus and his disciples actually walked, so in some ways the movie's set is more truly biblical than those of most movies about Jesus. But rather than try to re-create the buildings of Jesus's time, the producers used few props or sets at all. Most of the action takes place against a background of rocks and bare hills, with metal scaffolding set up as "stages." For some reason—perhaps an attempt to be "arty"—modern things like jets and tanks are sometimes seen against the stark background. Roman soldiers carry spears but also machine guns.

But the starkness does concentrate the audience's attention on the actors and the words they are singing (a factor that was also true of the Italian *Gospel According to Matthew* in the 1960s). Those words have been the cause of most of the controversy surrounding the play. While the lyricist Rice (who has identified himself as an atheist) obviously was familiar with the Gospels, he chose to make Judas almost a hero, an idealistic man who fears that his simple, saintly master is turning into a "superstar" with a horde of blind followers who have "too much heaven on their minds," which could bring down the wrath of the Roman troops that have occupied the land. He fears Jesus may actually begin to believe that he is divine. He agrees to betray Jesus to the chief Jewish priests, who see Jesus as a troublemaker. Then, seeing Jesus crucified, Judas kills himself, lamenting that he has been "used" by Jesus—and God. In the Bible we are told that Judas did betray Jesus and afterward killed himself. The Bible provides no glimpses into Judas's motivations, which is why Rice and other writers have felt free to "explain" Judas and excuse his acts. *Superstar* was not the first nor last attempt to make audiences "understand" Judas. Casting black singer Carl Anderson as Judas was an interesting choice, since in the highly race-conscious 1970s, a black character almost had to be a "good" character. In other words, a black Judas was one that audiences simply could not think of as a real villain—misunderstood, maybe, but hardly evil.

By making Judas such an important character, the movie rel-egates the apostle Peter to a fairly minor role, even though the Gospels show him as very much the leader—or at least the most outspoken—of Jesus's followers. The movie does include the har-rowing scene of Peter denying that he knows Jesus. But Peter takes a backseat not only to Judas but also to Mary Magdalene, who is presented as a sort of "groupie" who travels with the disciples and clearly adores Jesus. It is implied that the former prostitute's love for Jesus might be more than spiritual. There is no such "love interest" in the Gospels, but perhaps scriptwriters feel the need to include one in any play or movie. Practically every Jesus movie since *Superstar* has at least hinted at a love interest between Jesus and Magadalene, something that bore (rotten) fruit in *The Last Temptation of Christ*.

If the movie's Judas is rather unbiblical, so is its Jesus. He is fully human (something the Bible teaches) but hardly the divine Son of God, even though he can perform miracles of healing. Like so many "modern" Jesuses, he seems troubled with doubts about his mission in life. In fact, he seems downright self-absorbed—typical of a 1970s hippie, perhaps, but certainly not of the Jesus of the Bible. He seems likeable enough, and idealistic, yet hardly the sort of person that people of any age would elevate into a superstar.

Still, he has his finer moments, notably in the scene of driving the money changers from the temple. In this scene, Jesus shows a righteous rage that most other movie Jesuses lack. When his voice wails, "You have made it [the temple] into a den of thieves!" the words have conviction. In this scene and many others, Rice's lyrics are clearly rooted in the Bible. Fearing arrest, the disciple Peter denies knowing Jesus, a scene as touching in the play as it is in the Gospels. The third time he cries/sings out, "I don't know him!" we sense rage, exasperation—and guilt. After his denial, a sad and accusing Magdalene sings, "Peter, you've gone and cut him dead." The playful, festive song "Hosanna, Hey-Sanna" catches some of the joyous flavor of Jesus's entry into Jerusalem—and also the crowd's shallowness. The bass-voiced priest threaten-ingly sings to Jesus, "Tell the rabble to be quiet, / we anticipate a riot," and Jesus sings back joyously and defiantly that "the rocks and stones themselves would start to sing" if the people were hushed. In fact, moments like these make a viewer understand the advantage the sung word has over the spoken word. *Superstar* at least gives a hint of what a truly powerful opera about Jesus Christ might be like.

The villains of the piece are, as in the Gospels, the Jewish priests, a group of selfish bureaucrats who gladly collaborate with the Roman occupiers and who are quick to crush "dangerous" people like Jesus, people who might call down the wrath of Rome. The movie was charged with being anti-Semitic by the Anti-Defamation League of B'nai B'rith and the American Jewish Committee, both of which issued warnings that the film could provoke anti-Jewish sentiment. Universal responded to such criticisms with a prepared statement saying that the movie was "a rock opera, a musical entertainment, not a religious tract." The statement said that charges of anti-Semitism were not supported by the film itself. Of course, the stark fact is that the New Testament *does* show the Jewish authorities in Jerusalem as being the prime causes of Jesus's death.

Another villain of the Bible provides comic relief in the movie. The cynical, decadent Jewish ruler Herod is described in the Bible as mocking Jesus after trying to coax him into performing a miracle (see Luke 23:6–12). This is what Herod does in the movie, singing his sneering words "prove to me that you're no fool, / walk across my swimming pool" while Jesus silently endures the mocking. (The scene with the pudgy, shirtless, frizzy-haired Herod is extremely funny, especially as a contrast to the plight of the about-to-be-crucified Jesus. As in Luke's Gospel, Jesus says not one word to the effete Herod.) The film's Pontius Pilate, like the Pilate of the Gospels, is hesitant to crucify Jesus, whom he knows is innocent, and he has Jesus scourged in the hope this will satisfy the priests and the fickle rabble that has turned against Jesus. Pilate finally caves in and orders Jesus crucified ("Die if you want to, you innocent puppet!"). The flogging administered to Jesus seems tame compared to what Jesus endured in *The Passion of the Christ* many years later, but it was relatively brutal for its time, at least giving audiences a hint of what a real flogging was like. In fact, Pilate counts off the thirty-nine lashes as we see Herod initially enjoying the spectacle but finally repulsed by it. By relying on John's Gospel here, *Superstar* makes the audience a little more sympathetic to the cynical Pilate and a little more hostile to the priests. Barry Dennen, who played the Pilate role onstage and in the film, manages to convey Roman snobbery, frustration with the priests, and puzzlement over this obviously innocent victim.

Musically, the last piece in the movie has the title "John Nineteen Forty-One"—a Bible verse that mentions Jesus's burial in a garden tomb. This is an instrumental piece, and thus the story ends with Jesus's burial. The fact that Jesus is not resurrected is, of course, one of the prime reasons the play has offended so many Christians, since the resurrection is the cornerstone of Christian belief. Yet, curiously, the movie version provides an interesting twist on the ending of the play: we see the movie's cast members boarding the same bus on which they arrived at the beginning of the movie. But Ted Neeley, the actor who played Jesus, is not shown. What is the audience to make of this? Is he dead? Resurrected and taken into heaven? We aren't sure, though at least it is a more hopeful ending than the ending of the play. It is worth noting that when the play is staged today, Jesus often makes a "curtain call" at the end wearing a white robe—obviously a resurrected Jesus, not the dead-and-buried Jesus of the original play. Such an ending is inevitably used when the play is staged by church groups.

> In the play and movie, Pilate administers the flogging in the hope it will satisfy the Jews—he calls them "you vultures"—but they still want Jesus crucified, even after he is shown to them bloody and beaten. This reflects the version of the story in John 19:1–16, where Pilate has Jesus flogged, shows him to the people with the famous words, "Behold the man!" and hopes they will be satisfied. The other three Gospels leave out this detail, simply stating that Pilate had Jesus flogged as a prelude to crucifixion.

Though protests were small compared to the fuss years later over *The Last Temptation of Christ* and *The Passion of the Christ*, some Christian leaders did speak out against the "blasphemous" movie with its sympathetic Judas and its doubtful Jesus. In a thankfully isolated incident, a theater showing the movie in South America was bombed. Few people who identified themselves as Christians saw the movie. The review in *Newsweek* lamented the movie's "fatal foolishness everywhere." The review ended, "Lord, forgive them. They knew not what they were doing."[3] Unlike *Godspell*, *Superstar* was a success financially, but not to the level Universal expected.

A rather sad footnote to this film: the actor who played Peter found his career floundering and started a second career as an actor in pornographic films.

Gospel Road: *The Man in Black's Labor of Love*

Released March 1973
Twentieth Century-Fox
83 minutes
Filmed in Israel

Director: Robert Elfstrom
Producers: Johnny Cash, June Carter Cash
Screenplay: Larry Murray
Photography: Robert Elfstrom
Songs: Johnny Cash, Kris Kristofferson, Larry Gatlin, John Denver, Joe South, Don Reid, Harold Reid

Narrator: Johnny Cash
Jesus: Robert Elfstrom
John the Baptist: Larry Lee
Mary Magdalene: June Carter Cash
Peter: Paul L. Smith
Judas: Thomas Leventhal

The other "musical Jesus" movie of 1973 was radically different from the others and aimed at a radically different audience. This was *Gospel Road*, released in March, a labor of love undertaken by country music superstar Johnny Cash. The boozy, drug-taking Cash had become a Christian and recorded numerous gospel songs. Along with his wife, June Carter of the near-legendary country-gospel musical Carter family, Cash acted as producer of this film, in which he is shown visiting Holy Land sites associated with Jesus, performing several songs about Jesus's life, and narrating episodes from the Gospels. The eight songs were by Cash himself and several other noted singer-songwriters, including John Denver, Larry Gatlin, and Kris Kristofferson. The Gospel episodes are acted in period costume, and June Carter has the role of Mary Magdalene—a far more chaste one than the rather sensuous Magdalenes of other recent biblical movies. Jesus, who does not speak, was played by the film's director and co-cinematographer, Robert Elfstrom. (Interestingly, he had served as cinematographer a few years earlier on a radically different musical film, the Rolling Stones's *Gimme Shelter*.) Elfstrom, like the Jesuses of *Godspell* and *Superstar*, was fair-skinned and totally un-Semitic in appearance.

One interesting touch in the filming of Jesus's crucifixion: we see a close-up of him on the cross, and then the camera pulls back to show us not ancient Jerusalem but a modern American city. The obvious theological point: Jesus died for all people, not just the inhabitants of ancient Israel.

Though the film had the backing of a major distributor (Twentieth Century-Fox), it was not well received by audiences, perhaps because the unusual format (mixing a Holy Land travelogue with reenactments from the Gospels) seemed more appropriate for a TV special than for a feature film. Cash, with his craggy face and resonant voice, was an appealing screen presence, but his legions of fans did not rush out to see this film. And even though the age of blockbuster Bible movies seemed to have passed, audiences didn't seem willing to pay for a low-budget "bathrobe play." In later years, however, *Gospel Road* has fared better as a "church film," and it is available in video format.

In closing this section dealing with three biblical movies of 1973, it is worth noting that one of the top-grossing movies of the year was *The Exorcist*—a film that drew a lot of fire from Christians for its depictions of priests as lacking in faith, as well as for the profanity and obscenity of the demon-possessed girl. Yet in some ways the movie gave audiences a sense of the power of evil, specifically, the power of Satan—something none of the three biblical movies of that year managed to do.

The Passover Plot: *The Politicized Jesus*

Released 1975
Golan-Globus Productions
108 minutes

Director: Michael I. Grampus
Producer: Menahem Golan
Screenplay: Hugh J. Schonfield, Millard Cohan, Patricia Louisianna Knop
Music: Alex North

Yeshua (Jesus): Zalman King
Yohanan (John the Baptist): Harry Andrews
Judah (Judas): Scott Wilson
Caiaphas: Hugh Griffith
Shimon (Simon Peter): William Burns

Most people in the 1970s were vaguely aware that *Jesus Christ Superstar* had been made into a film, but few were aware that *Godspell* had. And even more obscure than *Godspell* was *The Passover Plot*, a 1975 movie based on a controversial book by Hugh

Schonfeld. It deserves some attention, however, because in many ways it was a dress rehearsal for the political themes of *The Last Temptation of Christ* in the next decade.

In Hugh Schonfeld's book, Jesus is not the divine-human Jesus of the Gospels. He is a committed Zealot, the Zealots being the Jews who were dedicated to driving out the Romans who had occupied their homeland. According to the Bible, at least one of Jesus's disciples was a Zealot (Simon, according to Luke 6:15), and many Bible scholars see hints that others among the disciples (Peter, James, John, and Judas Iscariot) may at least have been sympathetic to the Zealot cause. The Zealots were, of course, willing to use violence, and some were not above slitting Roman throats, robbing Roman couriers, and always encouraging any would-be Messiah who might possess the charisma to lead a successful revolt. We have no idea whether the apostle Simon was a *former* Zealot, or a lukewarm one, or perhaps only one who flirted with the cause. We do see clearly in the Gospels that Jesus is what tradition has called him, the Prince of Peace, rejecting violence totally, telling his followers to turn the other cheek, assuring the Roman governor Pilate that the spiritual kingdom is "not of this world." In other words, the Jesus of the Bible not only is *not* a Zealot but also is very much opposed to the way of violence. So he is assuredly not the Jesus of the book or movie *The Passover Plot*.

The movie was a U.S.-Israeli coproduction, with many Israelis among its cast members. TV actor Zalman King played Jesus—or rather *Yeshua*, for the movie was at least accurate in calling the various characters by their original Aramaic names. Yeshua comes across as an intense and crafty revolutionary leader, arranging to be crucified, then having himself drugged so he can survive the crucifixion, recover, then gain a vast following by appearing to be "resurrected." Instead of being the traitorous villain, Yehudah (Judas Iscariot, that is) is Yeshua's right-hand man and co-conspirator in the plot. The title, of course, comes from the plot taking place near the Jewish feast of Passover. Yeshua knows he is descended from the royal bloodline of David, and he cagily sets up his last days and (near) execution so as to appear to be the Messiah the Jews had long awaited.

Hugh Schonfeld's book has drawn fire from Christians, especially evangelicals, over the years, since it rehashes some centuries-old theories about what "really" happened on Good Friday and Easter. There were some mild protests against the movie, but in fact it was not distributed widely and few people saw it. Rather surprisingly, this nearly overlooked film did receive one Academy Award nomination, for best costume design.

The 1970s was, as already noted, a poor decade for biblical movies. While the big screen neglected the Bible—or contorted it—the small screen gave it some prominence. There were four TV miniseries in the 1970s centered on important biblical characters, and one of them, *Jesus of Nazareth*, is one of the finest biblical movies ever made. It will be discussed further in the chapter. For now, let's consider the obvious advantage of doing a biblical story as a TV miniseries: more time is available. The typical movie in a theater runs about two hours, and pushing it much beyond that tests an audience's patience (and comfort level). In the past people would line up to see an epic-length film like *The Ten Commandments* or *Ben-Hur*, but it's doubtful that audiences now or in the 1970s would do so. Certainly the failure of the 1965 *Greatest Story Ever Told* is partly attributable to its great length. But a made-for-TV movie or miniseries allows people to settle into their favorite chair in complete comfort.

The first of the biblical movies made for television was *The Story of Jacob and Joseph*, shown in 1974 and directed by the noted Greek director Michael Cayonnis. The story stuck reasonably close to the Jacob and Joseph sagas in Genesis, showing the destructive sibling rivalry between brothers Jacob and Esau, then the even more intense quarrel between Jacob's favorite son, Joseph, and Joseph's eleven envious, malicious brothers. It was not up to the level of the later *Jesus of Nazareth*, but all in all it was a fine production, one that still holds up well on video. The Australian actor Keith Michell was fine as the wily Jacob, and English actor Alan Bates lent his voice as narrator. The Joseph story with its elements of sibling hatred and forgiveness has fascinated filmmakers since the beginning of film, and from early in the silent era there were short movies with titles like *Joseph Sold by His Brothers*. But this 1974 production was the first color-and-sound film of the story that most people were able to see. It is commendable that these timeless stories were made available to a wide audience.

Equally commendable was the much longer (four-hour) 1976 TV movie *The Story of David*, shown on two nights, with Timothy Bottoms as the spunky shepherd boy David and Keith Michell as the adult David. The fine British actor Anthony Quayle did well as the ill-fated King Saul. The lovely Jane Seymour played the role of Bathsheba, the married woman with whom David commits adultery, and the movie covered in painful detail the sordid story of the fatal feud between David's sons Amnon and Absalom, as well as Absalom's rebellion. As in *The Story of Jacob and Joseph*, the script stuck very closely to the Bible, and the acting was fine. The movie is available on video and is certainly more watchable (and more biblical) than the 1951 blockbuster *David and Bathsheba* and the 1985 failure *King David*. Both of those movies suffered from an obvious problem: David's life story is the longest of any man in the Bible (including Jesus), and there is no way to really do it justice in a normal-length movie. But a multipart TV movie did fine with the David saga. Both *The Story of Jacob and Joseph* and *The Story of David* were scripted by Ernest Kinoy, a talented writer who later gained fame as one of the writers of the 1977 miniseries *Roots*. Obviously an important part of having a quality movie based on the Bible is having a competent writer who respects his source.

So in two separate years, TV viewers got a chance to see worthy presentations of the lives of some of the most important Old Testament figures—Jacob, Joseph, and David. Regrettably, the most important Old Testament figure, Moses, did not fare so well on the small screen. Of course, a TV movie attempting to follow the Moses saga of Cecil B. DeMille's *Ten Commandments* was almost doomed to disappoint.

For millions of movie viewers around the world, Charlton Heston is the definitive Moses, and *The Ten Commandments* directed by DeMille still reigns as the ultimate Old Testament movie (if not the ultimate Bible movie). So Oscar-winning actor Burt Lancaster must have felt at least a little intimidated at taking on the role of Moses. But then, the aim of the 1975 TV miniseries *Moses the Lawgiver* was relatively modest. Instead of trying to duplicate *The Ten Commandments* with its big-name director, huge cast of stars, and awesome (and expensive) special effects, the TV Moses saga would be relatively low-key, with only a few big-name actors, the rest mostly Italians, directed by an Italian and (surprise!) filmed partly in Italy, a country with landscapes often serving as backdrops for biblical movies (most recently *The Passion of the Christ*). It was not popular with viewers, even though it is still available on video today. (Lancaster was a professed atheist, by the way.) Another biblical made-for-TV movie, *Jesus of Nazareth*, would prove to be much more popular.

> *The Omen*, the first apocalyptic horror movie, was originally titled *The Antichrist*.

The year 1976 saw the release of a new genre of film: the apocalyptic horror movie, based (very loosely) on the book of Revelation. *The Omen* dealt with an evil Beast/Antichrist figure who (so the audience hopes) will be defeated by the forces of good. It is a stretch to call such movies biblical, for they don't draw their *plots* from the Bible. Rather, they are rooted in the Bible's handful of prophecies about the Beast, the Antichrist, the man of sin, and so on. Essentially they are horror movies with a slight amount of religion mixed in. They seem to draw upon audiences' vague feeling that the Bible is—or might be—correct in its prophecies of a wicked being who seeks world domination, and such a being seems more real-world possible than, say, a vampire, an alien monster, or some other stock character from horror movies. It is also more horrifying, since the Antichrist can, if he reaches maturity, do harm on a global level, not just commit a few random murders. Christian author Hal Lindsey's 1972 book *Satan Is Alive and Well and Living on Planet Earth* was tremendously popular, and not just with Christians. His frightening look at the rise of Satanism and his predictions about the Antichrist and the end times reached a wide audience. Speculation about the end times was "in the air," and Hollywood was not slow to profit from it. *The Omen* was hugely popular and would be remade in 2006.

Jesus of Nazareth: *All-Star, Long, and Truly Impressive*

Originally aired April 1977
ITC
Approx. 382 minutes (6 hours and 22 minutes)
Filmed in Tunisia and Morocco

Director: Franco Zeffirelli
Producer: Sir Lew Grade
Screenplay: Anthony Burgess, Suso Cecchi D'Amico, Franco Zeffirelli
Music: Maurice Jarre

Jesus: Robert Powell
Mary Magdalene: Anne Bancroft
Simon Peter: James Farentino
Judas Iscariot: Ian McShane

John: John Duttine
Matthew: Keith Washington
Nicodemus: Laurence Olivier
Mary, Jesus's mother: Olivia Hussey
Joseph: Yorgo Voyagis
John the Baptist: Michael York
Herod Antipas: Christopher Plummer
Caiaphas: Anthony Quinn
Pilate: Rod Steiger
Joseph of Arimathea: James Mason
King Herod: Peter Ustinov
Zerah: Ian Holm
The Magi: Fernando Rey, James Earl Jones, Donald Pleasance
Barabbas: Stacey Keach

The lukewarm reception of *Moses the Lawgiver* was not repeated with the next biblical movie filmed in Italy with an Italian director. In fact, *Jesus of Nazareth* proved to be one of the most popular biblical films ever made—and also the longest.

It helped that the director was the very talented Franco Zeffirelli, a noted director of operas who had also directed the movies *Romeo and Juliet* and the medieval religious epic *Brother Sun, Sister Moon*. Though Zeffirelli is a homosexual (something not widely known at the time *Jesus of Nazareth* aired, of course), he is also an ardent Catholic, so he brought to the project not only his skill in directing a historical spectacle but also a reverence for the subject. He intended to make the definitive movie about the life of Jesus and was given the broadcast time to do it in more detail than any previous movie based on the Gospels.

He had an all-star cast at his disposal—Anne Bancroft (very touching as the aging prostitute Mary Magdalene), Rod Steiger (as Pilate), Laurence Olivier, James Mason, Anthony Quinn, Ernest Borgnine, and many other faces audiences would instantly recognize. Most importantly, he had the right actor for Jesus, the lean-faced Robert Powell, who seemed to have stepped right out of a medieval painting. Powell's eyes could seem at different times warm, intense, authoritative, or sad; in short, he had a face that could show the full range of emotions of the Jesus of the Gospels. But more than a few viewers thought that Powell—blue-eyed and fair-skinned—hardly looked like a Jew of first-century Galilee.

Worth noting: the director has stated that his stage productions and films are part of his "crusade against boredom." He likes his productions to look stunning, and they are. He has even said that he has the same sort of visual motivation as Cecil B. DeMille—"but in good taste."

Given the length of the miniseries, the script could not only include most of the key events of the Gospels but also give some glimpses into the workings of the Jewish religious bureaucracy that finally condemned Jesus as a blasphemer and asked for his death. Like the Gospels, the movie is not anti-Semitic (there are plenty of noble Jewish characters in the movie) but antihierarchy. The bad guys are the priests and other Jewish leaders who, in theory, ought to welcome the Messiah, not condemn him. But the leaders are portrayed as human beings, not as cardboard villains. Scriptwriter Anthony Burgess had done a lot of research into the political and religious situation in first-century Palestine, and it paid off. At the risk of sounding blasphemous, the movie actually improves on the Gospels by showing us how native Jews and the occupying Romans related to each other. In other words, it shows us the social world of those times, something the Gospels did not bother to explain because the first readers of the Gospels knew the situation firsthand.

Olivia Hussey, who played Mary, was actually younger than Robert Powell, who played her son Jesus.

One interesting note: in the earliest portion of the film, Joseph and Mary are shown to be about the same age, both barely out of their teens. The Gospels say nothing whatever about their ages, but in Catholic tradition, Joseph is depicted as much older than Mary, since he (so tradition says) was a widower with several children when he married Mary. The movie is probably correct in showing Mary and Joseph to be roughly the same age, and it is rather satisfying to see young Joseph responding to the jarring news that his virgin fiancée is to bear the Son of God. The movie also shows scenes from the childhood of Jesus—scenes not from the Bible, because the Gospels tell us almost nothing of Jesus's childhood except that he "increased in wisdom and in stature and in favor with God and man" (Luke 2:52 ESV).

The movie is beautiful to look at, as everyone expected of its visually oriented director. But it also has a gritty, realistic feel, and

The one film Jesus of the 1970s who seemed to please audiences: Robert Powell in the 1977 TV miniseries *Jesus of Nazareth*. Perhaps the long running time of a miniseries is the solution to the old dilemma: how to do justice to the life of Christ on film.

the actors seem a tad sweatier and dustier than the folks in some of the older biblical films like *King of Kings*. Thanks to Burgess's and Zeffirelli's obsession with historical detail, the costumes and hairstyles were probably as close as possible to the real dress of first-century Jews. Zeffirelli uses some clever editing also: cutting between two different caravans to Bethlehem, one the richly dressed Magi on their camels and one Joseph's homely band on their donkeys. The Magi arrive from different lands, then converge, all led by the star that is visible even in daylight.

The movie has some wonderful touches, some of them explaining elements in the Gospels that puzzle readers. One example: In Herod's palace, Roman officials tell Herod that a census will be taken. Herod is not pleased. One Roman explains to the others that the census might be made more acceptable to Jewish prejudices by having people return to their ancestral homes. This isn't a historical certainty, but it does provide one explanation of why Joseph of Nazareth was compelled to pack himself and his pregnant wife off to another town.

A movie this long could include neglected parts of Jesus's life, such as the story of Simeon. Joseph and Mary take the child to the temple, where he is circumcised. The aged Simeon hears the baby's cries and seeks him out. He says, "Now I can die contented, Lord, according to thy word."

John the Baptist is well played by the British actor Michael York, who had made a career of playing refined, effete men. Playing the fiery wilderness prophet was a definite change of role, and he rose to the task. John baptizes in the shallow Jordan River, denouncing the vile Herod Antipas. Herod and his wife pass nearby, and she cannot believe Herod lets John be. John literally spits while he speaks. Some of the Zealots think John might be useful to their cause. John preaches that the repentant heart is what matters to God. Some of the Pharisees protest, but John tells them that being sons of Abraham is not enough. Later, after John's execution by Herod (well played by Christopher Plummer), John's disciples bury him, a biblical event never shown in films but important since some of Jesus's followers were first followers of John.

The movie has time to show some of the personality clashes among the disciples, notably some of the disciples' contempt for the money-gouging tax collector, Matthew, who eventually becomes one of the band. At Matthew's house, Peter and the other disciples stay outside. Inside, Jesus tells the parable of the prodigal son, aiming it both at his disciples and at the riotous-living guests in Matthew's circle. This is a good scene, with Jesus's face extremely expressive, as are those of the disciples. Peter enters when Jesus finishes the story, asking Jesus's forgiveness. Jesus brings Peter and Matthew face-to-face. Later, Judas introduces himself as a son of privilege, a scholar who translates Hebrew, Greek, and Latin. We sense he looks down on fishermen and carpenters. He asks to be a disciple. Jesus says yes, but there is an agonized look in his face, as if he knows what Judas will become.

Some elements of the film are questionable. For example, there is no temptation scene after Jesus's baptism, even though Christians have always considered this a crucial part of the gospel message. Also, the film distorts one Bible passage that makes Jesus's mother, Mary, look bad: in the Gospels, Jesus's mother and brothers seek him out, leading Jesus to point out that whoever are his followers are his true family. In the movie, a man goes to visit Mary and kisses the hem of her robe, saying, "You are his mother." Mary says, "Anyone who obeys our Father in heaven is his brother, his sister, his mother."

But these dubious bits get lost in a sea of good things. For example, Jesus is often seen praying or lost in thought, as if communing with the Father. This is obvious enough in the Bible but seldom seen in biblical movies. Powell's delivery of Jesus's teaching is as powerful and expressive as in any film about Jesus. In the scene of the woman about to be stoned for adultery, Jesus sounds dead serious when he tells the forgiven woman, "Go, and sin no more." At work in Nazareth, Joseph tells young boys that "a man skillful in his work will stand before kings"—a paraphrase from Proverbs, reminding us that pious Jews often quoted the Scriptures to their families and that Jesus no doubt grew up in such a home. Our first sight of Jesus is a close-up when John looks up from baptizing and locks eyes with Jesus. When, at the Last Supper, Jesus tells Judas to go and do what he must do, Judas leaves with a half smile, as if Jesus knows what he is doing and approves of it. The Supper is lit only by lamplight, with the men seated on the floor, beautifully photographed. Watching Jesus on the cross, Nicodemus quotes the Isaiah passage beginning "He was despised and rejected" (Isa. 53:3). With that quotation we are on firm biblical territory, aware of how the first Christians applied so many Old Testament prophecies to the life of Jesus.

Zeffirelli was aware, as is anyone making a movie about Jesus, that accusations of anti-Semitism would be heard. He defused these by making the Sanhedrin a divided group—or, more accurately, by having two fair-minded men, Nicodemus and Joseph of Arimathea, speak on Jesus's behalf. It helped that these two were played by respected actors James Mason and Laurence Olivier. The chief priest Caiaphas, played by Anthony Quinn, does not seem quite as anti-Jesus as he is in the Gospels, but finally he does condemn Jesus as a blasphemer. Most of the wickedness of the Jewish hierarchy is centered in the fictional character Zerah, a scribe who negotiates with Judas for Jesus's betrayal and in fact tempts Judas into it. It is Zerah who gives the actual order to turn Jesus over to Pilate. So the burden of guilt is taken from the priests and the Sanhedrin and loaded onto one man, Zerah. Later, when Pilate offers the people the choice between releasing Jesus or the revolutionary Barabbas, it is not the priests' hirelings but the Zealots who work up the crowd and get them to yell for Barabbas. When Mary Magdalene calls out to release Jesus, one of the Zealots slaps her and says, "Shut up, you slut!" From a theological point of view, none of this is very important. What is important is that the innocent Son of God was condemned to death wrongly, whoever brought it about.

Regarding the trial and crucifixion of Jesus, the movie seemed pretty violent and realistic on its first broadcast in 1977. Watching it now, after having seen the realism of Mel Gibson's *Passion of the Christ*, it seems a bit tepid. The bare-chested soldiers who flog Jesus are not as brutal as Mel Gibson's, nor do we see the blood flow, but Jesus's agony is apparent on his face. The soldiers mock him, putting on him a robe and the crown of thorns. We see the gashes on Jesus's back, but they are not deep. People in 1977 would not have accepted the violence in Gibson's movie, so the violence in *Jesus of Nazareth* was bloody enough for its time.

Zeffirelli the Catholic made a film that pleased Catholic viewers and evangelical viewers as well. Some viewers complained that he took a few liberties with the Gospels—for example, it pours rain at the time of Jesus's crucifixion, something not mentioned in the Bible, though the Bible does say there was "darkness" (Luke 23:44), which could be attributed to an eclipse—or a downpour. Other viewers noted that the Pharisee teacher Nicodemus pays a visit to Jesus in daylight—even though John's Gospel mentions the detail that he came to Jesus at night (John 3:2), presumably so his fellow Pharisees would not see him speaking to Jesus. But these and other divergences from the Bible were mostly minor. Oddly, the miniseries generated more controversy *before* it aired than after, for some conservative Christians were disturbed to hear that Zeffirelli was aiming to focus on the *human* side of Jesus. Given the unorthodox Jesuses of the movies of the 1970s, the anticipation of another "revisionist" Jesus is probably understandable. At any rate, the murmuring was loud enough that General Motors backed off from its position as sole sponsor of the miniseries.

It is interesting that the film does at times seem to "demythologize" the New Testament—almost. For example, early in the program young Mary is heard talking to the angel Gabriel, who is not seen or heard. Mary's mother observes Mary standing in the moonlight talking to . . . nothing. Nonetheless, we have no doubt she really was visited by an angel, especially since his words about the aged Elizabeth conceiving a child prove to be true. Near the end of the movie, there is some tension because Mary Magdalene reports to the disciples that she has seen the risen Jesus—but several minutes pass before Jesus is actually shown on-screen again, making us wonder, briefly, if the movie is never going to show him.

Spread out over several nights (and with numerous commercials), *Jesus of Nazareth* ran eight hours. In its video version (with commercials removed, that is), it is a little over six hours, making it, as already noted, the longest biblical film ever made. Despite its length, it was immensely popular at its first broadcast in April 1977 (the first segment was shown on Palm Sunday) and also in later rebroadcasts, and in video format it has done well in both sales and rentals. It cost $18 million, more than any previous TV movie, but it paid off handsomely. On the film's first showing, the evangelical magazine *Christianity Today* praised its acting and cinematography and, more importantly, its fidelity to the Gospel accounts, adding that "the depiction of the Resurrection is the best ever filmed."[4] Several years later, in a review of the many films dealing with the life of Jesus, the magazine still had high praise for the Zeffirelli film, giving it high marks for somehow striking the right balance between Jesus the man and Jesus the Son of God.[5]

> As the actors' names roll at the end credits, the demon-possessed boy whom Jesus healed is referred to as "Obsessed Boy"—implying that he was not demon-possessed but rather what we would today call mentally ill.

Il Messia (The Messiah): *Rossellini's Neglected Swan Song*

Released in Europe in 1978
145 minutes
Filmed in Italy

Director: Roberto Rossellini
Screenplay: Robert Rossellini, Sivia
  D'Amico Bendice
Photography: Mario Montuori
Music: Mario Nascimbene

Jesus: Pier Maria Rossi
John the Baptist: Carlos de Carvalho
Mary: Mita Ungaro
Mary Magdalene: Antonella Fasano

This was the last film of noted Italian director Robert Rossellini, who is probably best remembered for his extramarital affair with actress Ingrid Bergman, whom he eventually married. He was well loved in his native country, directing films of every type. What drew him to the story of Christ is hard to determine, since he was a professed atheist. He directed a film version of the book of Acts, released in 1969. He completed *Il Messia* (*The Messiah*) in 1975, but it was not released until 1978, a year after his death. Though released in Italy and several other countries in Europe, it has never had a general release to theaters in the U.S. It does rate a mention here because it was done by a high-profile director who seemed drawn to the Jesus of the Gospels despite his own lack of religious belief. Unlike another atheist director, Pier Paolo Pasolini, whose 1966 *Gospel According to Matthew* followed the Bible very closely, including the miracles and the resurrection, Rossellini simply wanted to show Jesus as a good man and great moral teacher. Jesus teaches people while going about his job as a carpenter—something not mentioned in the Bible, though a possibility. One interesting aspect of the film is that it opens centuries before Jesus's life, showing how the people of Israel longed for a Messiah. In fact, it compresses the entire history of Israel into about twenty minutes, beginning with Israel's leader Samuel giving in to the people's request to anoint them a king so they can be like other nations. Bible readers know that most of the kings of Israel were disasters, so obviously something better was needed than an earthly king. Jesus of Nazareth was not, of course, the political Messiah-king they expected.

Rossellini was part of the wave of European directors whose films fell under the category of neorealism. In a nutshell, these films have a gritty, earthy quality, far removed from the gloss associated with studio-made films, especially those from Hollywood. Rossellini went back to his neorealist roots in this film, which is not a bad thing, for showing us the real Jesus plying his trade as a carpenter reminds us that the Son of God lived as a real man among real men, earning his living by the sweat of his brow.

How does a neorealist deal with events the Gospels report as supernatural? Underplay them, of course, or omit them entirely. At Jesus's baptism he gets in line with the other people, and when John baptizes him there is no divine light, no dove, no voice of God from heaven, saying, "This is my beloved Son, in whom I am well pleased" (Matt. 3:17 KJV). Jesus leaves, and John continues baptizing.

Having grown up in the Catholic culture of Italy, Rossellini couldn't help but devote a large place to Mary, Jesus's mother. Interestingly, in this film it is Mary who is the source of the idea of "the kingdom of God," a phrase frequently used by Jesus in the Gospels. Mary says, "The kingdom of God is here, but people have forgotten, because they have forgotten how to do good"—words not found in the Bible but certainly not at odds with it.

The movie has no temptation scene—which is also true of the more reverent *Jesus of Nazareth*. Apparently modern filmmakers have trouble accepting the reality of Satan, which is remarkable considering that in this same decade the general public flocked to see movies like *The Exorcist*, in which Satan is undeniably real.

Rossellini's film assumes that the Gospels as we have them are not accurate—that is, they give us some of the true sayings of Jesus (those about love, mercy, not being judgmental) but mingle those with the views of the disciples. For example, in the movie, when a disciple of John the Baptist comes and asks Jesus if he is the Messiah, it is a disciple, not Jesus himself, who tells him, "Tell John that the blind see and the lame walk"—words the Gospels attribute to Jesus. But in the movie, Jesus scolds the disciple who spoke those words and adds, "Tell John that the poor have the good news preached to them." This Jesus is underplaying his own ability to work miracles. The movie does show miracles, but they are so understated that the director almost seems embarrassed by them. Jesus is crucified and resurrected, but these scenes are not depicted with much drama. Clearly what was important for Rossellini was Jesus the teacher, not the miracle worker or the Son of God raised from the dead. In other words, this is a Jesus that a liberal could love—one who can "save" people by working some moral influence on their lives. This Jesus the gentle teacher does not seem to be the controversial figure of the Gospels—just a simple, country carpenter-preacher who gets into trouble because his own disciples and the catty Pharisees like to raise a ruckus.

The film was released on video in 1999, and so far its appeal has been to movie buffs who want to watch it to see how Rossellini fared directing his last film. It is in Italian with English subtitles, which is an obstacle to watching it (although *The Passion of the Christ* also had subtitles, and audiences did not seem to mind). It is also expensive and thus unlikely to be stocked at video rental stores. It will be interesting to see, as time passes, how the Christians who view it will react.

Jesus: *A Church Film That Somehow Sneaked into Theaters*

Released October 1979	**Jesus:** Brian Deacon
Warner Brothers	**Peter:** Niko Nitai
117 minutes	**John the Baptist:** Eli Cohen
Filmed in Israel	**Judas:** Eli Danker
	Pilate: Peter Frye
Directors: Peter Sykes, Joseph Krisch	**Mary Magdalene:** Talia Shapira
Screenplay: Barnet Bain	**Narrator:** Alexander Scourby
Music: Nachium Heyman	

The final biblical film of the 1970s ended up in theaters almost by accident. An evangelical Christian production company known as the Genesis Project set itself the lofty goal of filming the entire Bible—or at least the narrative portions of it. The resulting films and videos, called the New Media Bible, would be "church films," intended for sale or rental to Christian groups, not for showing in commercial theaters. But to generate interest in (and funding for) the massive project, the producers decided to release to theaters a movie about the life of Jesus. Obviously the popular TV miniseries *Jesus of Nazareth* of 1977 was a tough act to follow, but the producers were no doubt hoping that audiences had been too long deprived of a satisfying normal-length, big-screen movie about the life of Christ.

The result had the simple title *Jesus* and was released in 1979, running just under two hours. It was billed as "a documentary taken entirely from the Gospel of Luke," and though the narration and dialogue were in contemporary English, occasionally the script slipped in a "thou" and "thee" from the King James Version. The movie was filmed in Israel, with a mostly Israeli cast but with English actor Brian Deacon in the role of Jesus. Deacon, brown-eyed but not very Semitic looking, was a more appealing and more biblical Jesus than any of the actors in the three 1973 "Jesus musicals." (The very shaggy-haired John the Baptist was extremely Semitic in appearance, as were Jesus's disciples. In fact, most cast members were dark-skinned Yemeni Jews—supposedly the people of our time who most closely resemble the Jews of Jesus's day.) Jesus is reasonably well acted but perhaps a bit too laid back. At certain points more drama (and perhaps more special effects) would have been welcome: at the healing of a demon-possessed man, Jesus's transfiguration, the healing of a blind man, and especially Jesus's cleansing of the temple (a scene put over with great intensity in *Jesus Christ Superstar*). In the scene of Jesus's temptation, Satan is represented by a literal snake slithering among stones.

Narration for *Jesus* was provided by British actor Alexander Scourby, whose resonant, dignified voice has been immortalized in audio versions of the King James Bible.

Sticking so closely to the text of the Bible, *Jesus* is a faithfully biblical movie, and it did attract a fair number of Christians, who had gone more than a decade without seeing a satisfying biblical movie in a theater. Though it was released by a major distributor (Warner Brothers), the film boasted no big-name stars, and with minimal advertising to promote it, it was not a hit with the public at large. In fact, it was not even released nationwide, being shown in only 250 theaters in the South and West. Reviews, in the few places they appeared, were lukewarm. A wealthy Texas couple had donated $3 million to finance the movie but did not recover its cost. A few Christians griped about some very minor details, such as the fact that Jesus did not wear a crown of thorns. The producers responded that this was because in Luke's Gospel, the basis of the film, the crown of thorns is not mentioned.

However, in the years since its release, the film quite possibly has been viewed by more people than any other biblical movie, since it is widely used by evangelists and missionaries and reportedly has been dubbed into more than six hundred languages. A version in Hindi, one of the chief languages of India, has reportedly been seen by 21 million viewers. In fact, the film's distributor, Campus Crusade for Christ, may not be exaggerating when they claim the movie has been viewed by more human beings than any other film ever made (4.7 *billion*, but a disclaimer is necessary: most viewers did not *pay* to see the film). The video versions of the film follow up Jesus's resurrection with a call to conversion. It is likely that this relatively low-budget film has surpassed Cecil B. DeMille's lavish silent epic *The King of Kings* in its number of viewers. For many new converts in faraway corners of Africa, Asia, and Latin America, Brian Deacon's Jesus may be the only film Jesus, the only "live" Jesus, they've ever seen. In the U.S., the film has had a trans-denominational appeal, being widely used as an evangelistic tool by Roman Catholics, Nazarenes, Southern Baptists, the Salvation Army, Assemblies of God, and numerous others. Some Christian groups have bought huge quantities of the video and sent them out to friends and family members—sometimes anonymously. Catering to a world where people seem to have shorter attention spans, Campus Crusade has released a shorter (eighty-three-minute) version of the film and also an even shorter version for viewing by children. Campus Crusade founder Bill Bright, who originally conceived the film as part of his 1976 "I Found It!" evangelistic campaign, was immensely pleased with the film's success.

At the same time *Jesus* was filmed, the producers used the same cast, crew, and sets in a much longer church film, *The Gospel of Luke*. This followed New Media Bible's policy of having a narrator read every single word of the Bible text while the actors spoke their lines (in "voice-under," at a lower volume than the narrator) in the actual language of Jesus and his disciples, Aramaic. Twenty-five years later, a far more commercially successful film, Mel Gibson's *The Passion of the Christ*, would feature dialogue in Aramaic.

As we near the end of this chapter on biblical movies of the 1970s, it's revealing to consider why the 1979 movie *Jesus* was not produced by one of the Hollywood studios. John Heymann, a friend of Bill Bright and a major name in Hollywood talent management, had approached the big studios about doing a straightforward, Bible-based film about the life of Jesus, something that had not been seen in theaters since 1965's *Greatest Story Ever Told*. Heymann was told the project sounded dull. Would he be willing to give the story a new twist, such as giving Jesus a love interest or having the story told by a sister of Jesus? Heymann claimed later that he was unwilling to "crap up" (his words) the basic story of the Bible, so he had to turn to private backers to get the movie produced. He wanted to present the Bible "as is"—a commendable goal for people spreading the gospel, but not one that Hollywood found appealing. In the 1970s, a decade of phenomenal Bible sales, a decade of amazing vitality among evangelicals, a decade when TV viewers tuned in to some fine biblical miniseries, Hollywood only seemed interested in producing "crapped-up" biblical movies. More of such films would follow in the decade ahead. In the same year that *Jesus* was released, a low-budget mockery of the Bible and religious people caught the public's fancy, turning "crapping up" into a highly profitable art form.

Monty Python's Life of Brian: *Tasteless, Controversial, and Profitable*

Released August 1979
Handmade Films
94 minutes
Filmed in Tunisia

Director: Terry Jones
Executive Producer: George Harrison

Photography: Peter Biziou
Music: Eric Idle, Michael Palin, Geoffrey Burgon
Writers and cast: Graham Chapman, John Cleese, Terry Gilliam, Eric Idle, Michael Palin, Terry Jones

Someone stumbling into this film at the very beginning might think he was seeing a traditional and very reverent biblical movie: It opens with a choir, a night sky, one bright star, three figures on camels in the distance. (It is similar—probably deliberately—to the opening of *The Greatest Story Ever Told*.) The three men pass through the narrow streets of an ancient village to a stable. The reverent spell is broken immediately when the mother falls off her stool when the three greet her. The mother (obviously a man in drag) orders them out, wanting no astrologers around, until they tell her about the precious gifts. She says the baby's name is Brian (Cohen). The three men exit, then change their minds and take back the gifts, finding the *real* nativity nearby. Then the movie's silly credits roll, with cartoonish images of ancient Roman statues over a James Bond–type theme song.

Strictly speaking, *Monty Python's Life of Brian* does not belong in this book, since it is not a movie based on the Bible. But it warrants discussion, having come at the end of a decade in which really good theatrical movies based on the Bible were not to be

had. Somehow this low-budget comedy drew people to the theaters, and few of those who paid for tickets were offended by its
mockery of religion.

A little background is in order: *Monty Python's Flying Circus* was
a comedy program shown on the British Broadcasting Corpora-
tion network. It found a cult following in America, especially with
the younger crowd, who appreciated the British comedy troupe's
mix of bawdiness with surreal whimsy—a mix of G-rated and
R-rated humor that the British seem to fancy. Monty Python had
already had some modest success with its movie *Monty Python
and the Holy Grail* (which took some slaps at religion, including
a cartoonish white-bearded God speaking
from heaven). The giant media conglomer-
ate EMI planned to produce *Life of Brian*,

> Many of the
> Tunisians who served
> as extras in *Life
> of Brian* had been
> extras for *Jesus of
> Nazareth*, and some
> were brassy enough
> to tell the director,
> "Mr. Zeffirelli
> wouldn't have done
> it that way."

but when some staffers read the script,
it was dropped—too controversial, they
said. The Monty Python gang panicked and
flew member Eric Idle off to California in
a quest for backers. It turned out that the
moneybag behind the film was another
Brit, ex-Beatle George Harrison, who was
a great fan of Monty Python and just had to
come to their rescue. He put up $4 million
of his own money, claiming that when the
Beatles broke up, Python comedy "kept me
sane." So his production company, Handmade Films, backed the film, which was
made in a short time in Tunisia, not far from the locales where
the hugely popular *Star Wars* had been filmed two years earlier.

What exactly was the controversial movie all about? Essentially
it is the tale of Brian Cohen, who lives with his shrewish mother
in Judea at the time of Jesus's ministry. Brian (the name was
obviously chosen because it doesn't seem even remotely Jewish,
although Cohen certainly does) is a bit of a doofus, allying himself
with the anti-Roman revolutionary groups in Judea, and somehow
finding himself hailed as Messiah by some mind-numbed people
who are apparently determined to find themselves a Savior even
if no one is really qualified.

Why did this offend so many people? Partly because religious
people are shown not as saints or seekers after truth but as being

extremely gullible, unreasoning, and (worst of all, in the modern world) intolerant, ready and willing to brand someone else as an unbeliever or heretic and persecute them. A scene of some women trying to stone a blasphemer is indeed funny, but it presents religious believers as sadists who simply enjoy persecuting an innocent party. The crowd that gathers outside Brian's home in Nazareth speaks every word in unison, all individuality lost in the mass religious mentality. The movie isn't really blaspheming God or Christ, as its critics charged, but mocking religious people in general.

In the desert, crowds gather to hear Jesus. The words "About Tea Time" appear on the screen. He speaks familiar words from the Sermon on the Mount. (An actor named Kenneth Colley had the small role of Jesus, seen from a distance.) Toward the rear of the crowd, Brian tries to shush his carping mother. Several other listeners get into a petty quarrel, insulting each other. They can't hear correctly, one reporting that Jesus said, "Blessed are the cheese-makers." Brian's mother gets bored and tells him to follow her, there's a stoning nearby. Without mocking Jesus directly, the movie makes the people who went out to hear him look very silly—and cruel. Later, a certain Matthias son of Deuteronomy of Gath (a silly name, but "biblical" in a broad sense) is to be stoned for blasphemy. The priest presiding over the stoning gets irritated that one of the women throws a stone before he gives the signal.

In traditional movies about the life of Jesus, the Romans are shown as tyrants and oppressors. Not here. In the film, an anti-Roman group of Jews plots to kidnap Pilate's wife. Ranting on about the Romans, one asks, "What have the Romans given us?" One says, "The aqueduct," another "the roads," "peace," "baths," and so on. The movie implies that the Jews were fools for wanting to boot out the Romans—conveniently overlooking the Romans' violence and heavy taxation. Brian, as it turns out, is half Roman himself: Brian's mother tells him his father was really a Roman centurion named Naughtius Maximus, not Mr. Cohen. Brian won't accept it—he shouts to her that he is "a kike, a Yid, a Red Sea pedestrian, and proud of it." (The script is playing on a centuries-old rumor that Mary was no virgin and that Jesus's father was a Roman soldier.)

For writing anti-Roman graffiti on walls, Brian is brought before a dorky (and gay) Pilate, who has a speech impediment. This key figure in the story of Jesus's trial is made to look like a buffoon.

Quite without meaning to, Brian develops a following of people who think he has the secret to eternal life. They follow him into the desert. The movie is obviously spoofing people who are determined to find a miracle anywhere. Brian won't admit he is the Messiah, but finally he caves in, but tells them to "f— off."

Back at his house in Nazareth, Brian beds Judith, one of the Zealot women, then the next morning opens the window, stark naked (frontal) and sees a huge crowd of admirers awaiting him in the streets. His grumpy mother tells them to go away—"There's no Messiah in here—there's a mess, all right, but no Messiah!" Then they hail her as the Messiah's mother: "Blessed art thou among women," and the like. Softened up, she allows Brian to speak to them. Brian tells them they don't need him or any messiah, they each need to work it out for themselves—a rather shallow piece of liberal thinking about religion, but one probably shared by most of the people who loved the movie.

Brian ends up being among those condemned to be crucified. A very polite soldier has the condemned line up neatly with their crosses on their left shoulders. One of the crucified men protests having a Samaritan in their midst. The centurion tells them not to fuss, they'll all be dead in a day or two—which was pretty true of crucifixion. The Zealots show up, but instead of rescuing Brian from the cross, they read a pompous declaration against the Romans. Before leaving, they sing "For He's a Jolly Good Fellow." One of the crucified men tries to perk things up with a song, "Always Look on the Bright Side of Life." The other crucified men join in, of course, even doing a sort of chorus line kick, despite their limited mobility. Thus one of the most important events in human history, the crucifixion of the Messiah, is made a figure of fun. In 2004, many people watching the crucifixion in *The Passion of the Christ* shed tears. Watching *Life of Brian*, they laughed.

Some of the movie's humor is not particularly antireligion. For example, Jerusalem has a Caesar Augustus Memorial Sewer. The Zealots spend most of their time bickering over the use of "sexist language" (a hot topic of the late 1970s) and hiding whenever someone knocks on their door. In fact, the Monty Python crew could have easily made a movie spoofing ancient Rome that would've offended no one. But they chose to set the film in Jerusalem at the time of Jesus, and people were offended even before the movie's release. In fact, fearing censorship in their native Britain, the group chose to premiere the film in America.

It opened in New York on August 17, 1979. On August 19, Rabbi Abraham Hecht, president of the Rabbinical Alliance of America, claimed to be speaking for a half million Jews when he described the film as blasphemous. The Roman Catholics' film-monitoring office gave the film a "C" (condemned) rating and urged faithful Catholics not to see it. Several Protestant leaders also condemned the film. All the fuss bore fruit—not what the critics hoped, however. Thanks to the notoriety, the film that had been scheduled to open in two hundred theaters opened in six hundred. Back in the United Kingdom, the Church of England's Social Responsibility Board circulated anti-*Brian* literature and urged people to pray for the film to fail. While the film went uncensored nationally in the UK, some cities and counties actually banned the film under a law allowing "unhealthy" films to be banned. There was no censorship in the U.S., where seeing the R-rated film became a badge of hipness. Saying "I saw *Life of Brian*" was a way of saying "I'm cool, I'm not uptight about religion, and you people take yourselves way too seriously." Even people who had no intention of seeing the film heard about the men singing on their crosses, about the smutty jokes and profanity, and, most memorably, about the full frontal nudity of the main character.

In 1979 lots more people saw *Life of Brian* than saw the fine film *Jesus* discussed earlier. The smashing success of *Life of Brian* and the modest success of *Jesus* (which was not even released nationally but only in the South and West) seemed to point the way to the secular 1980s, a decade of truly bad biblical movies.

7

REVISIONISM AND CONTROVERSY

The 1980s and 1990s

The last chapter should have made it clear that the 1970s were not good years for biblical films, the few standouts in the decade being a handful of made-for-TV productions, especially *Jesus of Nazareth*. The decade ended with the good but not profitable *Jesus*—and the highly profitable but religion-mocking *Life of Brian*. The 1980s would see even fewer biblical films, which tells us that producers did not see them as an investment that would pay off.

We are probably still too close to the 1980s and 1990s to evaluate them objectively, but a few observations are in order. The culture seemed to be getting more secular in many ways, even though more conservative churches tended to grow. Many people predicted that the AIDS epidemic would lead to more traditional sexual morals, but that didn't happen. Pop music became more blatantly sexual, with lyrics to rap songs grating on the ears of anyone born before 1960. Television became more permissive in subject matter, and movies even more so. As more and more people bought personal computers and logged on to the Internet, sexually explicit pictures and videos could be had for the asking, and people could engage in something an earlier generation could not have imagined: cybersex. The scandal involving President Bill Clinton and former intern Monica Lewinsky made the news sex-saturated for several months.

Several new versions of the Bible were big sellers at the end of the century, even though polls showed that the population at large—and also people who described themselves as Bible read-ers—was woefully ignorant of the Bible. One surprise hit of the 1980s was *The Closing of the American Mind*, a book lamenting the lack of education taking place on college campuses. The book stated that in times past the Bible had been part of the educated person's education, but, alas, no longer. William Bennett's *Book of Virtues* and *The Moral Compass* were big sellers among people favoring traditional morals. Psychiatrist M. Scott Peck's books *The Road Less Traveled* and *People of the Lie* were huge sellers, and many people saw them as bridging the gap between psychology and religion (although many Christians regarded his books as "spirituality lite"). But in the same period, pop singer Madonna's book *Sex* was a huge seller also. Some "me-centered" books from the 1970s got updated (but were no less selfish), including *Pull-ing Your Own Strings* and *How to Be Your Own Best Friend*. On the Broadway stage, one of the most popular plays of the 1980s was *Joseph and the Amazing Technicolor Dreamcoat*, based on the Joseph saga in Genesis—but unlike Genesis, the bouncy musical did not once mention the name of God. Apparently theatergoers could accept a Bible story, so long as God wasn't involved in it.

The year 1995 marked the hundredth anniversary of filmmak-ing—or, more precisely, the hundredth anniversary of the Lumière brothers of Paris showing the first projected films to a paying audience. One person who commemorated the centennial was Pope John Paul II, who in a speech referred to the film industry's profound influence on people's attitudes and choices, although anyone with any spiritual sensitivity would agree that the influ-ence is often harmful. But in an effort to accentuate the positive, the Vatican at that time published a list of forty-five "Important Films," a list that included several films discussed in this book: *The Life and Passion of Jesus Christ* (1905), *Intolerance* (1916), *Ben-Hur*

(1959), and *The Gospel According to Matthew* (1966). Not all the films on the list were religious, for it also included *The Wizard of Oz*, *Citizen Kane*, *Fantasia*, *Schindler's List*, *2001: A Space Odyssey*, *Stagecoach*, and *It's a Wonderful Life*.

Interestingly, one of the most honored films of the period would be *Gandhi*, released in 1982 (and, incidentally, included in the Vatican's 1995 list of "Important Films"). *Gandhi* told the story (somewhat sanitized) of a leader who was not only not American and not European but also not even a Christian but rather a Hindu. Apparently producers could not, or would not, make a biblical character into a hero, but they could do so with a practicing Hindu. But it is worth noting that in the same year *Gandhi* was released, one of the top-grossing movies was *Porky's*, a truly vile bit of losing-one's-virginity trash directed at teens (and so success-ful it spawned two sequels). In fact, most of the popular films of the 1980s would fall into the category of mindless fluff—not all as vulgar as *Porky's*, fortunately. Some of the hits: *Airplane*, *Stir Crazy*, *Cannonball Run*, *Trading Places*, *Ghostbusters*, *Gremlins*, *Back to the Future*, *Batman*, *Raiders of the Lost Ark*, and *Who Framed Roger Rabbit*. A handful of adult (in the good sense) films were popular: *Out of Africa*, *Witness*, *The Last Emperor*, *Tender Mercies*, *The Ele-phant Man*, *Driving Miss Daisy*. And, surprisingly, one winner of the best picture Oscar was *Chariots of Fire*, in which one of the lead characters was an outspoken Christian.

The new decade of the 1980s began promisingly with a three-hour TV movie, *The Day Christ Died*. The credits for the movie said it was "suggested by" the popular book of that title by Jim Bishop, an author noted for his exhaustive research into history, including *The Day Lincoln Was Shot*. The TV movie did what *The Passion of the Christ* would do in 2004: cover the arrest and trial of Jesus, though not nearly so well. The biggest problem with the film is that its main character was rather badly played by actor Chris Sarandon, who appeared sullen and uninspiring. Actor Keith Michell, who in the 1970s had played in some fine TV movies about Jacob and David, did much better as Pilate. The movie did stick reasonably close to the Gospel accounts, and when it aired on March 26, 1980, its ratings were decent but not high enough to encourage TV or movie producers to plan more biblical films. The movie is barely remembered today, while *Jesus of Nazareth* from 1977 still sells well in video format. There would be a very long gap between *The Day Christ Died* and the much better TV movie *Jesus* of 1999.

King David: *A Royal Charisma Deficit*

Released August 1985	**Bathsheba:** Alice Krige
Paramount	**Michal:** Cherie Lunghi
114 minutes	**Abner:** John Castle
Filmed in Italy	**Nathan:** Niall Buggy
	Joab: Tim Woodward
Director: Bruce Beresford	**Abcalom:** Jean-Marc Barr
Producer: Martin Elfand	**Ahimelech:** Hurt Hatfield
Screenplay: Andrew Birkin and James Costigan	**Samuel:** Denis Quilley
	Jonathan: Jack Klaff
Photography: Donald McAlpine	**Ahitophel:** David De Keyser
Music: Carl Davis	**Uriah:** James Lister
	Goliath: Luigi Montefiori
David: Richard Gere	**Young David:** Ian Sears
Saul: Edward Woodward	

Back in 1951, the biblical movie *David and Bathsheba* was the top-grossing film of the year. *King David*, dealing with the same man and including the story of his adultery with Bathsheba, proved unpopular with audiences and critics. Why so, considering David is one of the most interesting characters in the Bible, the 1985 movie starred Richard Gere (one of the most desirable male stars of his era, as Gregory Peck was when he played David in 1951), and it was directed by a rising star in the cinema, Australian Bruce Beresford? Had the movie audience become so secular that masses of people were no longer drawn to the saga of a biblical king? Or was it simply a bad movie?

In the first place, no movie has yet been made that quite does credit to the long story of David. We know more about him than any character in the Bible, thanks to the mass of colorful details related in 1 and 2 Samuel, 1 Kings, and 1 Chronicles, not to mention the various psalms that are attributed to him (including the famous "Shepherd Psalm," number 23). His story is so appealing that there must be truth in it, since no storyteller would have dared to invent it. He is the shepherd boy who with one stone and a sling defeats the armor-clad hulk Goliath. He is the harpist and singer who soothes the melancholy soul of the brooding King Saul, later becoming Saul's most devoted friend—one Saul wishes to kill out of jealousy. He is the fugitive living abroad among outlaws. He

According to the Bible, David was "goodly to look at"—and so was Richard Gere, but Paramount's 1985 *King David* was not an audience-pleaser, nor was it overly faithful to the Bible. Still, David's rivalry with Saul was handled well in the film.

has a deep emotional bond with Saul's son Jonathan. He marries many women and fathers many children, who quarrel among themselves, one raping his sister, one brother avenging her dishonor with murder. He faces rebellions, including one led by his favorite son. He impregnates the wife of one of his most devoted soldiers, then arranges for the soldier to die in battle to cover up his guilt. He dances with joy when the ark of the covenant is brought into Jerusalem, but God denies him the privilege of building a holy temple. He is a flawed and fascinating character, all charisma, surrounded by a cast of minor characters who are fascinating in themselves, not a dull moment in his long story. One wonders what Cecil B. DeMille, master of the biblical epic, might have done with the David saga. In the 1930s, DeMille had his writer (and mistress) Jeanie Macpherson prepare a script titled *Thou Art the Man: The Story of David*. DeMille and Macpherson had struck gold with their collaboration on *The Ten Commandments* (1923) and *The King of Kings*. DeMille nixed the David project after Twentieth Century-Fox released the popular *David and Bathsheba*. *Thou Art the Man* is one of the great might-have-beens in film history.

The two-hour 1951 *David and Bathsheba* could not cover all the facets of the amazing David, and thankfully it did not try. It concentrated on his failed marriage with Saul's catty daughter Michal and on his adultery with the married Bathsheba. David's bigger story was attempted in the four-hour 1976 TV movie *The Story of David* (see page 211), which was reasonably faithful to the Bible and is still watchable today. *King David* tried to compress the David epic into two hours and inevitably failed. Yet its intentions were good, and for all its flaws, the film contains good things.

An entire chapter could be written about the fine-tuning of its script. Apparently Paramount's executives did not like the many direct quotations from the Bible that were in the original script, especially quotations from some of the psalms attributed to David. So all the dialogue that sounded "too biblical" was dropped, alas. (A sign of the secular times: in the past, biblical movies could include dialogue taken directly from the Bible and assume that most people in the audience would find it familiar. Not so in the 1980s and afterward.) The executives also insisted that the movie "soften" David's image as a warrior—which would pretty much mean changing his life story completely. Director Bruce Beresford did as well as he could with the final script.

The movie opens with the words on the screen, "Israel, 1,000 years B.C.," which is historically correct. Israel's spiritual leader

> Director Bruce Beresford had shown himself capable of handling religious subjects in the film *Tender Mercies*, about a washed-up country singer who finds contentment with a Christian woman. Making the story of David fit into a normal-length movie would prove a greater challenge.

Samuel barges into King Saul's court, angry that Saul has spared the life of the captured Amalekite king. Samuel takes Saul's own sword and tells Saul he has disobeyed God by sparing the wicked Amalekite king. Samuel beheads the Amalekite king. Samuel recalls he did not want to give Israel a king, for God was their true king. He holds up the head of the Amalekite king and tells Saul this is what becomes of earthly kings. Saul admits he has sinned and asks forgiveness. Samuel walks away and Saul grasps his robe, tearing it. Samuel tells him God has torn away the kingdom and will give it to a worthier man. This incident is biblical, as is the next scene, in which God tells Samuel not to mourn for Saul but to go to Jesse of Bethlehem to choose a new king. Samuel looks over each son while looking at two "seer stones" he holds in his hand. (These stones are not mentioned in the Bible, where God himself is speaking to Samuel and telling him which son to choose as king.) Samuel tells Jesse that God does not see as man sees. Finally the youngest, David, is called in from the pastures. Samuel looks at his stones and sees David is the one. Samuel tells him God has chosen him to be shepherd of Israel and to defend the honor of the Lord.

Jonathan, Saul's son, hears David is a good musician and singer and wants to take him to Saul. David recalls Samuel's prophecy that he would someday be brought to Saul's service. The brothers are surprised to see David in the camp. David is brought to Saul, where the king seems to be having a mental and spiritual breakdown. David sings and plays Psalm 23. Saul, his eyes squinched and arms crossed over his chest, seems to be soothed.

Inevitably the film includes the famous battle with Goliath. A Philistine warrior walks out; his brushy circular helmet is striking. He is taunting the Hebrews and their "unseen God." Their God is obviously weak, since he cannot send a mighty man against him. The challenge: one man against Goliath, and whoever wins, wins the day. With no introduction regarding the confrontation, David simply strides out. (Wouldn't it have been more dramatic to have Saul and others telling David not to be so foolish as to fight the giant, as in 1 Samuel?) Goliath's face is almost completely covered in armor, except his eyes and nose. David fires off two stones against him, but they bounce off Goliath's shield. He puts down the shield and comes at David with a curved sword. David's stone hits its mark. (In the Bible, David's first stone does the job.)

David closes the giant's eyes and says, "So be it, Lord." He cuts off Goliath's head. The Israelites cheer, and the Philistines flee in panic. Sadly, the episode of Jonathan swearing eternal friendship to David is not included at this point.

Next we see the adult David, Richard Gere. David and Jonathan return to the city, both embracing Saul. The moment is spoiled for Saul when women begin chanting, "Saul has slain his thousands, and David his tens of thousands." Saul's jealousy of David inevitably follows.

David marries Saul's pretty daughter Michal. Omitted is the story of Saul hoping to get rid of David by stating that the bride price for marrying Michal is four hundred Philistine foreskins—which David brings (see 1 Sam. 18:20–27). Also, 1 Samuel makes it clear that Michal really was in love with David, so their contentiousness right after their wedding in the movie does not seem right. The two instances of Saul hurling his spear at David while David played the harp are also omitted. And no movie has yet tried to depict Saul "prophesying," since the Bible suggests he went into ecstatic trances (see 1 Sam. 10:11; 18:10; 19:23).

The priest Ahimelech reads David the story of Jacob wrestling with God. They talk about seeing God face-to-face, which only Moses had done. David wants to see him too, remembering that as a boy he felt God's presence around him. Ahimelech takes David to see the ark of the covenant, telling him only the priests are allowed to see it. David wants to know why it is kept hidden in the sanctuary when it should be in a more accessible place. David vows to God to make a temple someday to house the ark. Ahimelech learns that someone at the sanctuary has let Saul know David is hiding out there. He sends David away before Saul arrives. The priests are singing a hymn when Saul arrives asking for David. Ahimelech says he does not know where he is but admits he had been there. They will not tell him which direction David went. Saul orders Abner to kill the priests until they answer his question. Abner hesitates, but Saul insists that the priests who live off the people's offerings are not anything special. No one will obey the order until one soldier steps forward, a Gentile. Ahimelech continues chanting as the soldier kills them one by one with his sword. When Ahimelech sings praise of David, Saul himself spears him through the heart. The incident at Nob is found in 1 Samuel 21–22. In the Scriptures Saul does not actually go to Nob and kill the priests but has them sent to him. It is indeed a Gentile, Doeg the Edomite, who alone will do the killing. The passage does not say that Saul himself killed Ahimelech or anyone else.

David is in exile for six years, attracting all the malcontents. He takes three new wives, who bear him several children, including Amnon and Absalom. David decides that since Saul is after him, maybe he should pay him a visit. He steals into Saul's camp at night and finds Saul in a cave sleeping. The next morning Saul awakens and senses David was there. The next morning David shouts at Saul from a hill, showing that he took Saul's sword in the night. He gives it back, proving to Saul he was not well guarded and saying, "The Lord delivered me into your hands, and I spared your life." Saul for the time being feels love for David, even though Abner suggests nabbing David while they have the chance. In 1 Samuel 24, David does not take Saul's sword but cuts off a piece of his robe. Obviously the filmmakers thought that the sword would be more dramatic.

Disguised as a blind beggar, David is admitted into the walled Philistine city of Gath. Achish, the local chieftain, is amazingly cynical and effete. David asks Achish for refuge. David tells him he will gladly help him fight against any enemies—except Saul. Achish tells him the love of enemies is nice for poets but not for kings. This is radically different from the account in 2 Samuel 21, where David has to play the role of a madman to prevent Achish from killing him. However, it does square somewhat with chapter 27, in which Achish and David come to trust each other.

Alas, one of the most colorful incidents in David's life is made to look silly in the movie. David dances when the ark is brought into Jerusalem. Exactly how he danced we are not told, but the movie has Gere making a fool of himself, looking neither graceful nor devout. Apparently the producers considered it a chance to show off Gere's fine physique, but audiences laughed. The bringing of the ark is recounted in 2 Samuel 6. The movie omits the serious incident of Uzzah falling dead after touching the ark to steady it.

The adultery with Bathsheba begins when David sees her bathing nude on her rooftop. Bathsheba is brought to David. She tells him she is married to Uriah. David asks why they have no children after five years of marriage. She tells him they have no relations at all. David tells her he can give her the children she desires.

She says no, not as long as Uriah lives. So David sends a sealed order to place Uriah in the thick of the fighting. David and Bathsheba marry as soon as possible after Uriah's death. None of this nonsense about Uriah not touching her is in the Bible. The 1951 movie was closer to the truth when it related that Uriah would not sleep with her while he was home on leave.

For this affair, David is confronted by the prophet Nathan. Alone with the king, Nathan tells him the story of the ewe lamb as if it were an actual legal case. Nathan uses the actual words "Thou art the man" (2 Sam. 12:7 KJV). Nathan tells him that God has blessed David so richly, including numerous wives, yet he murdered Uriah and took his only wife. David falls on the floor in agony. Nathan tells him he will not die, nor Bathsheba—Nathan calls her "the wife of Uriah"—be taken from him, yet the punishment will be that he will feel the sword in his house forever. The words of Psalm 51 are heard. This section follows 2 Samuel 12 very closely, even to the accuracy of Nathan calling her "the wife of Uriah."

David's favorite son Absalom murders his half brother Amnon, and David reluctantly sends Absalom into exile. Absalom (now with a beard) laments the corruption of his father's court, with his father under the thumb of Bathsheba, and he promises he would bring justice to the land. Joab advises David that Absalom is a traitor, but David will not hear of it. Joab tells him that his love has made him blind to the threat. Absalom marches out with an army, but David's men rise to meet him. He flees in a chariot, Joab firing arrows at him. He is dangling in midair when caught in a tree limb. Joab kills him with a sword. When messengers bring news of Absalom's death, David falls prostrate, going into his "Absalom, my son, my son" lament. Nathan is appalled, asking him when he intends to obey God instead of his own emotions. The Absalom incident is at least true to the spirit of the Bible, though incorrect in some details. In 2 Samuel 18, Absalom is riding a mule when his hair is caught in the tree, and Joab kills him with three spears, not a sword. And it is not Nathan but Joab who reprimands David for lamenting over the traitorous Absalom (see 2 Samuel 19).

As the film continues, the old David, confined to bed, designates Solomon his heir. He reminds Solomon that God speaks to man through the heart, not through the prophets. His last words are, "I am waiting, Lord; hide your face no more." These are a far cry from the last words recorded in 2 Samuel 23, which state that a reverent king is like the sun shining and that God will bless all his descendants because of his eternal covenant with David. However, 1 Kings 2 claims to record David's last instructions to Solomon, which include telling him to obey all the Lord's commands written in the law of Moses. In fact, the movie has made it clear that the emotional David has never been too happy with the law of Moses, seeing it as strict and merciless.

As all these details indicate, the movie in its two-hour running time chose to omit some incidents from David's life and alter others. For the most part the Bible was followed closely, though Bathsheba lamenting that her husband, Uriah, has no physical relations with her is rather implausible. The movie omits all the dealings of David with Saul's son Ishbosheth and the war between David's and Saul's partisans, and also Abner switching sides from Saul's family to David and being murdered by Joab (see 2 Samuel 2–4). The movie also omits any mention of Mephibosheth, the lame son of Jonathan who was brought to live with the king (see 2 Samuel 9). The famous visit of Saul to the medium ("witch") of Endor, when she calls up the spirit of Samuel, is missing, as is David's marriage to Abigail, who abandons her foolish husband. Several other key stories are omitted, such as David fleeing Jerusalem to escape Absalom, Shimei's cursing of David, the rebellion of Sheba, the killing of Saul's descendants, and the like. The movie originally ran over three hours, but Paramount ordered it reduced to two, so perhaps some of the key incidents were cut for time's sake.

King David was to be shot in Morocco, but when the Moroccan Muslims learned that the film was glorifying a Jewish king, they nixed the project, and the movie was shot in Italy.

Despite its many omissions, the movie does give us a general impression of what David was like, but unfortunately Richard Gere does not seem to have the depth that the biblical David has. One simply cannot imagine Gere as the man who wrote some of the deeply spiritual psalms. In the 1951 film, Gregory Peck did at least seem to have more substance. In fact, the Golden Raspberry Foundation gave one of its "Razzie" awards to Gere for what they considered the worst acting job of 1985. Actually, the most interesting character in the movie is the luckless, aging Saul, well played by Edward Woodward. The prophets Samuel and Nathan, alas, come across as merciless religious fanatics. The movie's ending is troubling, with David telling his son to trust his own heart, not the prophets. This is a very modern sentiment—"trust your own feelings, no matter what others tell you"—and one not even remotely in keeping with the Bible, where trusting our own feelings usually leads us into trouble. Film critic John Simon called the film "Goliath's revenge."

David's story would be told again, and much better, in the 1997 movie *David* made for Turner Network Television, part of that network's Bible Collection. Not counting the animated 1999 *Prince of Egypt*, *King David* was the last attempt to tell an Old Testament story in a theatrical film. Its failure did not encourage the making of others.

The Last Temptation of Christ: *Oy, Such Controversy!*

Released August 1988
Universal Pictures
156 minutes
Filmed in Morocco

Director: Martin Scorsese
Producer: Barbara De Fina
Screenplay: Paul Schrader
Photography: Michael Ballhaus
Music: Peter Gabriel

Jesus: Willem Dafoe
Judas: Harvey Keitel

Mary Magdalene: Barbara Hershey
Peter: Victor Argo
John: Michael Been
James: John Lurie
Mary, mother of Jesus: Verna Bloom
John the Baptist: Andre Gregory
Martha: Peggy Gormley
Mary, sister of Lazarus: Randy Danson
Saul/Paul: Harry Dean Stanton
Pilate: David Bowie
Girl Angel: Juliette Caton
Zebedee: Irvin Kershner

Controversy can lead to profits—but it doesn't always. Almost everyone remembers hearing about this highly controversial 1988 film, but relatively few people saw it. Even the secular critics, who seem well disposed toward anything controversial, were not very kind to the film, despite its being directed and scripted by some high-profile people in the industry. People who have never seen it may well wonder: was it really as bad—or as shocking—as everyone seemed to think? I hope this section of the book will answer those questions as well as shed some light on the cultural atmosphere of the 1980s.

In the first place, *The Last Temptation of Christ* is based *not* on the Bible but on a novel by Greek author Nikos Kazantzakis, who also penned the popular *Zorba the Greek*. This is clear enough at the very beginning of the film, which begins with a black screen and these words from the book: "The dual substance of Christ—the yearning, so human, so superhuman, of man to attain God . . . has always been a deep inscrutable mystery to me. My principle [sic] anguish and source of all my joys and sorrows from my youth onward has been the incessant battle between the spirit and the flesh . . . and my soul is the arena where these two armies have clashed and met." Then these words appear: "This film is not based upon the Gospels but upon this fictional exploration of the eternal spiritual conflict."

Fair enough: we have been warned already that we are witnessing a "fictional exploration," not a movie based on the Bible. (Incidentally, the book was very controversial when first published in Kazantzakis's native Greece.) But the movie still has to be seen as a "biblical movie" for the simple reason that most of the human race regards the Gospels as the only valid sources for what we know about Jesus. Call it a "fictional exploration" if you will, but you still risk offending people if your "exploration" ventures too far afield from the sources, namely, the Gospels. (For the record, author Kazantzakis also wrote his own version of Homer's *Odyssey*, another classic. But this offended no one, for who has any life stake in *The Odyssey*? The Gospels of the Bible are another matter entirely.)

The controversial elements begin immediately. Jesus narrates, describing his period of hearing "voices." We then see that he makes crosses for the Romans to use in executions—in fact, he is the only Jew around who will perform this service. Jesus carries a crosspiece to a crucifixion, while some call him "traitor." The tattooed, gold-bedecked Mary Magdalene spits in his face. The Latin placard *"Seditio"* (treason) is affixed to the cross. The Roman soldier reads the list of offenses to the people who watch. Jesus actually aids in the nailing while the victim recites a psalm, then screams in agony.

We hear Jesus's voice again: "God loves me. I know he loves me; I want him to stop." Jesus makes crosses to spite God, hoping to crucify all would-be Messiahs. Jesus's mother asks him if he hears God's voice or the devil's. This is a very, very confused Jesus. Later, in a scene that was much talked about, Jesus waits in a room while the prostitute Mary Magdalene fornicates with her customers. Jesus seems like a sleazy voyeur, though we learn later that he and Mary were once in love—childhood sweethearts, in fact—but Jesus's sense of mission made his marriage impossible. Later he saves Mary from stoning—not because of adultery but because she has fornicated with a Roman on the Sabbath.

Can this confused, voyeuristic Jesus work miracles? At times, yes. Jesus bites into an apple, tosses the seeds on the ground, and an apple tree in full fruit suddenly appears. Jesus seems awed by the miracle. It is exactly the kind of pointless, showy miracle that the Jesus of the Bible did *not* do. However, later in the movie some genuine miracles from the Gospels are shown: Jesus heals several demon-possessed men, who are near naked and caked over with mud. The crowd is even more impressed by the healing of a blind man. Jesus also performs the miracle of turning water into wine at the wedding at Cana.

Later, the most dramatic of the miracles: Jesus goes to the tomb of Lazarus. Jesus and the others cover their noses as the stone is rolled, everyone being hit by the stench. (It is refreshing to see that Jesus has a human nose.) He goes to the entry to the tomb and softly calls to Lazarus: "In the name of the prophets and my Father, I call you here." There is suspense—nothing happens, then suddenly Lazarus's pallid hand shoots up. Jesus touches him; the two clasp hands. Jesus leads him out, with Lazarus still unsteady on his feet. Jesus is as awed by the miracle as the others are.

So the story does follow the Bible, at least at times. Jesus is baptized by John (a very wacky character, just shy of being a mental case), then goes into the desert, where he encounters Satan in the form of a cobra, a lion, and a flame. One temptation—the one referred to in the title—is to marry, raise a family, and live a normal life. This is not in the Bible, but perhaps Kazantzakis was right in speculating that every person with a divine sense of calling has faced this same temptation.

One scene that is well handled is the cleansing of the temple. We see the well-dressed money changers making a killing (and consorting with prostitutes, meaning the devout pilgrims' money is being paid out to whores). Peter reminds Jesus that the money changers are there for the temple tax (a good historical point, by the way). Jesus goes ballistic, overturning tables, tossing coins into the air. A riot almost ensues. One of the priests intervenes. With a statue of Caesar behind him, the priest reminds Jesus that the money changers have to be there so that heathen coins can be exchanged for the Jewish shekel, lest the temple be profaned. Jesus tells the priest he (Jesus) is the new law. The priest warns that such talk will get him killed. Jesus says that God is not tied to the temple; God is not an Israelite but belongs to the whole world—not words from the Gospel but a sentiment implied in Jesus's words that he would "tear down the temple" (John 2:19).

The Romans *did* crucify men nude—except for Jewish men, who were allowed to wear their loincloths. Whether scriptwriter Paul Schrader knew this is not known, but certainly word-of-mouth rumors about "seeing Jesus nude" gave the film some free advertising.

As in the Gospels, Jesus is arrested and brought before Pilate, played by former rock star David Bowie. Pilate is brushing down his fine horse, chatting amiably with Jesus, reminding him that he can send him to Golgotha where there are plenty of Jewish bones already. While the Pilate of the Gospels seems to show some interest in giving Jesus a fair shake, this blasé Pilate doesn't much care one way or the other. Jesus is stripped naked, beaten by the soldiers, then flogged. It is not quite as bloody as the same scene in *The Passion of the Christ* but fairly realistic. (It is jarring to see, briefly, Jesus's bare behind.) When Jesus is shown to the crowd, he wears a white robe, not red. Peter denies Jesus at this time. We see an overhead shot of Jesus carrying the crossbeam through the very narrow streets. Many people, mostly men, laugh. The walk to the cross, shown in slow motion, resembles medieval paintings, with Jesus streaked with blood, people jeering, even children pointing and laughing. Jesus is by no means stoic through all this. He is clearly in physical and mental agony. He sees the cross, and the audience recalls that he himself was a maker of crosses. Mary, Martha, Magdalene, and Jesus's mother are present. Jesus wears a loincloth when put on the cross but later he is seen to be nude, as are the other two men. (Their legs are bent, which is historically correct, so the camera never actually shows the groin.) He screams in agony when the nails are driven in. *INRI* is written on the placard. Golgotha is literally "the place of the skull" (which is what its name means), littered with skulls and bones. Most of the people present are mocking. Jesus says, though not aloud, "Father, forgive them." The genuine human agony shown on the cross is commendable, since most previous movie Jesuses did not seem to suffer much.

The film did not include the high priest Caiaphas or the blood-thirsty Jewish crowd in *Last Temptation*. (The novel did in fact include Pilate's handwashing and the crowd saying, "His blood be on us and our children.") Though controversy swirled around the film, no fuss was made about the film being anti-Semitic, since the Jewish priests are not the ones who bring about Jesus's death.

While Jesus is on the cross, the most controversial aspect of the movie takes place. Jesus looks down and sees a blonde girl, claiming to be his angel. She tells him she can stop all the horror, that he can get down from the cross and relive his life as a normal husband and father. He marries Mary Magdalene (from a distance we see them making love). She dies in childbirth (a common occurrence in ancient times), and he later marries Mary, Lazarus's sister, fathering children both by her and by her sister Martha. He is happy enough as a father and husband (or bigamist, rather). Then he meets Paul, a former Zealot, who killed Lazarus, since Lazarus was proof of Jesus's miracle-working power. (John's Gospel does say that the Jewish priests, not the Zealots, plotted to kill Lazarus for that reason.) Paul is now a Christian preacher, teaching that Jesus rose from the dead and can now give people eternal life and forgiveness from sins. Jesus mocks him and says he is an ordinary man, son of Mary and Joseph. Paul says his gospel message is good for the world, even if it isn't true, and that he doesn't even need the real Jesus. (Obviously the movie is taking a slap at traditional Christian teaching here.)

Later, an aged Jesus lies dying. His disciples come to him and tell him his "angel" was really Satan, tempting him away from his destiny of being crucified. So he goes back on the cross. His "normal life" was only a vision. He has passed the temptation test; he is worthy to be the Messiah. With an agonized smile, he cries out, "It is accomplished!"—words from the Gospels. His eyes shut, colors flash across the screen. A resurrection, or simply death? We are not sure. The movie did not seem willing to comfort us by affirming the resurrection, the key article of Christian belief—but did not deny it either.

Jesus (Willem Dafoe) marries Mary Magdalene (Barbara Hershey) in the infamous "vision on the cross" sequence from the oh-so-controversial 1988 *The Last Temptation of Christ*. In the same sequence he would later marry and father children by both Mary and Martha, the sisters of Lazarus. The controversy did not lead to huge profits.

Obviously the movie mixed the Gospels with pure fiction, some of it bordering on the pornographic. Director Martin Scorsese, educated in Catholic schools, claims his teachers never focused enough on the human side of Jesus, which is why he was drawn to Kazantzakis's book. This was also the stated motivation of screenwriter Paul Schrader, a graduate of conservative Calvin College. Early versions of the screenplay were leaked, and protests took place even before the movie was released. (Though credited to Schrader, the script got some extensive rewriting by Scorsese and former *Time* movie critic Jay Cocks.) Universal, aware that protests were planned, chose to release the film a whole month earlier than scheduled. No matter, the controversy raged anyway. Catholics were deeply offended. So was the National Association of Evangelicals; its spokespersons, after viewing *Last Temptation*, condemned the film, as did high-profile evangelical leaders Donald Wildmon, Jerry Falwell, and Bill Bright. The evangelical magazine *Christianity Today* said the movie's Jesus was "unlike anything in the Gospels (or even any liberal visions of Jesus)."[1] In an attempt at fairness, the magazine interviewed screenwriter Schrader in that same issue. Some of Schrader's statements in the interview: "All I was trying to do was provoke discussion about Christ," "When I first read the book, it struck me as a view of Christ that should be part of the debate," "I would say I've experienced a re-affirmation of my faith in recent years," and "How can we relate to a Christ who didn't feel the hungers we feel?"[2] Interesting sentiments, but the magazine's readers were probably not impressed. Secular magazines weren't kind to the film. *Newsweek* called it "part folly, part spellbinder,"[3] but reviews in general thought it more "folly." (Despite all the criticism, Scorsese was nominated for best director for 1988, though he did not win.)

> A proposed film *Christ the Man* was scheduled to begin production in 1989, directed by Paul Verhoeven and produced by Mel Brooks. It was scuttled, presumably because of the reception given *Last Temptation*. Controversial films about "the human side" of Jesus did not seem a good investment.

In response to all the fuss, two large theater chains chose not to show *Last Temptation*. The movie did manage to recoup its costs (it was shot on a fairly small budget in Morocco), but the controversy did not pay off in the same way controversy benefited the silly *Life of Brian* in 1979. In the *National Review*, critic John Simon stated that "it is too bad that various religious groups have seen fit to persecute it and thereby provide invaluable free publicity to a movie that could have died promptly of its own boring ineptitude."[4] His words were premature: it did die of its own ineptitude.

Hollywood seemed so taken aback by the failure of *Last Temptation* that no big-screen movie about Jesus would be produced for the rest of the century. Perhaps some Christians were relieved—better no movies at all about Jesus than movies that showed him confused, doubtful, and naked.

Twenty years later, what are we to make of this odd, misguided movie? I personally found it interesting, never boring—but not satisfying either. Willem Dafoe, who plays Jesus, does have a certain charisma at times. It is refreshing to see the Son of God struggling with real human doubts about his mission in life. But he seems a bit too self-absorbed to be the Messiah. He is far too emotionally dependent upon the more dedicated, stable Judas, whose sense of mission never wavers. He is not a Christ that people would hang their hopes upon. And the movie's Saul/Paul, the Zealot who commits murder, then creates the Christian creed out of falsehood, is truly offensive. (Paul was a Pharisee, not a Zealot.) The movie is simply parroting an old, old line of thought: Jesus was a simple preacher and miracle-worker, and the beliefs called "Christianity" were invented by Paul, who had no real concern for the real Jesus and who was legalistic and merciless while Jesus was kind and loving. In other words, if Christianity went wrong, it is Paul's fault, not Jesus's. It's an interesting idea but a very silly one, as any reading of the New Testament would prove. Paul's famous "love chapter," 1 Corinthians 13, proves he was not the unkind man depicted in this film. In fact, the small but important role of Paul in this film reminds us again that Paul has become the "Christian bogeyman" in modern thought, the judgmental man who condemned homosexuals and told women to be submissive to their husbands.

Though Paul was not depicted at all sympathetically in *Last Temptation*, he did fare well in two made-for-TV films of the 1980s, *Peter and Paul* (1981) and *A.D.* (1985). In the first film he was portrayed by the fine British actor Anthony Hopkins. These two films and a 1984 TV movie *Samson and Delilah* kept the 1980s from being a total washout as far as biblical films were concerned.

Eleven years would elapse before Hollywood released another biblical film—thankfully, one radically different from *The Last Temptation of Christ*. But there was hardly a famine of biblical movies in the 1990s, for they found an entirely new home: cable television. New cable channels grew up like mushrooms after a spring rain, catering to different tastes and audiences, so the Bible—as history, as entertainment, or both—got "cable-ized" in a big way, with programs popping up on the History Channel, Arts and Entertainment, and of course some of the religious channels. The channel most associated with some fine productions of Bible stories was, surprisingly, owned by a man who has been rather outspoken in his criticism of Christianity, media mogul Ted Turner of Georgia. Turner launched "superstation" WTBS and also founded the Cable News Network, Turner Classic Movies (which now owns the rights to a huge portion of Hollywood's best films), and Turner Network Television (TNT), which was the home of a series known as the *Bible Collection*. This was launched in 1994 with the fine *Abraham*, followed by *Jacob, Joseph, Samson and Delilah, Moses*, and *David*. The *Joseph* production won an Emmy Award as best miniseries of 1995. The productions have boasted some big-name talent, including Oscar-winner Ben Kingsley. In a decade when filmmakers in the U.S. and abroad showed zero interest in making films about the Bible, TNT aired some of the most faithful tellings of the biblical stories, plus released them all on video. This is indeed surprising, given that Turner's ex-wife Jane Fonda relates that during one of their first dates, Turner informed her that the Ten Commandments were completely outmoded in the modern world and needed replacing with his Ten Voluntary Initiatives. Supposedly he divorced Fonda because she became a Christian, and he told a United Nations environmental summit that Christianity was a huge problem in the world because it saw human beings as more important than sea otters. He has also referred to Christianity as a "religion for losers." Apparently this same man had no qualms about people tuning in to his cable channel to watch faithful depictions of characters from the Bible. The media world is full of surprises.

Another surprise would come at the end of the decade, when one of the world's best-known animation studios decided to retell the saga of Moses.

The Prince of Egypt: *Animation Extraordinaire*

Released December 1998	**Voices:**
Dreamworks Pictures	**Moses:** Val Kilmer
99 minutes	**Rameses:** Ralph Fiennes
	Zipporah: Michelle Pfeiffer
Directors: Brenda Chapman, Steve	**Miriam:** Sandra Bullock
Hickner, Simon Wells	**Aaron:** Jeff Goldblum
Executive Producer: Jeffrey Katzenberg	**Jethro:** Danny Glover
Producers: Penney Finkelman Cox, Sandra	**Seti:** Patrick Stewart
Rabins	**The Queen:** Helen Mirren
Songs: Stephen Schwartz	**Hotep:** Steve Martin
Story: Philip LaZebnik	**Huy:** Martin Short

How do you make a new film of the saga of Moses and the Exodus when it was done so superbly by Cecil B. DeMille in *The Ten Commandments*? One answer to that question is, "Don't even try." The 1975 TV miniseries *Moses the Lawgiver* (see page 211) only made the DeMille classic look better by comparison (ditto for the 2006 miniseries *The Ten Commandments*).

Along came Dreamworks, the film company founded by some of the biggest names in the entertainment industry: Steven Spielberg, Jeffrey Katzenberg, and David Geffen. (They are the "SKG" in the company's official name, Dreamworks SKG.) Dreamworks has produced some outstanding films, including some animated features that give the Disney company some serious competition. Dreamworks, being huge and rich, could afford to take a risk like doing the Moses saga in animated form. The result is a very good film and a very biblical one.

The film opens with these words: "The motion picture you are about to see is an adaptation of the Exodus story. While artistic and historical license has been taken, we believe that this film is true to the essence, values, and integrity of a story that is a cornerstone of faith for millions of people worldwide. The biblical story of Moses can be found in the Book of Exodus." An excellent beginning, and an honest one.

We see Hebrew slaves toiling away in front of sphinxes and other mammoth statues, with Egyptian taskmasters cracking their whips and yelling, "Faster!" The slaves sing to God, "Deliver us! Can you hear us cry?" A very dark Semitic-looking woman with a small boy and girl run furtively, the woman holding a newborn babe. They place the child in a basket in the river. A tender touch as the yawning babe clasps his mother's finger. The sister keeps watch along the shore. A splendidly dressed Egyptian woman finds the basket and is overjoyed. She is accompanied by a toddler whom she calls Rameses. (There is no mention of Moses's mother being brought in as a wet nurse, as in Exodus 2:6–10, or to the Egyptian woman realizing that it was a Hebrew child she was adopting.)

In depicting Moses as a "prince of Egypt," the film follows DeMille's *Ten Commandments*—and some very old Jewish traditions. The book of Exodus tells us nothing about the years between Moses's adoption and his adulthood. The tradition that he was raised as a prince of Egypt was voiced in the New Testament when the martyr Stephen spoke of Moses being "instructed in all the wisdom of the Egyptians" (Acts 7:22 ESV). The Jewish historians Philo and Josephus supply many details about these years of Moses's instruction in Egypt.

The film moves from Moses the infant to Moses the rambunctious young adult. Rameses and his adopted brother Moses race their chariots, even into the streets of a crowded city. The two are obviously bosom friends but also rivals. Some humor sneaks in: a chariot jostles a painter, who accidentally paints a ridiculous grin on the face of a pharaoh statue. Pharaoh Seti is obviously displeased with the rambunctious boys. The two court magicians, Hotep and Huy—one skinny, one fat—make their appearance. (The magicians in Exodus are unnamed, though they are called Jannes and Jambres in 2 Timothy 3:8.) Moses is mischievous enough to dump water on the two from a balcony. He is the instigator of their shenanigans, getting the more serious Rameses into trouble.

A captive Midianite girl brought in for the princes' amusement escapes from the palace. (It will turn out later that she is Zipporah, who will marry Moses.) Moses follows her, ending up in the Hebrew slaves' district. Miriam greets him as their long-lost brother. Aaron realizes this kind of talk will get them into trouble. As Aaron drags her away, she tells Moses he was set adrift in a basket in order to save him, and he should ask the "man he calls 'father'" about it. He returns to the palace, glorying in the lush life of the court. But gazing at a mural, he sees the whole story of the pharaoh's command to destroy the infants of the Israelites. The sight of infants being tossed into the jaws of crocodiles appalls him. (The animation of these hieroglyphic images coming to life is superb—and very frightening.) His father appears and explains that sacrifices had to be made, since the Hebrews were growing too numerous and potentially dangerous. And after all, "they were only slaves." This conversation is unbiblical, of course, as is the whole incident with Miriam and Aaron. Obviously the story in Exodus has gaps in it, and the movie does offer an explanation of why Moses would go down to watch "his people" at work.

Moses attacks and kills a slave driver for whipping one of the workers. (There is no mention of him hiding the man in the sand, as in Exodus 2:12.) Rameses tells Moses he can "forget" what happened, but Moses runs away into the desert.

In the desert, Moses tosses away his Egyptian jewels—but, significantly, he keeps the ring Rameses had given him. He makes his way to a well, drinking with some sheep. He chases off the men who are harassing some shepherd girls. He is made the honored guest of their father, Jethro, high priest of Midian. Jethro with his massive patriarchal beard is nicely drawn. Moses settles into life as a shepherd and the husband of Jethro's oldest daughter, Zipporah.

Moses goes looking for a lost sheep and hears a voice calling to him from a burning bush. He is told to take off his sandals. The voice of God says, "I am that I am" and that he has heard of the oppression of the Israelites. The burning bush allows for some fanciful animation. Omitted are the wonders of the leprous hand and the staff turning into a snake, though God does promise that the staff will do wondrous things. The mysterious incident of Exodus 4:24–26, Moses's near death at the hand of God, is omitted, of course.

In song, Jethro tells Moses to "look at your life through heaven's eyes," a very biblical sentiment.

Rameses, now Pharaoh, greets Moses warmly, though the magicians remind him of Moses's murder of a man. Rameses overlooks it, but Moses tells him that he must free the Hebrews. Moses's staff turns into a cobra, awing the people present, but then the two magicians call on the powers of Ra, Anubis, Horus, and the various other animal-headed gods and do some amazing tricks of their own. This is a grand excuse for some lavish animation. They sing to Moses, "You're playing with the big boys now." But Moses's snake devours the snakes of the magicians. Rameses orders the slaves' workload to be doubled. As in *The Ten Commandments*, Aaron is a mere bystander in all this, even though Exodus says he was Moses's mouthpiece.

The animators have a jolly time with the plagues: frogs, gnats, flies, death of livestock, boils, hail, locusts, and so on. Particularly effective is the "fiery" hail. But Rameses's heart is continually hardened. Part of his stubbornness is due to his old friend rejecting him. During the ninth plague, darkness, Moses warns him that something worse is coming. Rameses threatens another genocide of the Hebrews—not found in the Bible but an interesting touch.

The Hebrews mark their doorposts as Moses instructs them. The "death angel" is beautifully animated, particularly the sinister whirling light bypassing the homes where the Hebrews live. Moses shows up at the palace to find Rameses cradling his dead son. He gives Moses permission to leave.

Miriam sings the song "When You Believe," which was to win an Oscar for best song in a movie that year, with the words "There can be miracles when you believe." The Hebrews depart in a festive and thankful spirit.

Halted at the seaside, the Hebrews panic seeing the approaching Egyptian chariots. The pillar of fire appears between the troops and the Hebrews. Moses wades into the water and plants his staff in it, and the waters part—great animation. Aaron is first to go. The seabed is not flat but rocky, so the journey through is not easy. An interesting touch: in the wall of water on either side, the people can see huge fish, even a whale. The pillar of fire disappears, and Rameses spurs his men on. The waters fall down upon them, though Rameses survives, tossed up on the shore, screaming out, "Moses!"

There is no victory song as in Exodus 15, though we do see Miriam holding a tambourine (see v. 20). The story quickly moves to Mount Sinai, with Moses descending with the stone tablets of the Ten Commandments. The movie ends with no conflict, no incident of an orgy around the golden calf idol.

The older and younger pharaohs in the film are referred to as Seti and Rameses, the same names used in *The Ten Commandments*. The Bible never mentions the pharaohs' names, but scholars are fairly certain that the pharaohs of Exodus were indeed named Seti I and Rameses II.

An item that deserves mention is that most of the characters in this movie are very dark-skinned—which almost certainly was true of both the Hebrews and Egyptians at this time in history. Most biblical movies have made no attempt to "dark up" the actors to make them more true to history, but animated characters can be any shade the artists choose.

Film critic Roger Ebert of the *Chicago Sun-Times* raved about the movie, pleased that an animated film could move beyond the usual category of children's entertainment. Ebert even felt that the animation allowed the movie to improve in many ways on Cecil B. DeMille's classic *The Ten Commandments*, that somehow the parting of the sea in *The Prince of Egypt* looked more "real" than the famous scene in DeMille's film.

The movie was a huge success, even though it has much less comedy than the usual animated film. The two court magicians are threatening but also very funny, and there is some horseplay early in the film between the young Moses and Rameses. But for the most part it is very serious, and the film's success proved that animated films do not always have to be mindless fluff.

One other item worthy of note: Several Jewish and Christian religious advisors were brought in to give their input into the production. They must have served well, for the film generated no controversy and seemed to please everyone who saw it, religious or not. It remains to be seen whether Dreamworks or other Hollywood film factories will attempt another animated feature film based on the Bible.

8

A NEW MILLENNIUM, WITH *PASSION*

S ince we are only a few years into the new millennium, it is hard to look at these years objectively. Based on the mostly dismal biblical films of the 1980s and 1990s, a person might have assumed that few if any biblical films would be made in the new century, and certainly no one would have predicted that a film about the crucifixion of Jesus would be a great success. Audiences and trends are unpredictable, to say the least.

One trend left over from the last century is still with us: a fascination with "spirituality" without commitment to one particular set of beliefs. More and more people in polls describe themselves as "spiritual but not religious"—which, if you think about it, could mean darn near anything. Apparently a huge segment of the population believes there is some vague "higher power" in the world (or perhaps some other galaxy), a Someone or Something that is basically good—good, but not judgmental. And most people believe in some sort of afterlife, be it a heaven for everyone (good or evil) or being reborn on earth. In the past few years quite a few successful films have manifested this vague form of "spirituality":

The Sixth Sense, *Signs*, *Contact*, *What Lies Beneath*, *The Blair Witch Project*, *A.I.*, *What Dreams May Come*, and the Harry Potter and Lord of the Rings series. *End of Days* and *The Seventh Sign* showed there was still some life in the apocalyptic Antichrist thriller in the style of *The Omen*. (The opening credits of *End of Days* were shown imposed over the Greek text of the book of Revelation.) Television has its popular "spiritual" series, including *The Ghost Whisperer*, plus several "talk shows" involving a person who can supposedly communicate with audience members' deceased relatives. The long-running family drama *Seventh Heaven* was an inoffensive (but bland) look at the life of a minister's family. Many bestselling books served up "spirituality lite," such as *The Secret Supper*, *The Five People You Meet in Heaven*, *There's a Spiritual Solution to Every Problem*, and others. Many people are "spiritual dabblers," and probably some of those dabblers end up interested in the Bible at some point. Being interested in the Bible doesn't necessarily mean *believing* in it, however. Three big sellers in the new millennium were *The Da Vinci Code*, *The Jesus Papers* and *The Gospel of Judas*, all of them offering "revisionist" views of Jesus, catering to a centuries-old urge to prove the Bible itself misrepresents the "real" Christ.

One trend that began in the 1980s is still evident: namely, the release of almost all films in video format, meaning no individual film must ever be missed once it leaves the local theater. Some films that fared poorly in theaters do well as videos, and some video productions are never shown in theaters at all. (One film discussed later in this chapter was a theatrical spin-off from a series of popular videos aimed at preschoolers.) As I write this chapter, people in the film industry lament low attendance at theaters, overlooking the fact that people who skip the theater are still watching films on video or on cable channels. It is extremely unlikely movie theaters will cease to be, given the fact that going to a movie is a good way to get out of the house for a few hours, plus the fact that not even the hugest TV screen can compete with a theater screen.

The new millennium looked to be promising for biblical movies, for in the spring of 2000, two very fine movies about Jesus aired on television. The first, aired on Easter Sunday, was *The Miracle Maker*, done by a team of British and Russian animators, using the voices of some respected actors like Ralph Fiennes and Julie Christie. While animation doesn't sound like the ideal medium for communicating the gospel, the movie was extremely well done, reverent but not boring. (In 1999 *The Prince of Egypt* had proved that animation could be an excellent medium for communicating the Bible.) In one respect *The Miracle Maker* improved on previous movies about Jesus in showing Mary Magdalene *not* as a reformed prostitute but as a woman whom Jesus healed of her demons. The movie drew respectable ratings, and biblical movies of the new millennium were off to a promising start.

Even more popular with viewers was *Jesus*, which aired on May 14 and 21, 2000. While the movie was not nearly so long or comprehensive as *Jesus of Nazareth*, it did manage to include some Gospel stories usually not seen on film: Jesus stilling the storm, healing the Gentile woman's child, and giving the disciples power to heal and cast out demons. It also included Jesus's temptation—greatly enhanced by computer-generated images—which *Jesus of Nazareth* did not include. Most of the extrabiblical elements, such as Jesus weeping over the dead Joseph and Satan's appearance in Gethsemane, are handled well and add much to the story. In most ways the film is a worthy successor to *Jesus of Nazareth*. And in one sense it improved upon it: it humanizes Jesus more, showing him dancing at a wedding, laughing, cuddling children, and even at one point impishly playing "Who touched me?" with the disciples as they walk along. This Jesus seems to be the Son of God but is rather appealingly human also.

Jesus beat out the phenomenally popular quiz show *Who Wants to Be a Millionaire* in the ratings. It drew more than 21 million viewers and was the 1999–2000 TV season's highest-rated miniseries. For biblical movies, the new millennium looked very promising.

Jonah: A VeggieTales Movie: *Yeah, Bring the Kids*

Released October 2002	**Voices:**
Big Idea Entertainment	Phil Vischer
83 minutes	Mike Nawrocki
	Tim Hodge
Directors: Phil Vischer, Mike Nawrocki	Lisa Vischer
	Dan Anderson
	Kristen Blegen

Back in the 1970s, a comedy sketch on *The Carol Burnett Show* featured Carol as a bored housewife who claimed she wanted to be the author of a children's book about "animated vegetables." That got a hearty laugh from the audience, for no one could imagine children—or parents—taking an interest in "animated vegetables." As proof that truth is stranger than comedy sketches, VeggieTales has been a smashing success, its characters Bob the Tomato, Larry the Cucumber, Archibald Asparagus, and others known and loved by millions of children and parents. The VeggieTales video series was launched by Phil Vischer and Mike Nawrocki in 1993 with *Where's God When I'm S-Scared?* This set the tone for the series, mixing the goofy (and limbless) vegetables' comedy and songs with stories adapted from the Bible. Vischer and Nawrocki named their company Big Idea Productions, and their veggies became a smashing success with preschoolers, even earning the distinction of having the videos played on screens at the family-oriented Chuck E. Cheese's pizza restaurants. Needless to say, the video series has spun off into books, games, toys, and other products. For a Christian company that began on a shoestring, Big Idea has made quite a splash.

The popular videos made the jump to local theaters in 2002 with *Jonah: A VeggieTales Movie*, which used the comedy song/Bible story format that fans were very familiar with. The very British and very stuffy Archibald Asparagus has the title role of the reluctant prophet Jonah, who tries to run away from God but can't. He boards the ship of the Pirates Who Don't Do Anything, and the pirates (who are vegetables) later retell the Jonah saga as a flashback.

Suffice it to say that a "kid-vid" like this can't be critiqued in the same way as the other movies discussed in this book. The Bible has to get "tweaked" considerably to make it fit with the VeggieTales format of singing and clowning vegetables. In fact, some of the earlier videos in the series had to bend over backward to avoid sexual content. For example, in the VeggieTales version of the story of David's adultery with Bathsheba, nothing even remotely sexual is suggested. Ditto for the version of Potiphar's wife trying to seduce the virtuous Joseph. Fortunately, in the Jonah movie, the story could stick pretty close to the Bible, with Jonah (a stick of asparagus here!) refusing to obey God's command to preach repentance to the people of Nineveh, fleeing God (so he thinks) in a ship, then thrown overboard, swallowed by a whale, and coughed up on shore, where he wises up and decides to go preach to Nineveh.

Since the VeggieTales series was only launched in 1993, it is hard to know what moral and spiritual impact it will have on the many children exposed to it. Certainly parents are grateful for the "good, clean fun" that also manages to teach valuable moral lessons based on the Bible. We can assume—or hope—that the wiser parents will eventually expose their preschoolers to the Bible text itself so they can correct the "veggie-fied" versions in the videos. Some Christian parents have not taken to the VeggieTales, displeased with their "kidding" (pun intended) of the Bible stories, even if the producers' intentions are right. For every detractor, however, there seem to be many more devoted fans of the series.

The Jonah movie did very well in theaters, surprising the many childless people who had never heard of VeggieTales and probably thought the whole concept silly (just as many non-parents find Barney the dinosaur silly and annoying). In fact, it earned $26 million at the box office, almost double its cost, and another VeggieTales movie is scheduled for release. Most reviews praised the film's animation and humor, but one sign of the times was that some reviewers couldn't resist taking slaps at the film's "preachiness" and "air of moral superiority"—which these critics attributed to the film's connection to "the Christian Right."

What might it mean for the twenty-first century that the first theatrical movie based on the Bible was slanted toward preschool children, featured silly songs and lowbrow humor, and starred animated vegetables instead of human actors? Some might say that despite the movie's profits, it was a sign that the biblical movie had fallen on hard times. But the releases of 2003 and 2004 would be signs that the biblical film made for adults still was alive and well and perhaps even improving on the spectacles of the past in many ways.

The Gospel of John: *The Word, Verbatim*

Released September 2003
Visual Bible, International
181 minutes
Filmed in Spain

Director: Philip Saville
Screenplay: John Goldsmith
Producers: Garth H. Drabinsky, Chris Chrisafis
Photography: Miroslaw Baszak
Production Design: Don Taylor
Music: Jeff Danna

Jesus: Henry Ian Cusick
Narrator: Christopher Plummer
Peter: Daniel Kash
John the Baptist: Scott Handy
Andrew: Tristan Gemmill

John: Stuart Bunce
Nathaniel: Elliot Levey
Philip: Andrew Pieko
Nicodemus: Diego Matamoros
Mary, mother of Jesus: Diana Berriman
Thomas: Andy Velazquez
Samaritan Woman: Nancy Palk
Lame Man: David Meyer
Chief Pharisee: Richard Lintern
Mary Magdalene: Lynsey Baxter
Blind Man: Stuart Fox
Martha: Miriam Brown
Mary, Lazarus's sister: Miriam Hughes
Lazarus: Nitzan Sharron
Caiaphas: Cedric Smith
Pilate: Stephen Russell
Joseph of Arimathea: Jan Filips

Here is a film that broke new ground: a film released to theaters, based completely on one book of the Bible, with nothing omitted. Needless to say, the film was not a product of Hollywood, which would not have seen much commercial potential for it. It had the misfortune of bad timing also—being released not long before the surprise hit of 2004, Mel Gibson's much-anticipated *Passion of the Christ*. It may prove to have a long life in video format, however.

Behind the film is a Toronto-based company called Visual Bible, International, which is attempting to do what New Media Bible tried back in the late 1970s and early 1980s: film the whole Bible, or at least those parts of it that tell a story. The 1979 theatrical film *Jesus* was produced by New Media Bible and was the only Jesus movie of that decade to stick closely to Scripture. *The Gospel of John* would stick even closer.

In this situation, the "script" was already written—the Gospel itself. But screenwriter John Goldsmith, who is English, says that though the text was "given," it also had to be "reinvented" for the screen. He made choices as to what was actually spoken and what was narrated; for example, in the scene with Nicodemus, the words about God giving his only Son are narrated, not spoken by Jesus. Goldsmith says he chose to make the miracles happen off-camera, since the emphasis was not the miracle itself but its effect on people. The farewell discourses were a challenge, since

Jesus goes on talking for five chapters. Goldsmith chose to make it visually interesting by including flashbacks with the words. In places where the text says "the disciples said," he obviously had to delegate the words to one individual at a time. Connecting phrases like "he said" or "then he said to them" are eliminated. Goldsmith's resume includes adaptations of written classics for TV, notably several of Dickens's novels.

On the film's companion video, Miroslaw Baszak, the film's cinematographer, stated, "I tried to create a look that would have a certain timeless quality." Some of the scenes, such as the storm on the lake, were filmed in a studio, with computer-generated images (CGI) added later.

Don Taylor, production designer, stated that some shots of the huge temple set were actually CGI. Much of the film was shot on studio sets, not location. The "stone" walls were all styrofoam. The Sierra Nevada of Spain was used for most of the Jerusalem outdoor shooting. Over two thousand extras were employed.

Debra Hanson, the costume designer, researched what dyes would have been used in those times. The Pharisees really did wear elaborate embroidered clothing. She chose to have Jesus wear the lightest color clothes (symbolizing purity) in each shot. She learned that Jewish men covered their heads in the synagogue and that at a wedding (as at Cana) special clothes would have been worn. These clothes were not worn again in the film, however, since the disciples' everyday wear had to be simple and practical.

Actor Christopher Plummer (who played Herod in the 1977 *Jesus of Nazareth*) was narrator, and his voice has both warmth and dignity. But obviously the critical thing in this film was finding the right man to play Jesus. On the film's companion video, director Philip Saville said, "I wasn't going to look for someone who was handsome necessarily, but someone who passed as Jewish. . . . I think we found someone who had the drama, the fervor, the charisma." The choice was Scottish actor Henry Ian Cusick, who has worked with the Royal Shakespeare Company. He was born in 1969, so he was exactly the right age to play Jesus (since Luke 3:23 says Jesus was "about thirty"). Cusick says he saw Jesus as very manly and tough and a great public speaker, someone not intimidated by mobs. A frail, passive character, he says, could not have traveled so much and confronted people.

The film opens with these words: "The Gospel of John was written two generations after the crucifixion of Jesus Christ. It is set in a time when the Roman empire controlled Jerusalem. Although crucifixion was the preferred Roman method of punishment, it was not one sanctioned by Jewish law. Jesus and all his early followers were Jewish. The Gospel reflects a period of unprecedented polemic and antagonism between the emerging church and the religious establishment of the Jewish people. This film is a faithful presentation of that Gospel." Obviously the producers wished to defuse any accusations of a Jesus film being anti-Semitic. (Garth Drabinsky, one of the film's producers, is Jewish, incidentally.) The claim that John's Gospel was written two generations after Jesus is open to debate, since most scholars now believe it was probably written by the apostle John within thirty years of the events it describes. Several Bible scholars were consulted in making the film, and apparently they still held to the view that the Gospel was written long after the time of Jesus.

> When the Bible is going to be committed verbatim to film, an obvious question is, *which translation*? The American Bible Society's Good News Bible (also called Today's English Version), published in 1976, may seem an odd choice, since it is by no means one of the most popular versions. But in fact, it may have been a sensible choice, since so many of the versions on the market seem to be the favorites of either evangelicals or liberals—and the Good News Bible is not generally associated with either. It is also very clear and modern, and it makes no attempt to sound "King Jamesy."

The film has no credits. The story opens with the narration and the film's title over a shot of the sun over a seashore. A ragged John is baptizing by immersion in the river. The first shot of Jesus is his sandals as he makes his way to John. The Pharisees' garments contrast greatly with John's brown rags. John's actual baptism of Jesus is seen as a flashback, since the Gospel does not recount the baptism itself. Jesus's radiant face when he emerges from the water is very striking, with the light reflecting off the water as a kind of halo. Throughout the film, the narrator provides the bits of information that are parenthetical in the Gospel.

The wedding guests at Cana are very jolly, nearly intoxicated. Mary, interestingly, is dressed in blue, as in Catholic tradition. Jesus and his disciples are dressed in finery (relatively speaking), not their everyday garb. The servant's dumbstruck face at seeing the wine poured out of water jars is a nice touch.

Unlike in the other Gospels, Jesus goes to Jerusalem very early in the story. The cleansing of the temple occurs at this point. Close-ups of Jesus's eyes show his anger at the money changers before he goes almost berserk while the priests run about in alarm. Nicodemus is present at the cleansing and shows a smile of admiration. This segues into the next scene in which he visits Jesus. When Jesus speaks of the wind blowing, a literal breeze passes over them. The narrator provides the "God's only Son" passage, John 3:16.

The Samaritan woman at the well wears purple and is slightly sluttish looking, appropriate for what the Gospel says about her marital life. She is saucy in their first exchange. She runs away in alarm when the disciples approach.

Jesus and the disciples are walking some barren hills when the Roman official rides up on horseback, begging Jesus to heal his child. There is a moment of tension when Jesus says to him, "Go"—hesitation—"your son will live." The man's servants, also on horseback, meet him on the road. All the Romans on horseback add some visual interest, their red capes contrasting with the barren hills.

The incident of the man in the pool (see John 5) has rarely been shown in films. The pitiful man on his mat is a pathetic sight, not only lame and dressed in rags but also with his face contorted in pain. (The Good News Bible omits the mention of the angel stirring the waters, putting it in a footnote. The movie also omits it.)

Jesus is sitting on the temple steps when the Pharisees all close in on him together; it is a beautifully composed shot. Jesus is surrounded by them. He finally stands, defiant. Jesus seldom stands still for long while he is speaking, usually moving about, sometimes literally getting in people's faces. In this film he almost always carries a staff, using it for visual impact. The camera is very mobile in this movie.

The scene of the feeding teems with extras—not five thousand, perhaps, but it almost looks like it. The actual miracle of multiplying the loaves is not shown; Jesus simply hands the disciples one basket after another.

The computer-generated storm on the lake is frightening, as is the figure of Jesus when he is seen walking on the waters. The sun breaks through the cloud when Jesus sets foot in the boat.

John's Gospel is full of "I am" speeches by Jesus. These simply don't work well on film. They sound egomaniacal, and you wonder how the crowd could hear such talk and not respond with laughter immediately. But just when the scene with Jesus saying "I am the bread of life" begins to seem silly, some mockers denounce him, saying he is just the son of Joseph.

> A clever visual device: in Jesus's Jerusalem speeches, one particular Pharisee (Richard Lintern), tall and dark with a sort of turban, is the one who confronts him again and again. The Bible never individualizes the Pharisees, but having the same one appear again and again is a useful device.

The Good News Bible has not been used word for word but has been in many places made gender-inclusive; for example, John 6:56 has been changed from "Whoever eats my flesh and drinks my blood lives in me, and I live in him" to "All those who eat my flesh and drink my blood live in me, and I in them." And John 7:51 was changed from "we cannot condemn a man before hearing him" to "we cannot condemn people before hearing them." In John 12:43, "The approval of men" is changed to "human approval."

In places where the text says that "the people" said something, the movie individualizes it—one person speaks, sometimes followed by another, but always individuals, since having all the people say the same words would look ridiculous.

In the scene of the woman caught in adultery, the priests' servant shoves her to the ground after everyone has walked away. She looks so tearful and grateful that she seems about to kiss Jesus in gratitude. The woman is definitely not Mary Magdalene, a mistake other films have made.

Jesus's words about spiritual freedom (see John 8:31–57) are spoken outdoors to temple workmen. This is appropriate, since the scene ends with them picking up stones to kill him.

Just before the healing of the blind man, garish color fills the screen as a litter carrying a rich woman passes by, all gold and red. A stark contrast then is the blind beggar dressed in gray and brown. It is a bit jarring to see Jesus spitting into the mud in his hand. This is a good scene, with the man's hands shaking as he washes in the pool and gradually realizes he can see. The blind man seeing his aged parents for the first time is very touching; they all seem on the verge of tears.

The scene with Martha and Mary after Lazarus's death is very touching. Jesus's tears seem natural and unforced. When Lazarus is raised from the tomb, we see first his shadow on the rocks. After this great miracle, the priests determine to kill Jesus. The gray-bearded Caiaphas is appropriately nasty when he tells the council, "What fools you are!" Mary anoints Jesus's feet with perfume—meaning this is the one film that makes it clear that the anointing was her gesture of gratitude for the raising of Lazarus, at least in John's version.

Mary Magdalene is not mentioned in John's Gospel until 19:25, at the crucifixion, but the movie is obviously correct in showing her as a follower much earlier in the story. Luke 8:2 says that some women traveled with the disciples and specifically names Mary Magdalene.

The disciples are jarred to see Jesus strip to his loincloth and then wrap a towel around his waist. Their feet are realistically dirty. During the "farewell discourse," Judas is appropriately sullen and broody. Poor, simple Peter almost weeps when Jesus predicts his denial. Part of the farewell discourse is set on the roof of the house, with the hills and stars visible. They leave there, for as John 14:31 has it, he says, "Come, let us go from this place." When Jesus talks of being the true vine, they are in a literal vineyard. Much of this part of the discourse is spent walking by night, some of the men carrying torches. When Jesus speaks of persecution, there is a sepia flashback to the times he was nearly stoned. Even with all this and with cuts from one disciple's face to another, this section still drags.

As the discourse draws to an end, tension is built by cutting to Judas approaching with the soldiers. The soldiers do not literally fall to the ground (see John 18:6), which might have looked silly, but take a couple of steps back.

When Pilate and the other Romans appear, there is much scarlet on the screen. Pilate is a dour character but not cruel. His receiving room is all gold and red, very attractively contrasting with Jesus's plain white robe. He is taller than Jesus. He is amazed when the crowd asks for Barabbas instead of Jesus. Instead of the flogging, we see the Roman soldier wielding the whip. Jesus is on the point of collapse when Pilate has him brought out. Pilate's face registers surprise when the Jewish leaders shout that they have no king but the emperor.

Since there is no dialogue with the two thieves in John's Gospel, their crosses are nowhere near Jesus's. The two thieves scream when their legs are broken. All three of them hang far out from their crosses—out more than down. John weeps when he sees Jesus's side pierced. This is important because John 19 mentions it and states that "the one who saw this happen has spoken of it, so that you also may believe. What he said is true" (v. 35).

One oddity: according to the Gospel, Mary Magdalene goes to the tomb "when it is still dark," but it is clearly broad daylight. Couldn't they have made it appear to be just after sunup? This scene would've been more dramatic in dimmer light. And it is puzzling again why they filmed the last scene by the shore in broad daylight, since chapter 21 says it is just after sunrise, and dim light would explain why they did not recognize Jesus immediately.

The last image in the film is John's face, since "he is the disciple who spoke of these things, the one who also wrote them down" (21:24). It has long been accepted—though it isn't absolutely certain—that John was the "beloved disciple" mentioned several times in the Gospel.

Throughout the film, the acting is consistently good, and Henry Ian Cusick certainly has charisma, seeming more fiery and passionate than some of the more "laid-back" film Jesuses like Max Von Sydow (*The Greatest Story Ever Told*) and H. B. Warner (*The King of Kings*). At times, however, he seems almost too abrasive. And, as already noted, he has to deliver the various "I am" speeches in John's Gospel ("I am the bread of life," "I am the resurrection and the life," "I am the good shepherd"), which work well on paper but sound like egotistical ranting on-screen. No movie Jesus could ever please everyone, of course.

The movie is very long, although in video format (as with any movie), it lends itself to taking breaks. Many church groups are already viewing the film in Bible study settings, pausing now and then to discuss the Gospel and the film. The video edition contains special features, interspersing clips from the film with interviews with the Visual Bible's advisory committee of scholars. This section runs 100 minutes. It is very helpful, providing historical background on the times of Jesus. One of the scholars is Jewish.

When Mel Gibson's *Passion of the Christ* premiered in February 2004, few people were even aware that *The Gospel of John* had been released. *John* had technically been released in September 2003, since producer Garth Drabinsky arranged to have it screened at the Toronto Film Festival that month. But it was not generally released in U.S. theaters until January 2004, when theater owners and audiences were already bracing for *The Passion* in February. Certainly *The Passion* had the advantage of Gibson's name recognition, and all the prerelease controversy was free advertising, which paid off immensely. Both films are likely to have a long shelf life, and *John* is already selling well on Christian websites, along with Visual Bible's releases of *Matthew* and *Acts* (both of which use the New International Version of the Bible, the one favored by most evangelicals).

The Passion of the Christ: *Mel's Cross*

Released February 2004
Icon Productions
126 minutes
Filmed in Italy

Director: Mel Gibson
Screenplay: Benedict Fitzgerald and Mel Gibson
Executive Producer: Enzo Sisti
Photography: Caleb Deschanel
Music: John Debney
Makeup and Visual Effects: Keith Vanderlaan

Jesus: Jim Caviezel
Mary, Jesus's mother: Maia Morgenstern

John: Hristo Jivkov
Peter: Francesco De Vito
Mary Magdalene: Monica Bellucci
Caiaphas: Mattia Sbragia
Annas: Toni Bertorelli
Judas: Luca Lionello
Pilate: Hristo Naumov Shotov
Abenader: Fabio Sartor
Satan: Rosalinda Celentano
Claudia: Claudia Gerini
Cassius: Giovanni Capalbo
Simon of Cyrene: Jarreth Merz

Theological Consultant and Aramaic/Latin Translator: William J. Fulco, S.J., PhD

"I've had my career, and I'm bored with it. I created a secular utopia for myself in Hollywood, but it was empty. There are more important things. Civilization was changed forever by Christ. Whether you're a believer or not, his death affects you." These words were spoken by superstar actor-director Mel Gibson to an

Jesus Christ and superstar: actor-director-producer-writer Mel Gibson directing Jim Caviezel in the very controversial and very profitable 2004 film *The Passion of the Christ*.

audience of five thousand pastors at a prerelease screening of *The Passion of the Christ*. Some of them must have been awed to hear one of the most recognizable men in the world say he was "bored" with his phenomenal career. Others might have remembered that this was the same man who had played an incredibly foul-mouthed, violent character in the *Lethal Weapon* films and who had bared his behind in several others. Gibson and his *Passion* were proof that life is full of pleasant surprises.

One surprise was that when the film was released in February 2004, it was number one at the box office that weekend. Even more surprising was that after several weeks it went *back* to number one—on Easter weekend, of course. By all logic, the film should have failed—no big-name stars, a blatantly religious film in a blatantly secular age, dialogue in ancient languages, an R rating. The only thing going for it was Gibson's name, and it was radically different from anything he'd done before. Gibson said in many interviews that he expected the film to be "savaged by the critics"—and it was, though most admitted it had good things in it. Gibson also said the film could have been a "career-killer"—and an asset-killer too, since he sank $25 million of his own money into the $30 million film. He gambled and won.

In an interview with *The New Yorker* magazine, Gibson stated, "We're a bunch of . . . idiots and failures and creeps. But we're called to the divine. We're called to be better than our nature would have us be."[1] He observed that no Jesus film had ever properly captured the delicate balance between the horror and the beauty of Christ's sacrifice. Gibson didn't want an

> The many critics who railed against the movie's graphic violence, even calling it "obscene," really missed the point: such horrible violence done to an innocent prophet really *is* obscene—especially if he happens to be the Son of God.

ethereal depiction; he wanted to transport viewers to the foot of the cross. He wanted twenty-first-century audiences to understand all that was implied in the Gospels' bare words "They crucified him"—words that needed no explaining to first-century people, since most of them had seen men agonizing on crosses and knew just how bloody and excruciating the death was.

The film opens with the logo for Icon, Gibson's production company, accompanied by thunder. No credits are shown. On a black screen are these words: "He was wounded for our transgressions, crushed for our iniquities, by His wounds we are healed. Isaiah 53, 700 B.C."

The movie's first scene is, as some critics noticed, shot like a horror film: full-moon sky, an olive grove (the Garden of Gethsemane), Jesus standing and praying. He awakens Peter, James, and John and asks if they could not stay awake with him. They ask if they should call the other disciples; Jesus says he does not want them to see him like this. Then we see Judas and the priests agree on thirty pieces of silver as the betrayal price. Caiaphas, the high priest, flings the bag at Judas (in slow motion) and the pieces scatter. One of the priests' soldiers tells Judas to lead them to the spot.

Back in the garden, Jesus literally sweats blood (see Luke 22:44). The three disciples have never seen him in such a state before. The androgynous, pale, sinister Satan (played by a woman) appears, telling Jesus that no individual can carry the burden of the world's sin, for it is too heavy. Jesus prays using the words of Psalm 31, one of the "deliver me" psalms. He prays, "Let this chalice pass me by." (The use of "chalice" instead of "cup" puzzled some non-Catholic viewers.) Satan asks, "Who is your father? Who are you?" A serpent slithers from under Satan's cloak, then rubs against Jesus's hand. Jesus stomps its head, fulfilling the prophecy of Genesis 3:15. Immediately soldiers appear. Judas attempts to run, but one of the soldiers pushes him back, and he moves forward and kisses Jesus. The soldiers attempt to seize the three disciples. James and John get away; Peter resists, pulling out his sword and cutting one man's ear. Jesus is still while everyone else is in motion. Jesus heals the wounded man, who is obviously frightened at first that this man they came to arrest will hurt him, not heal him. Jesus calls to Peter, reminding him that those who live by the sword die by the sword. Peter drops the sword. As a preview of what is to come, the men beat and abuse Jesus, though he offers no resistance at all.

In a house somewhere in Jerusalem, Jesus's mother, Mary, awakens, disturbed. John bursts in and reports that they have seized Jesus. Along the way to Caiaphas's house, the soldiers slap and kick Jesus. Falling, Jesus sees Judas, who has visions of demons lurching at him. He follows to the high priest's house, as does Peter. (By fifteen minutes into the film, Jesus's face is already beaten and bloody and will remain so to the end, except for flashbacks.)

There is a flashback to Jesus working as a carpenter in Mary's house. It is a sweet scene, with Jesus joking with his mother about the very tall table made for a rich man and Mary insisting he take off his dirty apron and wash his hands before eating.

Pilate looks into his bedroom, where his wife tosses fitfully in her sleep. Pilate's head soldier, Abenader, reports that "Caiaphas has had some prophet arrested . . . some Galilean" and that the Pharisees hate him.

Annas, Caiaphas's father-in-law and former high priest, asks Jesus what line of kings he is descended from, and Caiaphas says he is merely the son of some obscure carpenter. An accuser is brought in and says Jesus casts out demons by the power of Satan. Another says he threatened to destroy the temple. But one council member, Joseph of Arimathea, sees contradictions in the accusations. Another man (Nicodemus) protests the proceedings at the late hour and says the whole proceedings are a travesty, but the priests force him out. But when Jesus is asked flatly if he is the Messiah, he replies bluntly, "I am . . . and you will see the Son of Man seated at the right hand of power and coming on the clouds of heaven." Caiaphas shouts, "Blasphemy!" and tears his robe. The council calls for his death. Caiaphas slaps Jesus and spits in his face; the others follow. Judas watches, disturbed, as does Peter. As they lead Jesus out, some people identify Peter as a follower of Jesus, but Peter denies who he is. As Peter screams out, "I've never seen him before," his eyes meet Jesus's. We see a flashback to the Last Supper, where Peter swears he will do anything for Jesus, even follow him to death, but Jesus predicts he will deny him three times that very night. After his denials, Peter weeps.

Judas tries to give the priests back the silver. They are not concerned about his remorse. He flings the money at them. In a surreal scene, two street children question what is wrong with Judas, and he sees them as demons, biting and clawing him. The next morning these children and others are still pursuing him, claiming he is "cursed." In their midst he sees Satan. Suddenly they all vanish. He sees a piece of rope tied to the head of a dead horse, abuzz with flies. He uses the rope to hang himself above the carcass. This is one film that makes no attempt at all to "explain" Judas's betrayal—as in the Gospels, he simply does it, the "why" not being important.

Pilate's wife tells her husband, "Don't condemn this Galilean; he's holy." Pilate contemptuously refers to "that filthy rabble out there." (Several of the Romans have shaved heads, including Pilate, which is pretty unhistorical.) The priests refer to Pilate by the title "consul," which is probably incorrect, though at one point Annas calls him "governor." (Pilate's actual title was "prefect.") Pilate's first words to the priests are, "Do you always punish your people before they're judged?" Pilate reminds them that the people hailed Jesus as a prophet only a few days earlier, so why do they now want him dead? Pilate's body language clearly says he detests the priests. He has Jesus brought in and orders his men out. Interestingly, he offers Jesus a drink. "Are you the king of the Jews?" he asks. Jesus replies, "My kingdom is not of this world."

Pilate reports to the priests that he finds no fault in Jesus. Then Pilate sends him to Herod, since he is a Galilean. Herod is a pudgy, effete sybarite, wearing eyeliner and putting on a ridiculous wig when Jesus is brought in. His mincing entourage finds the whole interview very funny. The priests present are irked to see him so flippant. Herod wants to see a miracle, then declares, "Take this stupid fool out of my sight—he's crazy." He thinks Jesus is no danger at all. As in Luke 23, Jesus says not a word to Herod.

Pilate and the Romans speak Latin; the Jews speak Aramaic. This is one major historical flaw in the film. Unless there was an interpreter present, they would have spoken to each other in Greek, the common language of the eastern part of the Roman empire.

Claudia, matronly and stately, comforts Pilate, who laments his eleven years of putting down rebellions. He fears being ratted on to Caesar if he does not crush Jesus. The only truth Pilate knows is that he must save himself. A Roman soldier reports that Jesus is back, not condemned by Herod. Pilate reports to the crowd that he will not condemn Jesus either. Pilate is agitated by the crowd's potential, so he orders his soldiers to take positions between him and the crowd. Then he offers to release a prisoner. Barabbas, a snaggle-toothed, brutal character, is brought in, also in chains. The high priest calls out, "Free Barabbas!" and the chanting is taken up by the fickle crowd. We see, fleetingly, that there are hordes of priests in Jerusalem, which was true. Barabbas walks through the crowd, disgusting even the priest who called for his release. Briefly the murderer and the innocent man make eye contact. The irony: Barabbas really was a dangerous revolutionary (see Luke 23:17–19), while Jesus was clearly not. The priests call for Jesus's crucifixion. Pilate tells them, no, he will flog Jesus instead.

He orders his men to make it severe but not to kill Jesus. The two Roman soldiers, both with shaved heads, are clearly jubilant at a flogging. Jesus, seeing them ready their rods, prays for strength. Clearly these lashes hurt. Some of the priests turn away from the spectacle, though Caiaphas and Annas remain. Satan walks behind them, with a subdued smirk, and briefly is seen over Annas's shoulder. Jesus seems to be on the verge of collapse. After the beating with rods comes the actual scourging. Jesus's hands quiver in anticipation. Before the soldiers begin, one dangles the studded cords in front of Jesus's face. Mary watches tearfully, and we see many of the watchers wince in pain. The scourgers seem to hope that one of their blows will kill Jesus. Both delight in being splattered with blood. Lying on the pavement, still enduring the scourging, Jesus sees Satan carrying a leering demon child. Meaning what? Making a mockery of Jesus's being the Son of God, perhaps?

> In old versions of the Bible, John's Gospel (18:40) calls Barabbas a "robber," a translation of the Greek *lestes*, but newer versions are probably correct in using "revolutionary," since *lestes* was often used for a Zealot.

We see a flashback to Jesus washing the disciples' feet the night before while reminding them that they will all endure persecution, but the Helper will come: "If they persecuted me, they will persecute you."

Pilate's faithful chief soldier Abenader rushes in, reminding them that they must stop, since Jesus must not be killed. Jesus cannot walk at this point but is dragged out, leaving a trail of blood. While Jesus is barely able to sit up, one of the soldiers plants the crown of thorns on his head, pushing it into his brow with a staff. Clearly this is their own doing, not Pilate's. They mock him as "your majesty, king of the worms." They put an old robe on him and a reed in his hand, then spit wine at him.

> Gibson has released an "edited" version of the film, with eight minutes of the worst violence cut. Most of those eight minutes are from the scene with the rods and scourge. Even with the eight minutes cut, the film is still awash in blood.

A flashback shows Jesus writing in the sand when the woman taken in adultery was about to be stoned. The people walk away, leaving their stones. The woman reaches out and touches Jesus's foot. We then realize that the woman is Mary Magdalene.

Pilate is appalled at Jesus's appearance, as is the crowd. He says, "Behold the man." But immediately the priests call out, "Crucify him!" Pilate protests, "Isn't this enough? Look at him!" Caiaphas immediately cries out, "Crucify him!" Pilate is perplexed. He reminds Jesus he has the power of life or death. Jesus tells him that power is from above and that the one who delivered him to Pilate is guilty of the greater sin. Then the priest delivers the crowning blow: if Pilate does not crucify Jesus, he is no friend of Caesar. Pilate washes his hands, saying, "It is you who crucify him, not I." Gibson had filmed a scene in which Caiaphas said the biblical words, "His blood be on us and on our children." But Gibson did not include the scene, fearing the accusations of anti-Semitism would be too intense.

A flashback to the Last Supper shows the disciples washing their hands before the meal. The contrast between Jesus smiling at the disciples and the bloodied face of Jesus next to Pilate is stark.

As Jesus and the two thieves are led out, already one of them is taunting him. As Jesus passes through the streets, he recalls Palm Sunday. He sees Satan amongst the faces of the crowd. Mary is watching on one side, Satan on the other. Jesus falls, shoved by one of the soldiers, who then beats him. The soldiers never cease

When the film was released in February 2004, *Newsweek* magazine ran a cover article titled "Who Really Killed Jesus?"—a question that has vexed filmmakers since Cecil B. DeMille in the 1920s, since any film that places the responsibility on the Jews will always provoke cries of anti-Semitism. *Newsweek* called Gibson's film a "powerful but troubling movie" and made the point—a valid one—that Pilate is seen in a very favorable light, even though in ancient histories he is described as inflexible, stubborn, and cruel. Obviously the film was following the Gospels, which do show Pilate as better than the secular histories made him out to be. Even bad men have days of sound judgment.

taunting him. Some of the bystanders pelt him with stones. He falls a second time, with the cross landing on him. Mary, nearby, recalls him falling as a child, with her rushing to his aid. Now she does the same, rushing to him in spite of the crowd. It is the last time they will touch. One of the Roman soldiers is touched by this scene.

Jesus falls a third time, and the lead soldier orders the others to cease, since obviously Jesus can't go on. One of them orders a bystander to carry the cross. The man refuses, but then women bystanders tell him that he should help a holy man. This is Simon of Cyrene (see Luke 23:26).

A young woman offers the fallen Jesus a cup of water. She also wipes his face. This is the Veronica of Catholic tradition. A soldier brutally slaps the cup from her hand and orders her away. Simon protests their brutality. One soldier spits out the word "Jew!" at Simon. As Jesus continues to fall, Simon urges him on, sympathetically.

Those who accuse the movie of being anti-Semitic should note: the depiction of the Romans makes us despise *their* anti-Semitism, even if the priests are shown in a bad light. The women of Jerusalem, as in the Bible, are clearly sympathetic to Jesus.

Jesus carries a "full cross," which is probably not historically correct, since only the horizontal timber would've been carried. Interestingly, the two thieves carry only the horizontals. Perhaps the producers knew that the audience would expect Jesus to be carrying the full cross through the streets.

Seeing the hill, Jesus flashes back to giving the Sermon on the Mount, when he spoke the words about loving one's enemies and persecutors. Then there is a flashback to the Last Supper, of Jesus breaking bread. Jesus speaks the words, "No greater love than this, that a man lay down his life for his friends."

At Golgotha, Jesus is so wounded that one arm has to be stretched in order to nail it down. We hear the arm being wrenched from the shoulder socket. At this point he says, "Father, forgive them." The soldiers go about their business like they are building a table, not dealing with a human being. The brutes drop the cross twice, sending Jesus into more agony. Obviously every small movement of the cross causes intense pain.

One thief, in pain but nowhere near as bloody as Jesus, taunts him. The Romans find this highly amusing. Caiaphas comes to the cross with the same taunt, daring Jesus to come down from the cross. The other priests mock him also (see Matthew 27:41–42). Jesus again says, "They know not what they do." As Caiaphas walks away, the other thief calls to him, "Listen, he prays for you." He then reminds the nasty thief that they deserve their punishment, but Jesus does not: "I have sinned and my punishment is just. . . . Remember me, Lord, when you enter your kingdom." Jesus promises him that he will be with him in paradise that day. But the other thief laughs in mockery. A crow lights on his cross and pecks at his eye—not biblical but an interesting touch.

Caiaphas and Mary make eye contact as he rides away. Cassius, the soldier who had been touched by Mary's devotion earlier, allows her and John near the cross. She can only touch his feet. Jesus says, "I thirst," and one soldier raises a sponge to him on the tip of a spear. Jesus commits Mary to John's keeping. The sky has become almost black with clouds. Jesus calls out, "My God, my God, why have you forsaken me?" Then, "It is accomplished"—which is the perfect translation. Then he says, "Father, into your hands I commend my spirit," he groans, and his head falls forward. We see a distant aerial view—a "God's-eye view" of the scene—then in slow motion a drop (God's tear?) falls to the ground and there is an earthquake, which rattles the Romans (see Matthew 27:54). Pilate even feels it in his palace, and it causes major damage in the temple.

In a kind of surreal landscape, Satan screams in agony. Clearly it was his hope that Jesus would not be crucified. His appearances throughout the ordeal must have been intended to make Jesus change his plan. (Some people who saw the film in theaters claimed that this scene passes so quickly that it appeared Satan was screaming in triumph. Having played it back several times on video, I can assure them that, no, this is not triumph but rage.)

Mary cradles the dead Jesus—a sight familiar from Michelangelo's *Pieta* sculpture. Briefly we see a close-up of the crown of thorns and the three nails that were removed from his body. There is no burial scene. The screen goes dark and we next see, from the inside of the tomb, the stone being rolled away, the grave clothes settling down to rest after being emptied—"deflated," as it were. We see Jesus, no longer bloody but quite hale and hearty, even though we see the nail hole in his hand (see John 20:20–27). The crucifixion scene was filmed with a "cold" filter, giving things a chilly bluish cast, but in the final shot, Jesus's resurrected body is bathed in warm light. The film ends. Biblically, this is perfect—the resurrection is the divine "payoff," and though the audience experienced discomfort watching the film (nothing compared to what Jesus himself endured), there is a sigh of relief—after the horror comes new life.

The film was given an R rating because of its graphic violence. It is indeed difficult to watch at times, as Gibson intended. It is a horror movie, but it shows a horror that actually happened. The "monsters" here are human beings, not demons or aliens. Satan, played by a woman, was certainly the most bone-chilling Satan ever seen on-screen.

The other actors were well chosen. Peter is burly and bluff and emotional. Judas looks sneaky and, later, guilt-stricken. The actress playing Satan is wonderfully sinister. Jim Caviezel, who played Jesus, was chosen by Gibson for his staunch Catholic beliefs. For the role as Jesus, his hairline was raised, he wore a prosthetic nose, and his blue eyes were digitally changed to brown on film. The cross he carried weighed 150 pounds, and during one of his falls he suffered a shoulder separation. For much of the movie his face, chest, and back are covered in fake blood and wounds, though realistic enough that the film's makeup received an Academy Award nomination.

Mary, Jesus's mother, is given a much larger role here than in any other biblical movie—a large role based on the brief mention in John's Gospel that she was present at the cross (see 19:25–27). The large role for Mary no doubt pleased Catholics, but it certainly did not keep most evangelicals away. (One does not have to be a Catholic to appreciate maternal love, obviously.) In the film Peter and John both refer to her as "mother." While the Gospels hint at a certain distance between Mary and her son during his ministry (see Matt. 12:46–47), clearly their differences had been settled or forgotten at the time of Jesus's crucifixion. Interestingly, the other three Gospels make no mention of his mother, only that Mary Magdalene and other women followers watched "from a distance." Incidentally, Maia Morgenstern, the Jewish actress who played Mary, was only six years older than the actor playing Jesus.

Regarding charges of anti-Semitism: None of the Gospels tries to excuse the Romans for their part in the drama. Crucifixion was a Roman punishment, not a Jewish one. Despite a somewhat favorable depiction of Pilate, Pilate's wife, and a couple of Roman soldiers, Pilate did assent to the execution, so he bears a huge responsibility, even if he did "wash his hands" of it. The Jewish authorities, not Jews in general, urged the death penalty. In reviewing the film, the *New York Times* stated that if the film seemed anti-Semitic, it was no more so than the sources—the Bible, that is.[2]

Mel Gibson reserved for himself a small role in the film: in the scene of the nails, it is Gibson's hand that drives the nail in, in keeping with his conviction that each of us caused Jesus's death.

Regarding the script, Gibson and writer Benedict Fitzgerald took a real risk with the decision to have the actors speak Aramaic and Latin. By doing so, however, the film avoided one problem that plagues every movie set in ancient times: what sort of accent should the actors have? *The Last Temptation of Christ* served as a fairly recent example of American accents jarring the ear of audiences. By having the actors speak the actual words the people probably spoke, the accent problem was solved. (Jim Caviezel, who played Jesus, was one of the few Americans in the cast, incidentally.)

The movie opened in theaters on Ash Wednesday, February 25, 2004. Even before it opened, accusations of "obscene" violence and anti-Semitism were in the air. But most people who actually saw the movie were touched. Billy Graham, representing evangelical Protestants, said he was "moved to tears" by the film and said, "I doubt if there has ever been a more graphic and moving representation of Jesus's death and resurrection."[3] In that he was correct. In writing this book, I viewed most of the earlier films showing Jesus's crucifixion, and I can only say they fall woefully short of showing the reality of crucifixion. We have gradually grown accustomed to violence on-screen, and the graphic realism seen

The accusations of anti-Semitism thrown at Gibson and his film were resurrected in July 2006 when the superstar was arrested in California for speeding and drunk driving. After being stopped by the police, Gibson spewed profanity and made some anti-Semitic remarks, for which he later apologized profusely.

in *The Passion* would never have been allowed in the years *King of Kings* or *The Greatest Story Ever Told* were released. Truth be told, the critics who obsessed about the film's violence were probably more put off by the fact that it was a blatantly religious film, but they didn't wish to sound intolerant of religion—evidenced by the fact that some of the same critics who thought *The Passion* too violent praised the violence of films like *Pulp Fiction* and *Kill Bill*.

In the online version of *Time* magazine, movie critic Richard Corliss wrote, "Mel Gibson's first achievement in *The Passion of the Christ* is to strip the biblical epic of its encrusted sanctimony and show biz. It takes hard men to work this Holy Land."[4] In the print version of *Time*, Corliss gave the film a mixed review, titled "The Goriest Story Ever Told."[5]

Interestingly, one magazine that called the film's violence "obscene" was the liberal *Christian Century*, which also accused the film of being anti-Semitic. In fact, the magazine stated that the movie was so horribly violent that the rating should have been not R but NC-17, today's equivalent of an X rating.[6] On the other hand, *Today's Christian*, an evangelical magazine, featured Gibson in its March–April 2004 issue and lavished praise on the film. The article noted that Gibson was a traditionalist Catholic, not an evangelical, and that in his personal life he had some "rough edges" (don't we all?). Still, he is a "passionate believer" who believes his life has been truly changed by the cross of Christ.[7]

A historical note: In 1919 a Roman Catholic group in the U.S. produced *The Eternal Light*, about the life of Jesus. It was screened in Boston but shut down by the state police because it was considered too violent. As the book of Ecclesiastes says, there is "nothing new under the sun" (1:9).

It might be useful here to let Gibson speak for himself. This quotation is from his foreword to a book of still photographs from the film:

> People often ask me why I wanted to make a film about the Passion of Our Lord. . . . [It] had its genesis during a time in which I found myself trapped with feelings of terrible, isolated emptiness. . . . The only effective resource for me was prayer. I asked God for his help. It was during this period of meditation and prayer that I first con-

ceived the idea of making a film about the Passion. I began to look at the work of some of the great artists who had drawn inspiration from the same story. . . . It is one thing to paint one moment of the Passion and be true to it, it is quite another to dramatize the entire mysterious event. . . . I wanted the effort to be a testament to the infinite love of Jesus the Christ, which has saved, and continues to save, many the world over. . . .

The film is not meant as a historical documentary, nor does it claim to have assembled all the facts. But it does enumerate those described in relevant Holy Scripture. . . .

My new hope is that *The Passion of the Christ* will help many more people recognize the power of His love and let Him help them to save their own lives.[8]

> Not since the 1966 film *The Bible . . . In the Beginning* had a biblical film been among the top-grossing films of the year.

Cynics might doubt the sincerity of such words, claiming they were aimed to catch the interest of Christians and make them want to purchase the video of the film. But Gibson's sincerity is hard to doubt, particularly given the risk he took with the film. The gamble paid off handsomely, however. It was the third-highest-grossing movie of 2004, and the presales of the video were the largest in history. The film ranks among the top ten (or at least top thirty, depending which authority you consult) moneymaking movies in history, when adjusted for inflation. For a film with subtitles, dialogue in Aramaic and Latin, and no major stars, this is quite an achievement. Part of *The Passion*'s success, of course, was that many people who had not paid for a movie ticket in years lined up to see it. In a sense it benefited from the lack of biblical movies in the past two decades.

Gibson's peers in the film industry did not take the movie to heart. True, it was nominated for three Academy Awards (makeup, music, and photography), but it won none. It is hard for fans of the film to imagine that Gibson was not nominated for best director or that the superb (often chilling) photography did not win an award. Gibson's use of flashbacks in the film was both artful and theologically sound—flashing back from the hill of Golgotha to the Sermon on the Mount, for example, and from the child Jesus stumbling to the adult Jesus falling under the cross.

One tribute to the film's great success was the decision by CBS to re-air in May 2004 its *Jesus* miniseries from 2000. But probably the best tribute of all is the "tear duct" tribute: many people who saw the film (this author included) wept. Few films in recent history have caused audiences to become so emotionally engaged in what happened on the screen. Numerous people testify to being converted due to seeing this film, and other stories report lukewarm believers experiencing a renewal of faith.

There are not a lot of Mel Gibsons around—stars with clout (and money) and the drive to put the Bible on screen. But at least the film sent the world a message: people will pay money for—and even invest their emotions in—a film that tries to do justice to a story with spiritual depth.

Aftermath of *The Passion*

In pop culture, success breeds imitation. Gibson's successful film sent people the message that "religion sells," a message that TV producers heard loud and clear. NBC aired the six-part miniseries *Revelations*, written and produced by David Seltzer, who had written the script for the successful 1976 film *The Omen*. Aired in April and May 2005, *Revelations* was essentially an updating of *The Omen*, with the story revolving around a possible Antichrist rising to power. The story's main characters were a Catholic nun, a skeptical Harvard professor, and a violent Satanist who is in prison. Seltzer did not identify himself as a believer in any particular faith, just someone who acknowledged a "higher power." The *Revelations* story included numerous quotes from the Bible, and the nun was made out to be an appealing character. NBC hoped the show might prove so popular that it could lead to an ongoing series, but this did not happen, although ratings were decent.

In January 2006, NBC premiered the short-lived series *The Book of Daniel*, about an Episcopal minister who literally talks to an on-screen Jesus. Daniel's family was seriously dysfunctional—he popped pills, his wife drank too much, his son was gay, and his daughter dealt in drugs. But most of the controversy surrounding the show was in depicting Jesus as a laid-back, "no sweat," totally nonjudgmental person who assured Daniel that whatever his family and others did, they were all "good" people. (Squaring that sentiment with the Bible's insistence in Romans 3:23 that "all have sinned and fall short of the glory of God" is not possible.) The show's writer was a professed homosexual, so the message of "true Christianity means total tolerance" wasn't surprising. The show came under fire from conservative Christian groups like Focus on the Family and the American Family Association, both of which urged Christians to call and email their local NBC affiliates. Several NBC stations did not air the show, and several sponsors withdrew. The show was canceled after four episodes. Non-Christian reviewers claimed the show simply wasn't very good—that the humor was lame, the religious message shallow, the characters not very interesting. NBC claimed the show was canceled due to poor ratings, not to pressure from Christians. The show did mark a first, as the producer intended: the first prime-time TV series to feature Jesus Christ as a regular character. However, he did not seem much like the Jesus of the Bible.

Worth noting: in this same period, people tuned in daily to watch psychologist Phil McGraw—Dr. Phil—dispense his often-blunt advice to people, telling them how to straighten out their lives. A psychologist can do so and audiences applaud, but ministers—and the Son of God—are not given that privilege.

In April 2006, ABC did something surprising: it aired a new two-part TV movie *The Ten Commandments* the same week it aired the 1956 *The Ten Commandments*. The new version was budgeted at $20 million, much more than the average miniseries, and was originally scheduled for "sweeps week" in February, but apparently ABC thought it not good enough for that. Most critics were very negative about the production, and apparently viewers were too, since it did poorly in ratings. Jewish reviewers noted that never once is the name "Israel" mentioned, nor does Moses say those famous words, "Let my people go." British actor Dougray Scott said he wanted to play Moses as "an ordinary man," and apparently viewers found him a bit *too* ordinary. A few reviewers did prefer it to the 1956 DeMille version, saying its Moses was a more "complex" personality—riddled with doubts about himself and God, in fact. Not surprisingly, though, when the 1956 version aired later in the week, it got higher ratings—an astonishing feat for a film released fifty years earlier.

Summer 2006 saw the remake of the popular 1976 apocalyptic thriller *The Omen*. Not coincidentally, ads for the film highlighted its premiere date of 6/6/06, reminding audiences that the Antichrist child in the film would bear the 666 "mark of the Beast" somewhere on his body. The sequel, unlike the original, fared very badly at the box office. But we will probably see more of these end-time scream fests that are really just horror movies with a tad of Revelation thrown in.

Happily, the fall of 2006 saw the premiere of two films with much more substance—and much more Bible—than *The Omen*.

One Night with the King: *Eye Candy, with Substance*

Released October 13, 2006
Gener8Xion Entertainment
122 minutes
Filmed in India

Director: Michael O. Sajbel
Screenplay: Stephan Blinn
Photography: Steven Bernstein
Music: J.A.C. Redford

Hadassah/Esther: Tiffany Dupont
Mordecai: John Rhys-Davies
Xerxes: Luke Goss
Haman: James Callis
Memucan: Omar Sharif
Hegai: "Tiny" Lister
Admatha: John Noble
Samuel: Peter O'Toole

The Old Testament's book of Esther is loved by Jews and mostly neglected by Christians, who have never been terribly inspired by this book that does not mention the name of God or even refer to prayer. (Note: in the expanded version of Esther found in Catholic Bibles, some apocryphal "Additions to Esther" do mention God, prayer, etc., but neither Jews nor Protestant Christians consider this expanded text to be inspired by God.) Jews connect the Esther story with their annual holiday of Purim (a relatively rowdy, secular celebration), and Christians mostly bypass Esther and concentrate on more inspiring parts of the Old Testament. That being said, the story of a virtuous Jewish girl who becomes queen of Persia and helps save her fellow Jews from genocide is an inspiring one, and has been made into more than one film, the most memorable (though hardly a great movie) being the 1960 *Esther and the King* (discussed on pages 145–51). This recent rendition of the Esther story is an improvement on the 1960 film in many ways.

The film's producer, Gener8Xion Entertainment, posted production notes online, stating that great films based on the Bible were not done by "zealots" and that audiences were not drawn to them because of "religious dogma or theological proselytization" but because they were simply great stories. In short, the company was making it clear that, quite unlike Mel Gibson's *Passion of the Christ*, *One Night with the King* was not the fruit of anyone's spiritual quest, nor was there even the slightest intention of converting anyone to biblical faith. The crew was a veritable "UN of religions," with Christians, Jews, Muslims, Hindus, Buddhists, Jains, and people of no faith working side by side—something the production notes touted as a fine thing.

The film's script was based, of course, on the book of Esther—and also on the novel *Hadassah* by Tommy Tenney and Mark Andrew Olsen (the novel was written with the intention of being turned into a film script). Tenney's name is fairly well known in evangelical and charismatic circles, as he is a noted pastor and author of *The God Chasers* and several other popular books. As usual with any transfer of the Bible to the screen, characters and plot points were added. One interesting element in this film is the use it makes of the Bible's mention that Haman, the villain of the book of Esther, was an "Agagite." Traditionally, Jews took this to mean that Haman was a descendant of the wicked Amalekite king Agag, who appears in 1 Samuel 15. In that account, Israel's king Saul had been commanded to exterminate the evil Amalekites, but Saul had failed to execute the captured Agag. The job had to be done by the prophet Samuel, who scolded Saul for disobeying the Lord's command to stamp out these rapacious, violent people. The account of Agag, Saul, and Samuel appears in the movie as a kind of prologue, with Samuel played by noted actor Peter O'Toole. (Blond and beardless, O'Toole hardly looks like an Israelite prophet.) It is an interesting prologue, although unlikely to have any real connection with the story of Esther, since Bible scholars think that the description of Haman as an Agagite may mean he was from a region called Agag, meaning he had no connection with the Amalekites or their king named Agag. However, the story provides Haman with a motive for his anti-Jewish malice: he wants to avenge the slaughter that Saul and Samuel brought upon his own people.

Fast-forward several centuries to the Persian Empire, where many Jews (conquered and deported earlier by the Babylonians) live in exile. We learn that the Jewish girl Hadassah is an orphan because her parents were killed by the marauding Amalekites. (This is a bit of a stretch, historically. The Amalekites aren't mentioned in the Bible after the time of King Hezekiah, centuries before the time of Esther, but they may still have existed that late in time.) As in the Bible, Esther is the ward of her kinsman Mordecai, who is a minor official in the court of the Persian emperor Xerxes. (The 1961 movie used—and horribly mispronounced—the biblical name Ahasuerus for the Persian king. The new film agrees with most Bible scholars in identifying the book of Esther's Ahasuerus with the king known to history as Xerxes.) Mordecai treats Hadassah as a beloved daughter, and he is well played by British actor John Rhys-Davies.

The film sticks close to the Bible in telling of how the Persian queen Vashti defies her husband's order to appear before him and his guests at a celebration. In fact, the film provides her with a motivation: she opposes Persia's ongoing war with Greece, and she sees the king's banquet as a "drunken war council." The king councilors see her defiance as a horrid violation of court etiquette (not to mention setting a bad precedent for wives disobeying their husbands!), so the order is given to search for a new and better woman to replace Vashti. Hadassah, who is told by Mordecai to keep her Jewishness a secret, is one of many attractive young women taken forcibly into the "charm school" where they will be trained to make as queenly an impression as possible, and finally one of them will be chosen as queen. Hadassah has the good fortune to be the favorite of the eunuch Hegai (played by a hulking, shaven-head, bullfrog-voiced wrestler—surely the most intimidating eunuch ever to grace the screen!). This tough character (with a surprising soft side) sees her as having more substance (she reads and seems to possess a *mind*) than the other young women. Some mild comedy is provided in showing how graceless some of the women are when they appear before the king. As in the Bible, Hadassah (who is now using the non-Jewish name Esther) wins the king's favor and his love, and is chosen as the next queen of Persia.

But disaster is looming: the villain Haman is plotting with Admatha, one of the Persian princes, to overthrow the king. Mordecai learns of the plot, passes the information on to Esther, and thus saves the king's life. Haman's own part in the plot goes undiscovered, however, and due to his hatred for Mordecai (and to the long Agagite tradition of hating all Jews), he plots to exterminate all the Jews in the empire. He especially despises Mordecai, who refuses to kneel to him when he passes in the street, and in a fine scene, Haman is humiliated by being forced to lead Mordecai on horseback through the streets, proclaiming him as one honored by the king (see Esther 6). Once Xerxes consents to the mass killing of Jews, he can't retract the order, even though his wise elderly advisor Memucan (played by the aging but distinguished Omar Sharif) advises against this genocide. Esther courageously defies court protocol (she can't enter the king's presence unless summoned). In the movie's most dramatic scene, she barges into the king's presence (she is wet from a pouring rain outside), while his court officials hold their breath, expecting him to allow her to be executed for her brashness. Instead, he is willing to listen to her, and she reveals Haman's wicked plans. As in the Bible, Mordecai tells her that in the divine scheme of things, she has been made queen of Persia "for such a time as this." The movie ends as the book does, with Mordecai being made the king's right-hand man.

Haman's anti-Semitic fanaticism is an interesting element in the movie, since (as most audience members should know) his rants sound suspiciously like the ranting of Muslim fanatics of today, spewing out their hatred for both Jews and Christians. Haman is a wild-eyed character, but one with enough charisma and zeal to whip up anti-Jewish feeling among the crowds. His inability to forgive or forget events that happened centuries ago is a trait shared by the more violent Muslims today. So the movie manages to be true to its biblical roots and, incidentally, connected to contemporary world events also.

The film's visual splendor impressed everyone who saw it. Filmed in Mogul palaces in Jodhpur, India, with unforgettable costumes by Indian designer Neeta Lulla, the film was a feast for the eyes. And for the most part, the movie's epic look was real, not computer generated—for example, the fifty-foot winged lion figures and thousands of extras are all real. Some clever use of aerial photography gives a sense of just how wide and wealthy the ancient Persian Empire was. Certainly the film had a more genuinely Persian look than *Esther and the King*, and the men (most of them bearded and long-haired) resemble men of ancient Persia much more than the short-haired, clean-shaven men in the 1961 film. (The blond Haman in that film looked laughably unhistorical!) On the safe assumption that the ancient Persians had skin and hair coloring and facial features similar to that of their descendants (today's Iranians), we can applaud the use of a cast that is relatively dark in coloration (a case where anthropology and the wise financial policy of hiring extras cheaply seemed to fit together nicely!). The day when biblical people on film all seemed to be fair-haired or at least fair-skinned Europeans and Americans seems to have passed (a case where historical accuracy and political correctness seem to work in harmony together).

The book of Esther is a violent one, but the film keeps most of its violence discreetly offscreen (in reaction to the achingly graphic violence of *Passion of the Christ*, maybe?). Such events as the butchering of Agag, the hanging of Haman, and the Jews' violent self-defense are referred to but not shown.

Although critics acknowledged the film's visual beauty, they were not so kind to the film as a whole. Roger Moore of the *Orlando Sentinel* called it "epic lite" and "talky imitation DeMille"[9] sentiments typical of many reviews in secular publications, though some were much more positive. Christian publications were generous with praise, and though the film hardly evoked the deep emotional response of *Passion of the Christ*, most Christian reviewers praised the positive presentation of maidenly virtue, marital love, and courage under pressure. The fact that the script was based on a novel by evangelical pastor-author Tommy Tenney added to the movie's credibility among evangelicals, of course. Also, it is a family friendly (meaning, *clean*) film, and lacking in the violence that kept many people from seeing *Passion*.

Although actress Tiffany Dupont doesn't show a great amount of depth, her Esther is an admirable character, Mordecai even more so, and old faithfuls like O'Toole and Sharif add some weight to the film. Rather surprisingly for a twenty-first-century film, the movie kept the sensuality to a minimum—interesting, especially in light of the 1961 film being such a "cheesecake" movie, with its gyrating, vulgar women and its men cavorting in skimpy full-leg-baring tunics. (The muscular king does seem to bare his chest fairly often, however.) The love story between Esther and the king has some substance to it, and the film is a reminder that it is possible to depict emotional intensity while keeping the characters fully clothed. The lavish wedding shown in the film seems like a fitting fulfillment of a chaste but nonetheless intense romance. And the fact that the king has a harem full of concubines at his disposal is mentioned rather discreetly.

The film does justice to the Bible's book of Esther, in fact, "improves upon" it, since God is mentioned quite often, and Esther and Mordecai seem to possess genuine faith in their God. In the tense minutes when the Jews' extermination seems imminent, Mordecai reads several comforting passages from the book of Isaiah.

Although the film was only a modest success in theaters, time will tell how well it fares in video format—and whether the film encourages other companies to produce commercial films based on the Bible. Any film following *The Passion of the Christ* is bound to be a letdown, of course, but at least the film is a sign that Mel Gibson didn't "raise the bar" so high that producers would shy away from putting the Bible on film anymore.

The Nativity Story: *Tried and True, and Gritty*

Released December 1, 2006	**Mary:** Keisha Castle-Hughes
New Line Cinema	**Joseph:** Oscar Isaac
100 minutes	**Elizabeth:** Shohreh Aghdashloo
Filmed in Italy and Morocco	**Herod:** Ciaran Hinds
	Gabriel: Alexander Siddig
Director: Catherine Hardwicke	**Anna:** Hiam Abbass
Screenplay: Mike Rich	**Joachim:** Shaun Toub
Photography: Elliot Davis	
Music: Mychael Danna	

The last film in our survey answers the same question that *The Passion of the Christ* answered: how do we tell a very familiar Bible story in a new and engaging way? *Passion* answered the question by showing the crucifixion of Jesus as it really was. *The Nativity Story* took a similar approach to the birth of Jesus—less dramatic and less profitable than *Passion*, but also less controversial.

The film opens with the eerie strains of the old Advent hymn "O Come, O Come, Emmanuel." A prophecy of the Messiah from the book of Jeremiah appears on the screen. The first scene is a sort of "flash-forward," showing evil King Herod's slaughter of the infants of Bethlehem following the birth of Jesus, obviously intended to let the audience know that this isn't going to be the typical "story of the first Christmas." The next scene is from Luke's Gospel, where the priest Zechariah offers a sacrifice in the temple and is told by the angel Gabriel that Zechariah and his aged wife will produce a son, who will be John the Baptist, forerunner of the

Messiah. This scene is well handled, for we hear Gabriel's voice but never see him, although the smoke from the incense wafts upward and almost, but not quite, appears in human shape.

From this point on, the film interweaves three stories: Mary and Joseph, the three magi (wise men), and the paranoid Herod. The magi are, the movie tells us, living in Persia—which is probably historically correct, although the New Testament doesn't actually tell us where they came from. The film gives them the traditional names—Gaspar, Balthasar, and Melchior—names not found in the Bible, incidentally. There is some gentle humor in the dialogue of the magi, one of them being at first reluctant to set out on a long, hazardous journey to faraway Israel (he thinks it may be a wild goose chase).

We get some glimpses of daily life in the village of Nazareth, where Herod and the Romans oppress through taxes and confiscation. Mary is played by sixteen-year-old Keisha Castle-Hughes, in a rare case of a film casting someone who is the probable age of Mary of Nazareth. Mary's parents, Joachim and Anna, betroth her to Joseph, a carpenter. Mary is not pleased, since she admits she does not love him—or really know him, for that matter. She submits to her parents' will (as most girls did in those days), but the betrothal goes amiss when Mary is told by the angel Gabriel that she will bear the Son of God. (This Gabriel is dark and bearded, an interesting change from the fair-haired, beardless angels usually seen in artwork and films.) Not sure whether to believe or not, and fearing what will happen if her miraculous pregnancy begins to show, Mary asks her parents if she can visit her aged cousin Elizabeth. When she arrives there, her faith in the angel's words is strengthened when she learns that Elizabeth is indeed pregnant, as the angel said. After the birth of Elizabeth's son, Mary returns to Nazareth, where the entire village, Joseph in particular, is scandalized to learn that Mary is pregnant. No one believes her story of the angel, and Joseph is perplexed about what to do. He has a dream in which the villagers, himself included, are about to stone Mary, but the angel intervenes and tells him not to be afraid to take Mary as his wife. (The movie makes it clear that the ancient world didn't treat unwed motherhood as lightly as we do today.) Joseph trusts Mary, but the villagers continue in their coldness toward her—and now toward him as well. The couple leaves for Bethlehem, Joseph's ancestral home, because of the

Romans' census, and as they depart, Joseph tells Mary, "They will miss us"—implying that the villagers won't be able to snub them while they are gone.

This touch of reality—an unwed pregnant woman facing the scorn of her hometown—isn't something we're accustomed to seeing in retellings of the Christmas story. Something else that is new here is that Joseph and Mary aren't really a couple, emotionally speaking, when they set out for Bethlehem. As they journey for a hundred miles and Mary sees what a decent and protective man Joseph is, she begins to love him. Joseph here is played, by the way, by a young actor—breaking the tradition of a million paintings (and Christmas cards) showing Joseph as a much older man than Mary. He is well played by actor Oscar Isaac (who is, incidentally, a professed Christian).

At the very point when they reach Bethlehem, Mary's labor pains begin, and Joseph makes a frantic search for shelter. They make their way to a stable in the nick of time, and in another bow to reality, the birth is painful (as all births were in the days before anesthetics). Some very ragged-looking shepherds come to the stable, having been told of the birth by the angel, and soon after the three magi arrive on their camels—the familiar "Nativity scene," and another case of tradition triumphing over the Bible itself, since Matthew's Gospel tells us that the magi found the family in a "house," meaning they had moved out of the stable at some point (also meaning that the shepherds and magi probably weren't present at the same time). But the script is willing to "bend" a little in order to show the exotically clad magi in the same scene as the ragtag shepherds. The magi, who had dined with the scheming Herod and knew he wanted them to tell him the whereabouts of the newborn Messiah, choose not to return to the paranoid king. Herod orders the slaughter of the infants of Bethlehem, but Joseph, warned by the angel, hurries out of the town with his wife and the newborn Jesus. As in the Bible, they journey to Egypt for safety, and the movie ends with Mary's song of praise to God, the familiar "Magnificat" found in Luke 1:47–55.

Obviously the script stuck very close to the stories found in Matthew 1–2 and Luke 1–2—appropriately so, since this was a case of the screenwriter being a professed Christian. Writer Mike Rich had done the scripts for *Finding Forester* and *The Rookie*. In an interview with *Today's Christian* magazine, Rich stated, "I wanted to make sure we were faithful to the tone and spirit of the Gospels. If you don't feel that pressure writing this type of story, you're not approaching it in the right way."[10] In many parts of the film, Rich did the most sensible thing and simply used the exact words of the Bible, notably in the words spoken by Gabriel. Rich submitted the script to several theologians and Christian leaders for their comments, and he leaned heavily on Bible scholar Raymond Brown's *Birth of the Messiah*. He spent almost a year researching the project, then a month writing it. The film apparently pleased the Roman Catholic hierarchy, because its world premiere was at the Vatican on November 26, 2006. Apparently the Vatican was not bothered that the film broke with the Catholic tradition in which Joseph was an older widower with children when he married Mary.

Prior to directing *Nativity*, Catherine Hardwicke was best known for directing *Thirteen*, a rather frank look at teen delinquency and promiscuity. It may seem an odd leap from that to *Nativity*, but perhaps not, since *Nativity* does deal with an unwed (but definitely *not* promiscuous) teen mother. (As it turned out, the actress playing Mary did, after the film wrapped, become pregnant at age sixteen by her boyfriend—a reminder that actors playing biblical roles don't always have biblical morals.)

Michael Wilmington, critic for the *Chicago Tribune*, described the film as "reverent without seeming too pious-minded."[11] Ty Burr of the *Boston Globe* stated approvingly that "if *Passion* was the Gospel According to Mel, *The Nativity Story* is strictly by the Book." Burr noted that *Nativity* followed *Passion* in bringing a refreshing realism to biblical films.[12] Most critics in the secular media gave similar reviews, praising the movie for being well produced, well cast, and tastefully directed but stopping short of giving it a heartfelt "hurrah." Reviews of the film in Christian magazines and websites were more enthusiastic.

Two minor criticisms of the film: in its attempt to show daily life in ancient Judea realistically, the film is perhaps a little too real—colors are so muted that the viewer almost wishes for some of the Technicolor "gloss" of old Hollywood movies dealing with the Bible. Another point is that the characters on occasion speak their prayers in Hebrew, so subtitles (as used in *Passion*) would have been appropriate in these sections. But all in all it is a satisfying film, proving that a much-told story still has some life in it.

The Nativity Story was released by a major distributor, New Line Cinema, a sign that major studios were, in the wake of the great success of *Passion of the Christ*, willing to turn again to the Bible for stories. *Nativity* was a fairly low-budget movie, filmed in Italy and Morocco (in fact, much of it was filmed in Matera, Italy, the same locale used in *Passion*), and its cast was mostly unknowns. *The Passion of the Christ*, *One Night with the King*, and *The Nativity Story* seem to indicate a pattern for twenty-first-century biblical films: use scripts that stick close to the Bible, aim for a realistic depiction of ancient times, aim for reverence toward the subject, and, for reasons of budget, film abroad with mostly unknown cast members, hoping that the appeal of the old, old stories will draw audiences.

Postscript: "The Book Was Better"

An old cliché of moviegoers is "I liked the movie, but the book was better." In the case of the biblical films, the book—or, rather, Book—is definitely superior. After all, the Book (so Christians believe) is God's own revelation to humankind, and any movie (or play or novel or artwork) based on the Book is still "second generation." As this survey of biblical films shows, some biblical movies depart radically from the Bible, which suggests their writers and producers felt no compulsion to stick close to the source material. A film like the 1951 *David and Bathsheba*, popular though it was, seemed to use the story of David as an excuse to put two gorgeous stars together in a film that basically condoned an adulterous relationship. On the other hand, some films—such as the 1949 *Samson and Delilah* and the 2006 *One Night with the King*—actually (dare we say this?) improve on the biblical material with a deeper spirituality. The story of Samson in Judges is hardly inspiring, and the book of Esther does not even mention God or prayer, yet the film versions had some spiritual depth. You might say that they applied the deep spirituality of the entire Bible to certain stories that, by themselves, were not spiritually rich.

But, one closing thought about biblical films: although none of them can truly substitute for the Word itself, they can fill in some knowledge gaps in the audience. When the authors of the four Gospels wrote their stories of Jesus, they did not have to describe a crucifixion in detail, since chances are their original readers had seen men dying on crosses and knew the horror of it. That isn't so for people in the twenty-first century, so the Gospels' bare words "they crucified him" can't have the impact they had for the original readers. A movie like Gibson's *Passion of the Christ*, criticized by many for its "obscene" violence, broke with film tradition by showing crucifixion in all its nastiness—in other words, anyone who saw the film came close to experiencing the horror that people in first-century Jerusalem would have seen. The film pretty much swept away the "painless" crucifixions of old movies and church pageants. Likewise, *The Nativity Story* brought audiences face-to-face with a harsh reality: Mary was a young teenager facing the scorn of her village and the doubts of her fiancé because she was pregnant out of wedlock—an uncomfortable situation our parents' generation would've understood well enough, but which our own (taking unwed motherhood in stride) has to be reminded of. A good biblical film can, in a few minutes of screen time, bridge the enormous culture gap between us and the people of biblical times. "The Book is better," yes, but biblical films can go a long way to singing "the Lord's song in a foreign land," as Psalm 137 puts it.

NOTES

Introduction

1. *Time* (February 29, 2004), online version.
2. *New York Times* (December 1, 2006), online archives.
3. Quoted in Jan Herman, *A Talent for Trouble: The Life of Hollywood's Most Acclaimed Director, William Wyler* (New York: Putnam's, 1995), 410.
4. Frank Capra, *The Name above the Title* (New York: Vintage Books, 1971), 463.

Chapter 1: Grainy, Silent Beginnings

1. Paul Johnson, *A History of the American People* (New York: HarperCollins, 1997), 690.

Chapter 2: From Full-Length to the Era of Sound

1. Cecil B. DeMille, *Autobiography of Cecil B. DeMille* (Englewood Cliffs, NJ: Prentice-Hall, 1959), 276.
2. Ibid.
3. Ibid., 282.
4. Ibid.

Chapter 3: The Lean Years

1. The entire Code can be viewed online at www.artsreformation.com/a001/hays-code.html.
2. Ibid.
3. DeMille, *Autobiography of Cecil B. DeMille*, 299.
4. *New York Times* (July 17, 1936), online archives.

Chapter 4: The Golden Age

1. DeMille, *Autobiography of Cecil B. DeMille*, 398.
2. Ibid., 399.
3. Ibid.
4. *Newsweek* (November 28, 1949), 71.
5. DeMille, *Autobiography of Cecil B. DeMille*, 400.
6. *New York Times* (December 22, 1949), online archives.
7. Philip Dunne, quoted in Gary Fishgall, *Gregory Peck: A Biography* (New York: Scribner's, 2002), 160.
8. *New York Times* (August 15, 1951), online archives.
9. Martin Scorsese, quoted in Gary Fishgall, *Gregory Peck*, 161.
10. *New York Times* (March 25, 1953), online archives.
11. DeMille, *Autobiography of Cecil B. DeMille*, 249.
12. Charlton Heston and Jean-Pierre Isbouts, *Charlton Heston's Hollywood: Fifty Years in American Film* (New York: GT Publishing, 1998), 56.
13. Charlton Heston, *In the Arena* (New York: Simon and Schuster, 1995), 133.
14. Ibid., 140.
15. DeMille, *Autobiography of Cecil B. DeMille*, 55.
16. *Time* (January 11, 1960), 64.

Chapter 5: The Silver Age

1. *Time* (January 6, 1967), online archives.
2. *Time* (January 5, 1970), online archives.
3. *New York Times* (November 1, 1960), online archives.
4. *New York Times* (December 1, 1962), online archives.
5. *Time* (February 29, 2004), online version.
6. *New York Times* (January 24, 1963), online archives.
7. *Newsweek* (January 28, 1963), 88.
8. Heston, *In the Arena*, 297.
9. *Newsweek* (February 22, 1965), 96.
10. *Time* (February 29, 2004), online version.
11. "Lights, Camera, Jesus," *Christianity Today* (22 May 2000), 62.
12. John Huston, *An Open Book* (New York: Da Capo Press, 1994), 322.
13. Ibid., 318.
14. Ibid., 322.
15. *Time* (October 7, 1966), 119.
16. Huston, *An Open Book*, 336.
17. Ibid., 329.

Chapter 6: Musical Mishaps and the Longest Bible Movie Ever

1. *Newsweek* (April 9, 1973), 109.
2. Ibid.
3. *Newsweek* (July 9, 1973), 82.
4. *Christianity Today* (May 20, 1977), online archives.
5. *Christianity Today* (May 22, 2000), 62.

Chapter 7: Revisionism and Controversy

1. *Christianity Today* (September 16, 1988), 41.
2. Ibid.

3. *Newsweek* (August 15, 1988), 57.

4. *National Review* (September 16, 1988), 55.

Chapter 8: A New Millennium, with *Passion*

1. Quoted in *Today's Christian* (March–April, 2004), 32.

2. *New York Times* (February 25, 2004), online archives.

3. *Today's Christian*, 30.

4. *Time* (February 29, 2004), online version.

5. *Time* (March 1, 2004), 64.

6. *The Christian Century* (March 3, 2004), 18.

7. *Today's Christian*, 31.

8. Mel Gibson in foreword to *The Passion: Photography from the Movie* The Passion of the Christ (Carol Stream, IL: Tyndale, 2004), ix.

9. *Orlando Sentinel* (October 13, 2006), online version.

10. *Today's Christian* (November–December, 2006), 23.

11. *Chicago Tribune* (December 1, 2006), online version.

12. *Boston Globe* (December 1, 2006), online version.

INDEX

J. Stephen Lang is the author of thirty-five books, including the bestselling *Complete Book of Bible Trivia*. He is also a devoted film buff. He holds the MA from Wheaton College and resides in Seminole, Florida.